BLOKHEDZ

A Street Legends Ink Production

Created by:
Mark & Mike Davis
"MadTwiinz"

Written by:
Mark & Mike Davis
Brandon Schultz

Pencils:
Mark Davis

Colors:
Mike Davis

Book Layout:
Kobina Yankah

Backgrounds (book 4):
Robert Crump

Lettering:
Comicraft's
Jimmy Betancourt

Rhymes:
Blak: Ali Vegas
Vulture: Axl

Poems:
Blak: Nicole Duncan - Smith
Essence: Nikia "Liberty" Scott

Graffiti Support:
Galo "Make One" Canote
Upendo "The Blak Krayon" Taylor

Executive Producer:
Michael Schultz

Producers:
Brandon Schultz
Nicole Duncan-Smith

Special Thanks to:
Morgan Bond
Riggs Morales

Edit Support:
Michael Bou
Karen Chung
Eric Wiggins

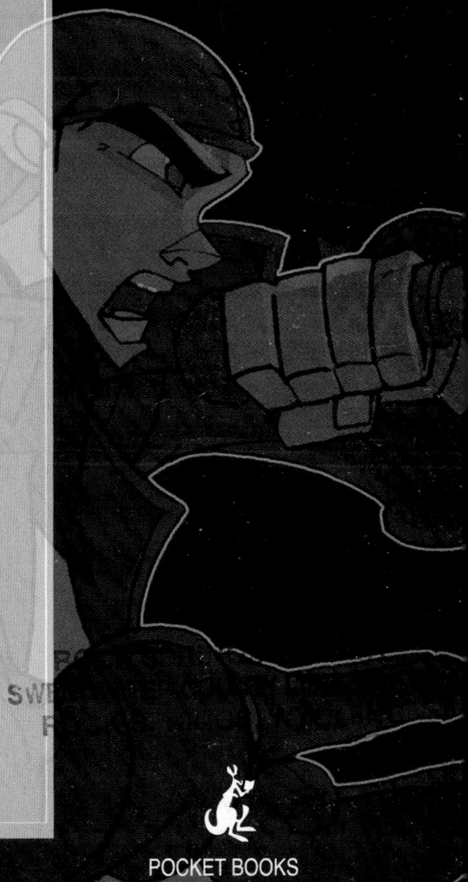

www.blokhedz.tv
www.simonsays.com

POCKET BOOKS
New York London Toronto Sydney

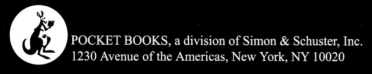

POCKET BOOKS, a division of Simon & Schuster, Inc.
1230 Avenue of the Americas, New York, NY 10020

Library of Congress Cataloging-in-Publication Data is available.

ISBN-13: 978-1-4165-4073-1
ISBN-10:   1-4165-4073-3

This Pocket Books trade paperback edition March 2007

10 9 8 7 6 5 4 3 2 1

POCKET and colophon are registered trademarks of
Simon & Schuster, Inc.

Manufactured in the United States of America

For information regarding special discounts for bulk purchases, please contact
Simon & Schuster Special Sales at 1-800-456-6798 or business@simonandschuster.com.

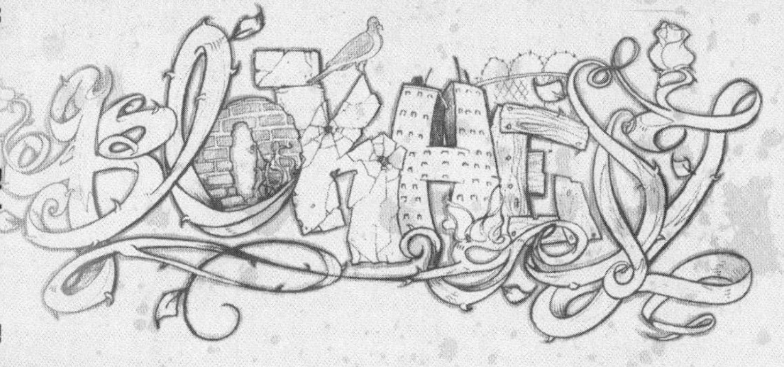

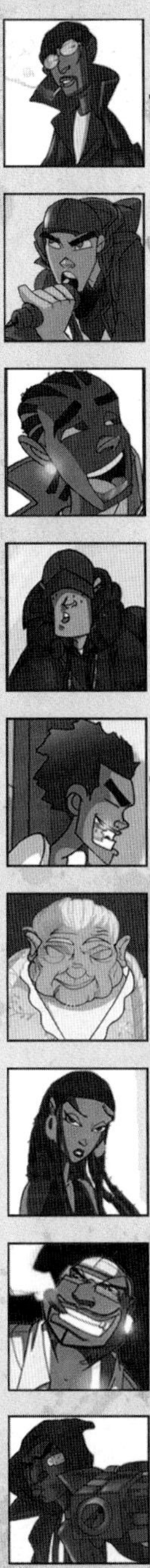
Konzaquence
Blak
Flash
Eatho
Skrap
Rosetta
Essence
Bloko
Vulture
Drop

THE SYNOPSIS

Empire City. A Manhattan-like metropolis on steroids. A city fallen in disrepair can only be saved by the gifted one. The problem: He's seventeen, with ambitions to be a rap star.

THE BACKDROP

Residents call it "The Jungle." The outsiders call it a hopeless abyss. BLAK calls it home.

Twenty years ago, E.C. was a thriving metropolis and its crown jewel was Monarch Housing Projects. Monarch was a mega-million-dollar development erected to appease the long-oppressed underclass. The Monarch development was supposed to show the progressiveness of the city's politicians.

What they told no one is that these projects were built on top of historical burial grounds. These burial grounds belonged to an indigenous nation whose name can only be translated as the "Original People." The Original People were a mystical and spiritual group who had special... some say even magical talents or gifts. Legends say that the elite leaders of the Original People had special gifts for spinning stories. They could influence others with the power of their words in a way that can only be described as supernatural.

When E.C.'s power brokers discovered the magnitutude of their mistake they swore to each other to keep this knowledge secret, fearing the political backlash. They turned Monarch over to the Housing Authority police and wiped their hands clean of the mess. Crime swelled, and Monarch began to fall into despair and disrepair.

According to the legends, the Original People's scrolls told of the construction of Monarch and warned that the power of their ancestors would live through a select few. That power could be used for incredible good or to perpetrate tremendous evil.

The power was in the hands of those bestowed with the gift. As with most myths, the scrolls predicted an anointed one who would use his power to save his city from the massive decay. It was said he would wear the mark of the lion. No one really gave the myth much credibility. Most people dismissed it as just another street legend.

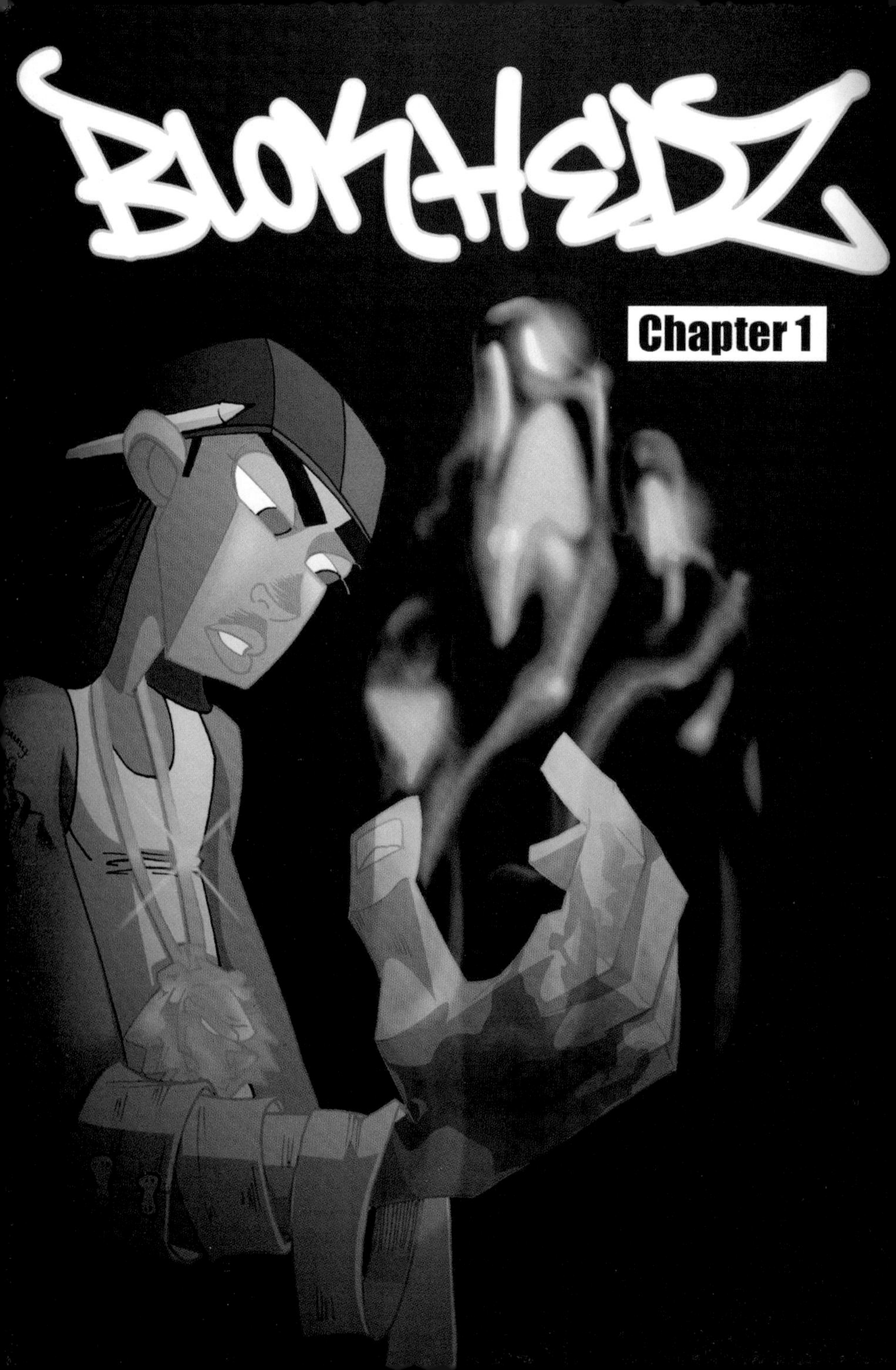
BLOKHEDZ
Chapter 1

WELCOME TO THE JUNGLE
WHERE EVERY BORN PRINCE DIE KING
MY OLDER BROTHER AND HIS LIVE TEAM

DRUNK 40'S AND LET THEIR EAH STEAM
COOKIN' CRYPT TO GET THEM FLY THINGS
A RODEO DRIVE DREAM AND A WISE SCHEME

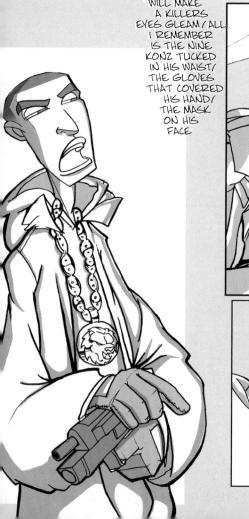

WILL MAKE
A KILLERS
EYES GLEAM/ ALL
I REMEMBER
IS THE NINE
KONZ TUCKED
IN HIS WAIST/
THE GLOVES
THAT COVERED
HIS HAND/
THE MASK
ON HIS
FACE

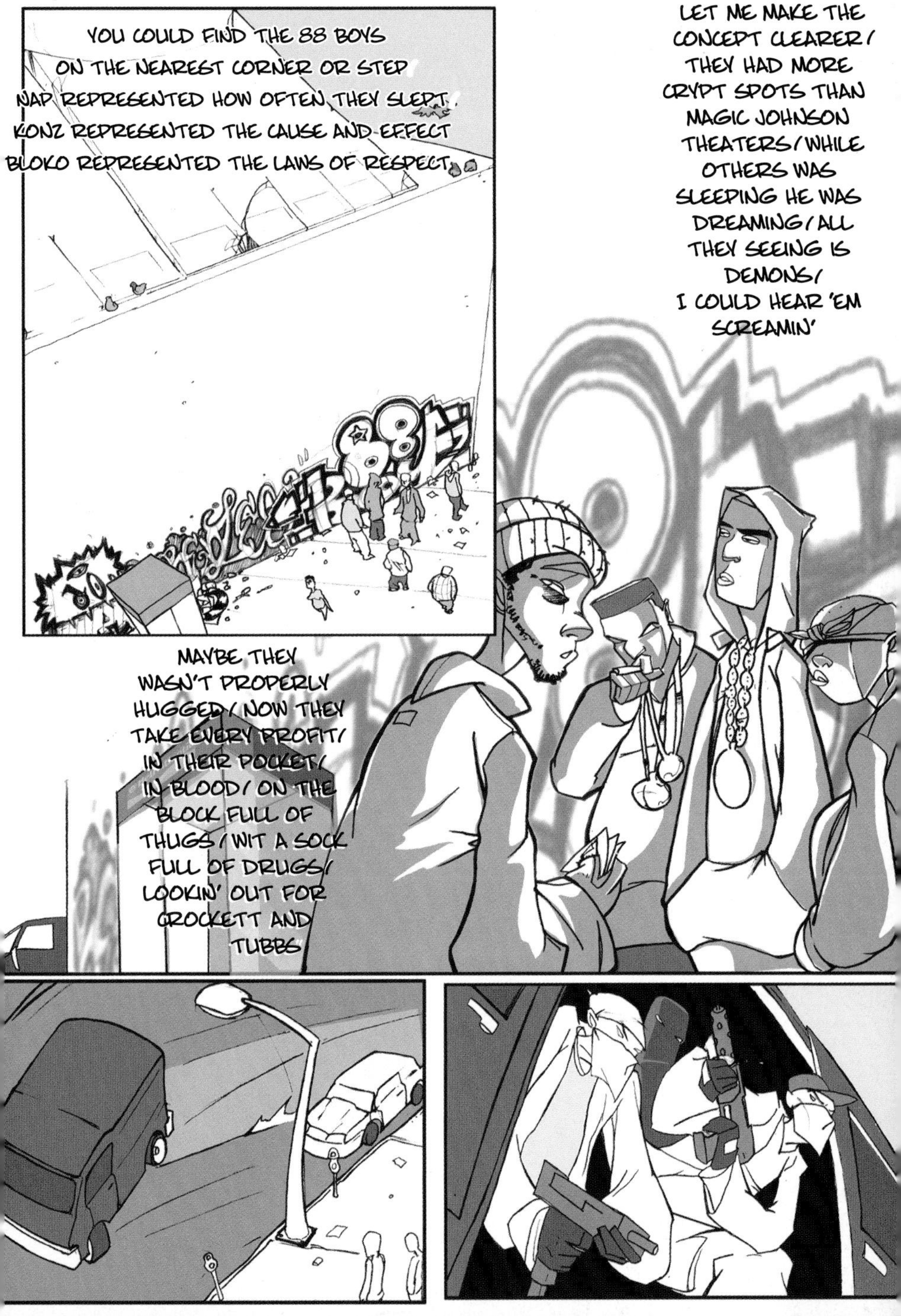
YOU COULD FIND THE 88 BOYS
ON THE NEAREST CORNER OR STEP
NAP REPRESENTED HOW OFTEN THEY SLEPT
KONZ REPRESENTED THE CAUSE AND EFFECT
BLOKO REPRESENTED THE LAWS OF RESPECT
LET ME MAKE THE CONCEPT CLEARER / THEY HAD MORE CRYPT SPOTS THAN MAGIC JOHNSON THEATERS / WHILE OTHERS WAS SLEEPING HE WAS DREAMING / ALL THEY SEEING IS DEMONS / I COULD HEAR 'EM SCREAMIN'
MAYBE THEY WASN'T PROPERLY HUGGED / NOW THEY TAKE EVERY PROFIT / IN THEIR POCKET / IN BLOOD / ON THE BLOCK FULL OF THUGS / WIT A SOCK FULL OF DRUGS / LOOKIN' OUT FOR CROCKETT AND TUBBS

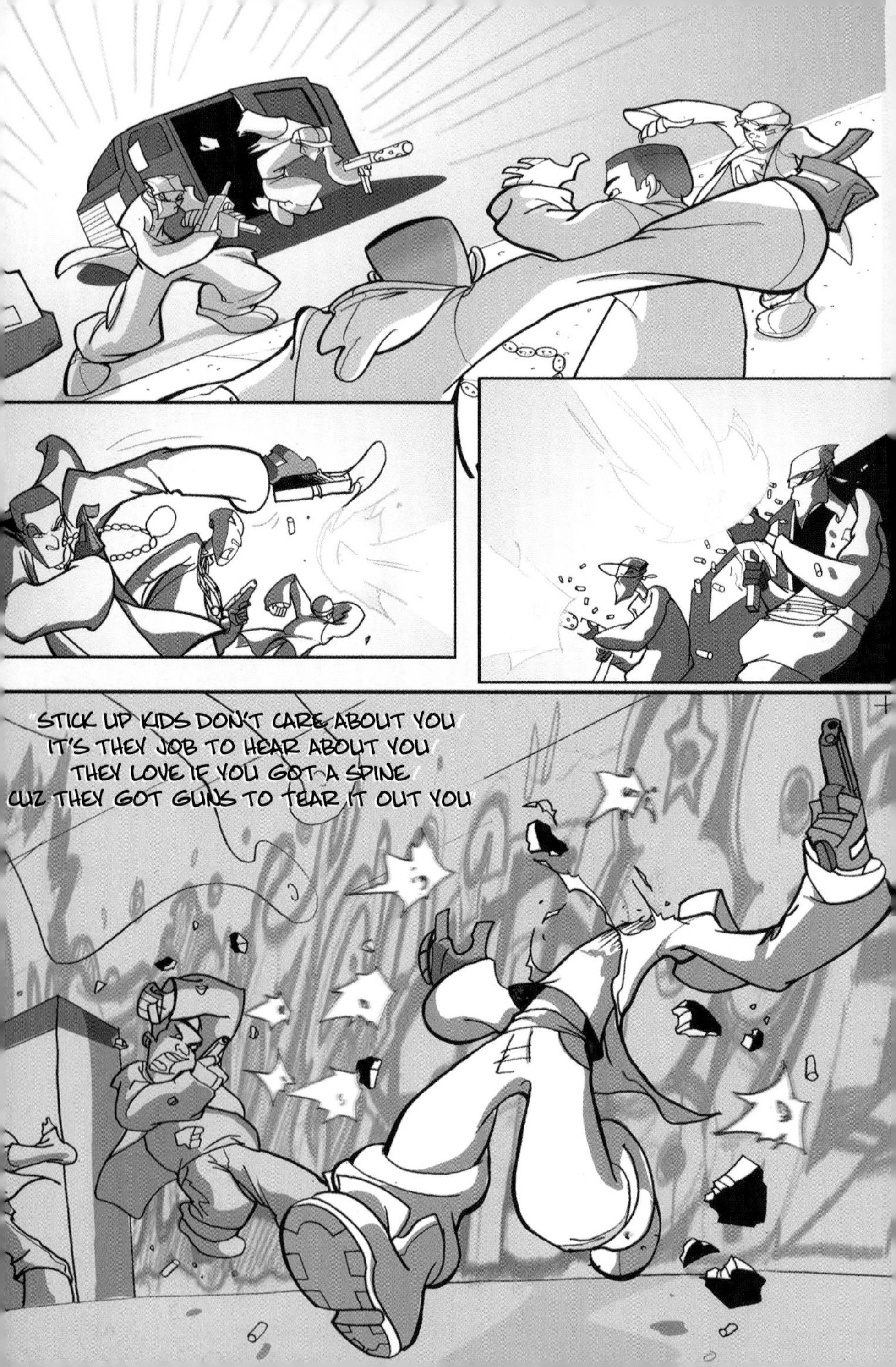
"STICK UP KIDS DON'T CARE ABOUT YOU/
IT'S THEY JOB TO HEAR ABOUT YOU/
THEY LOVE IF YOU GOT A SPINE/
CUZ THEY GOT GUNS TO TEAR IT OUT YOU"

ARRRGHH, THAT DON'T RHYME RIGHT.

RRIIIPPP

IT *AIN'T* BAD, BUT IT *DOESN'T* SOUND LIKE YOU.

I KNEW YOU WERE GONNA SAY THAT. IT JUST DIDN'T RHYME RIGHT, THAT'S ALL.

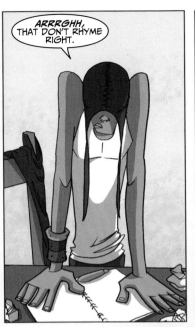

IT *DIDN'T* RHYME RIGHT CUZ THAT WAS MY LIFE, YO, NOT YOURS.

I GOTTA GIVE THE PEOPLE WHAT THEY WANT TO HEAR.

IF I HAD A NICKEL FOR EVERY TIME SOMEBODY TOLD ME: "YOU'RE NICE BUT WHY YOU SO CONSCIOUS?" I'M TIRED OF PEOPLE THINKING I'M SOFT. I WANT CATS TO KNOW IF THEY STEP TO ME, THEY GONNA GET DEALT WITH.

BLAK, YOU GOT TALENT THAT MOST PEOPLE WOULD KILL FOR. YOU WANNA BE A TOUGH GUY? TOUGH GUYS GET TOUCHED EVERY DAY.

YOU MAY NOT REALIZE IT, BUT YOUR WORDS HAVE POWER.

YEAH, YEAH, I KNOW.

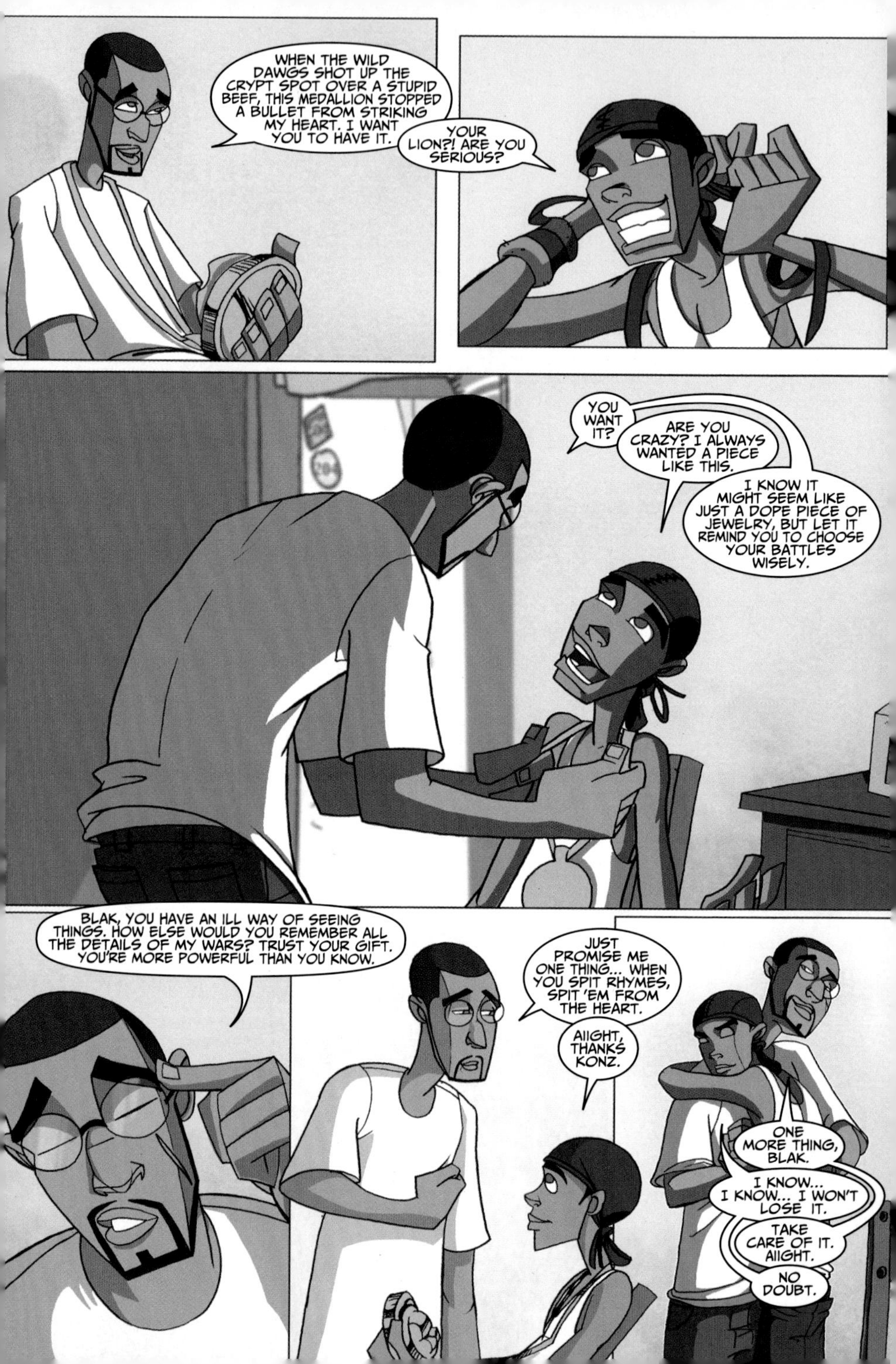
WHEN THE WILD DAWGS SHOT UP THE CRYPT SPOT OVER A STUPID BEEF, THIS MEDALLION STOPPED A BULLET FROM STRIKING MY HEART. I WANT YOU TO HAVE IT.
YOUR LION?! ARE YOU SERIOUS?
YOU WANT IT?
ARE YOU CRAZY? I ALWAYS WANTED A PIECE LIKE THIS.
I KNOW IT MIGHT SEEM LIKE JUST A DOPE PIECE OF JEWELRY, BUT LET IT REMIND YOU TO CHOOSE YOUR BATTLES WISELY.
BLAK, YOU HAVE AN ILL WAY OF SEEING THINGS. HOW ELSE WOULD YOU REMEMBER ALL THE DETAILS OF MY WARS? TRUST YOUR GIFT. YOU'RE MORE POWERFUL THAN YOU KNOW.
JUST PROMISE ME ONE THING... WHEN YOU SPIT RHYMES, SPIT 'EM FROM THE HEART.
AIIGHT, THANKS KONZ.
ONE MORE THING, BLAK.
I KNOW... I KNOW... I WON'T LOSE IT.
TAKE CARE OF IT. AIIGHT.
NO DOUBT.

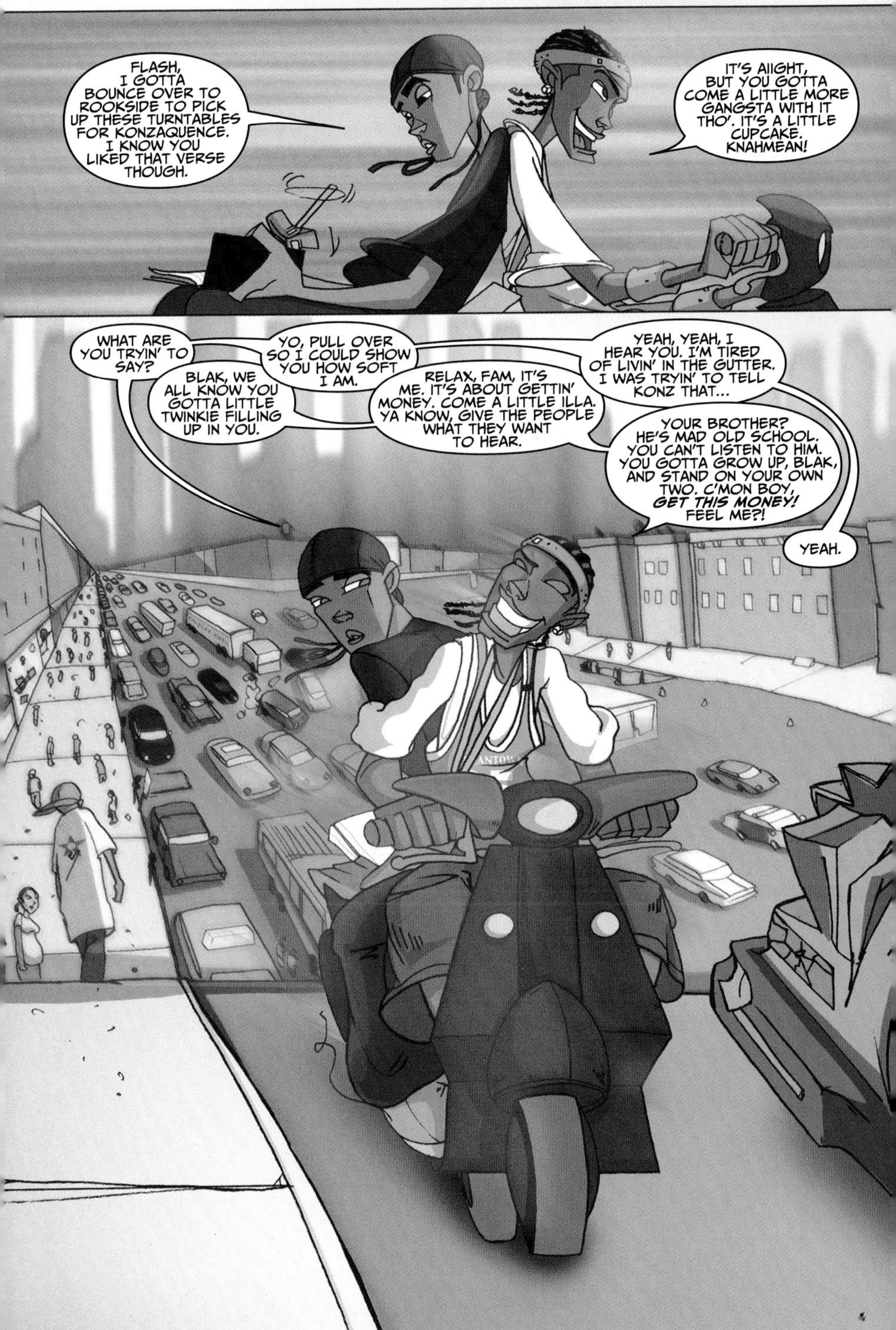
FLASH, I GOTTA BOUNCE OVER TO ROOKSIDE TO PICK UP THESE TURNTABLES FOR KONZAQUENCE. I KNOW YOU LIKED THAT VERSE THOUGH.
IT'S AIIGHT, BUT YOU GOTTA COME A LITTLE MORE GANGSTA WITH IT THO'. IT'S A LITTLE CUPCAKE. KNAHMEAN!
WHAT ARE YOU TRYIN' TO SAY?
YO, PULL OVER SO I COULD SHOW YOU HOW SOFT I AM.
BLAK, WE ALL KNOW YOU GOTTA LITTLE TWINKIE FILLING UP IN YOU.
RELAX, FAM, IT'S ME. IT'S ABOUT GETTIN' MONEY. COME A LITTLE ILLA. YA KNOW, GIVE THE PEOPLE WHAT THEY WANT TO HEAR.
YEAH, YEAH, I HEAR YOU. I'M TIRED OF LIVIN' IN THE GUTTER. I WAS TRYIN' TO TELL KONZ THAT...
YOUR BROTHER? HE'S MAD OLD SCHOOL. YOU CAN'T LISTEN TO HIM. YOU GOTTA GROW UP, BLAK, AND STAND ON YOUR OWN TWO. C'MON BOY, ***GET THIS MONEY!*** FEEL ME?!
YEAH.

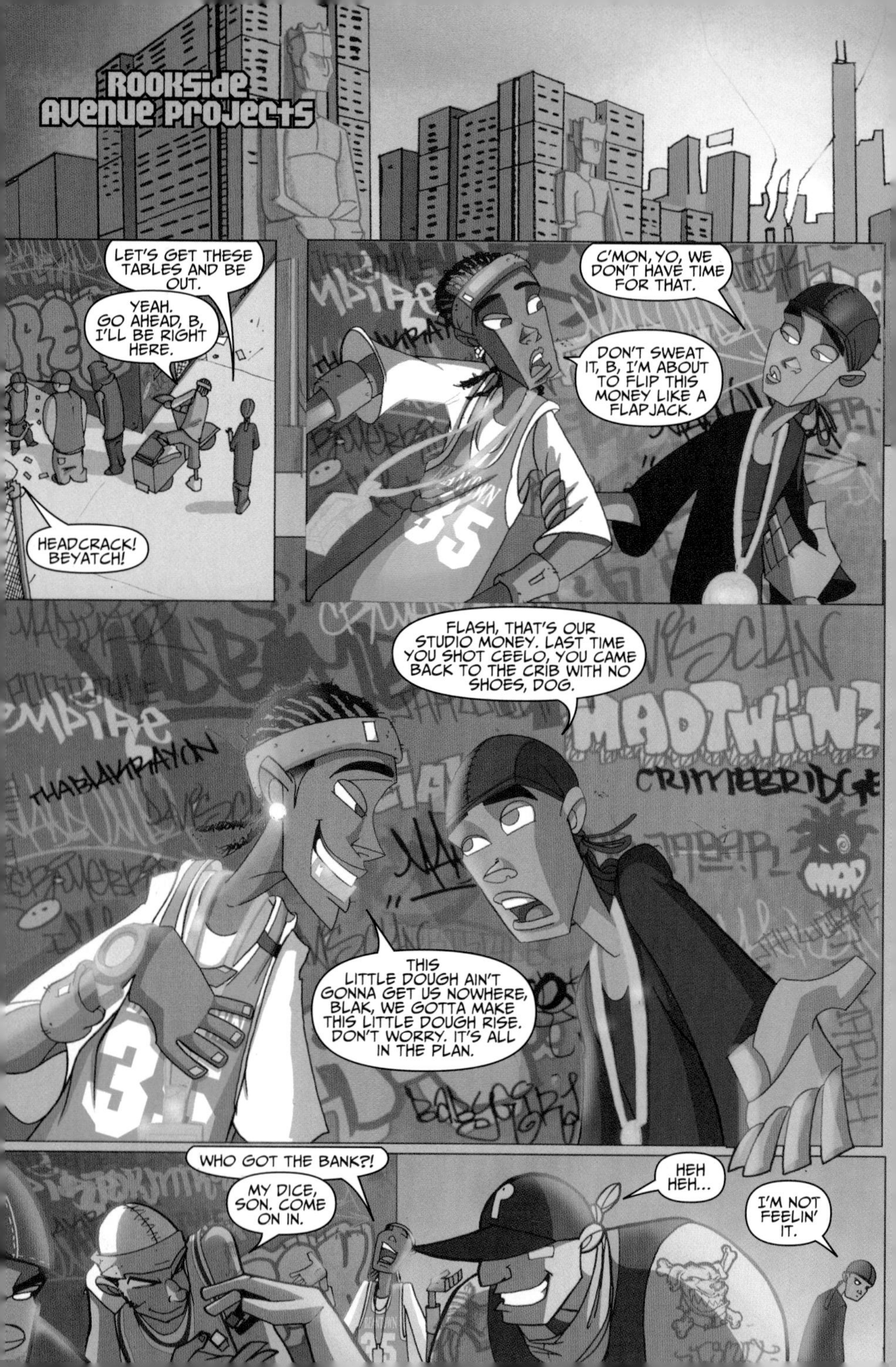
ROOKSIDE AVENUE PROJECTS
LET'S GET THESE TABLES AND BE OUT.
YEAH. GO AHEAD, B, I'LL BE RIGHT HERE.
HEADCRACK! BEYATCH!
C'MON, YO, WE DON'T HAVE TIME FOR THAT.
DON'T SWEAT IT, B, I'M ABOUT TO FLIP THIS MONEY LIKE A FLAPJACK.
FLASH, THAT'S OUR STUDIO MONEY. LAST TIME YOU SHOT CEELO, YOU CAME BACK TO THE CRIB WITH NO SHOES, DOG.
THIS LITTLE DOUGH AIN'T GONNA GET US NOWHERE, BLAK, WE GOTTA MAKE THIS LITTLE DOUGH RISE. DON'T WORRY. IT'S ALL IN THE PLAN.
WHO GOT THE BANK?!
MY DICE, SON. COME ON IN.
HEH HEH...
I'M NOT FEELIN' IT.

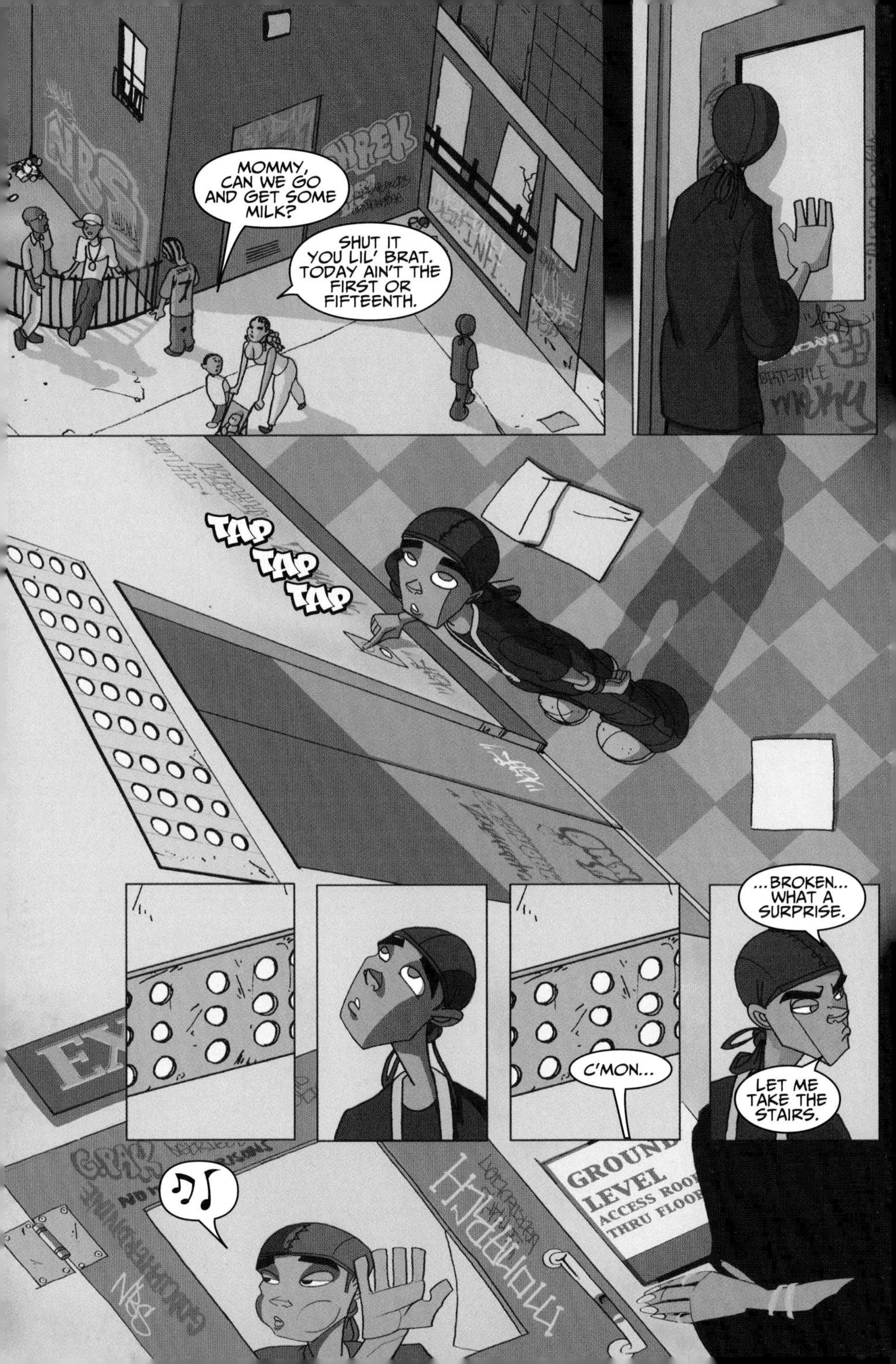
MOMMY, CAN WE GO AND GET SOME MILK?
SHUT IT YOU LIL' BRAT. TODAY AIN'T THE FIRST OR FIFTEENTH.
TAP TAP TAP
C'MON...
...BROKEN... WHAT A SURPRISE.
LET ME TAKE THE STAIRS.
♫♩
GROUND LEVEL ACCESS ROO THRU FLOO

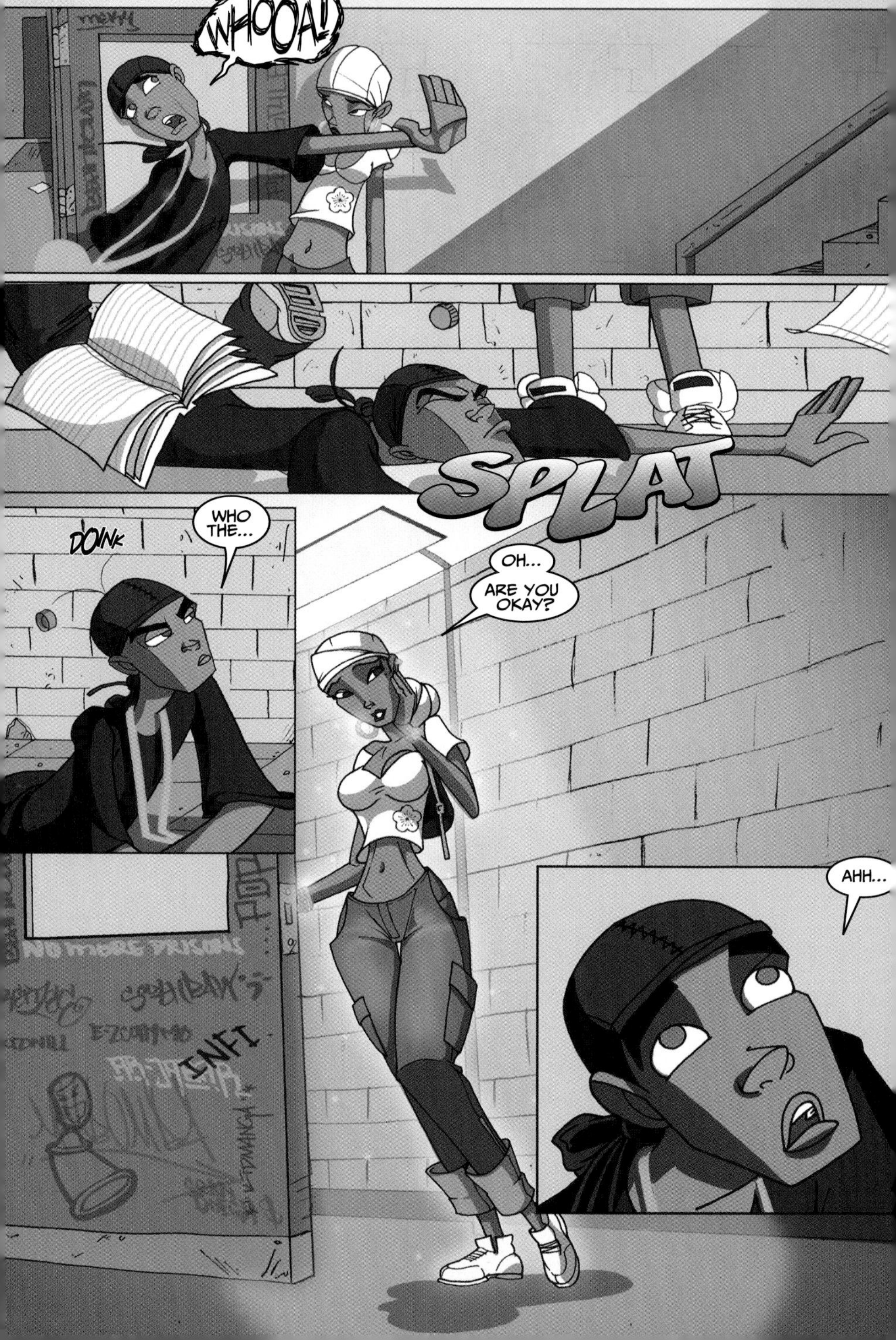

WHOOA!!
SPLAT
DOINK
WHO THE...
OH...
ARE YOU OKAY?
AHH...

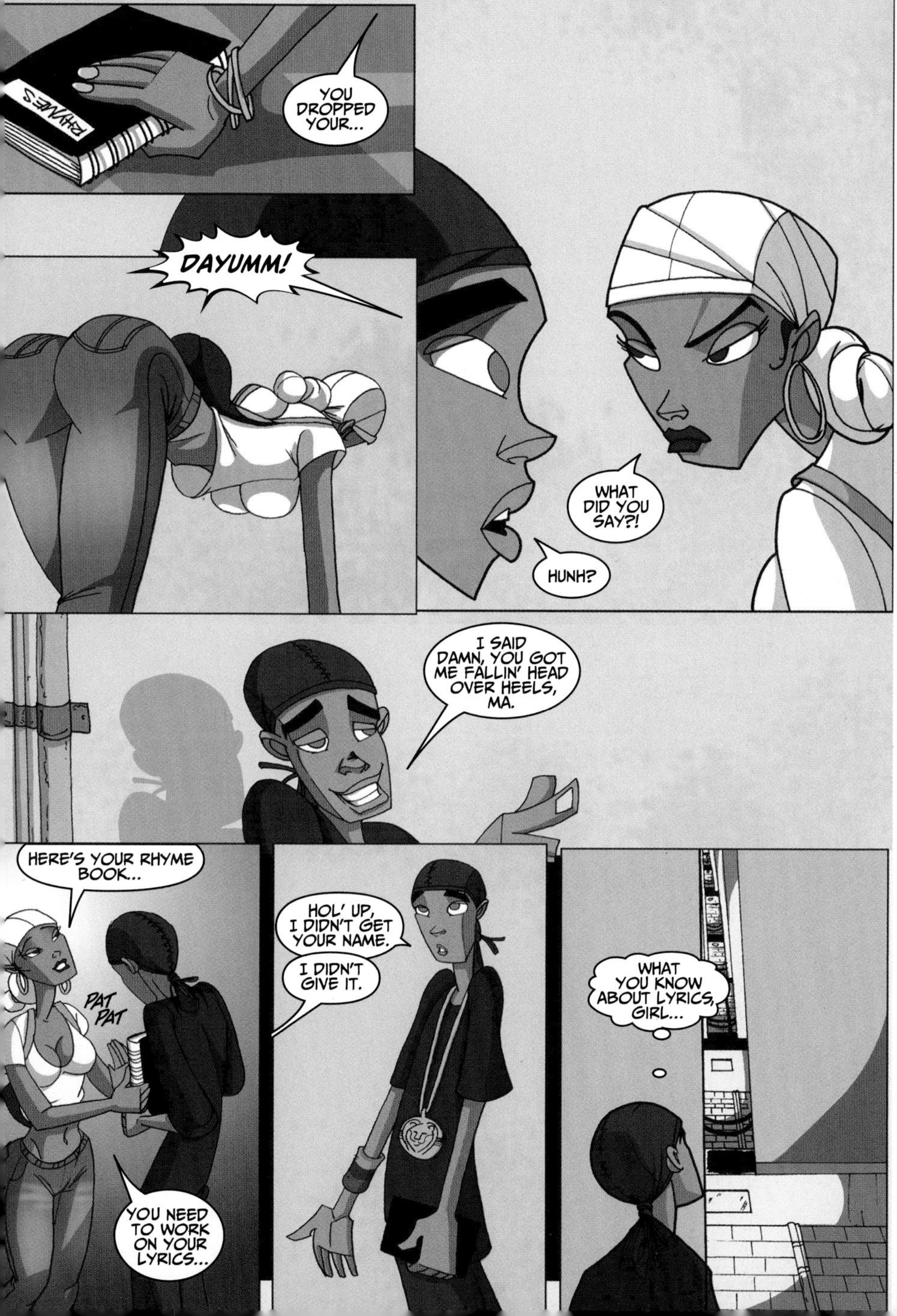
RHYMES
YOU DROPPED YOUR...
DAYUMM!
WHAT DID YOU SAY?!
HUNH?
I SAID DAMN, YOU GOT ME FALLIN' HEAD OVER HEELS, MA.
HERE'S YOUR RHYME BOOK...
PAT PAT
YOU NEED TO WORK ON YOUR LYRICS...
HOL' UP, I DIDN'T GET YOUR NAME.
I DIDN'T GIVE IT.
WHAT YOU KNOW ABOUT LYRICS, GIRL...

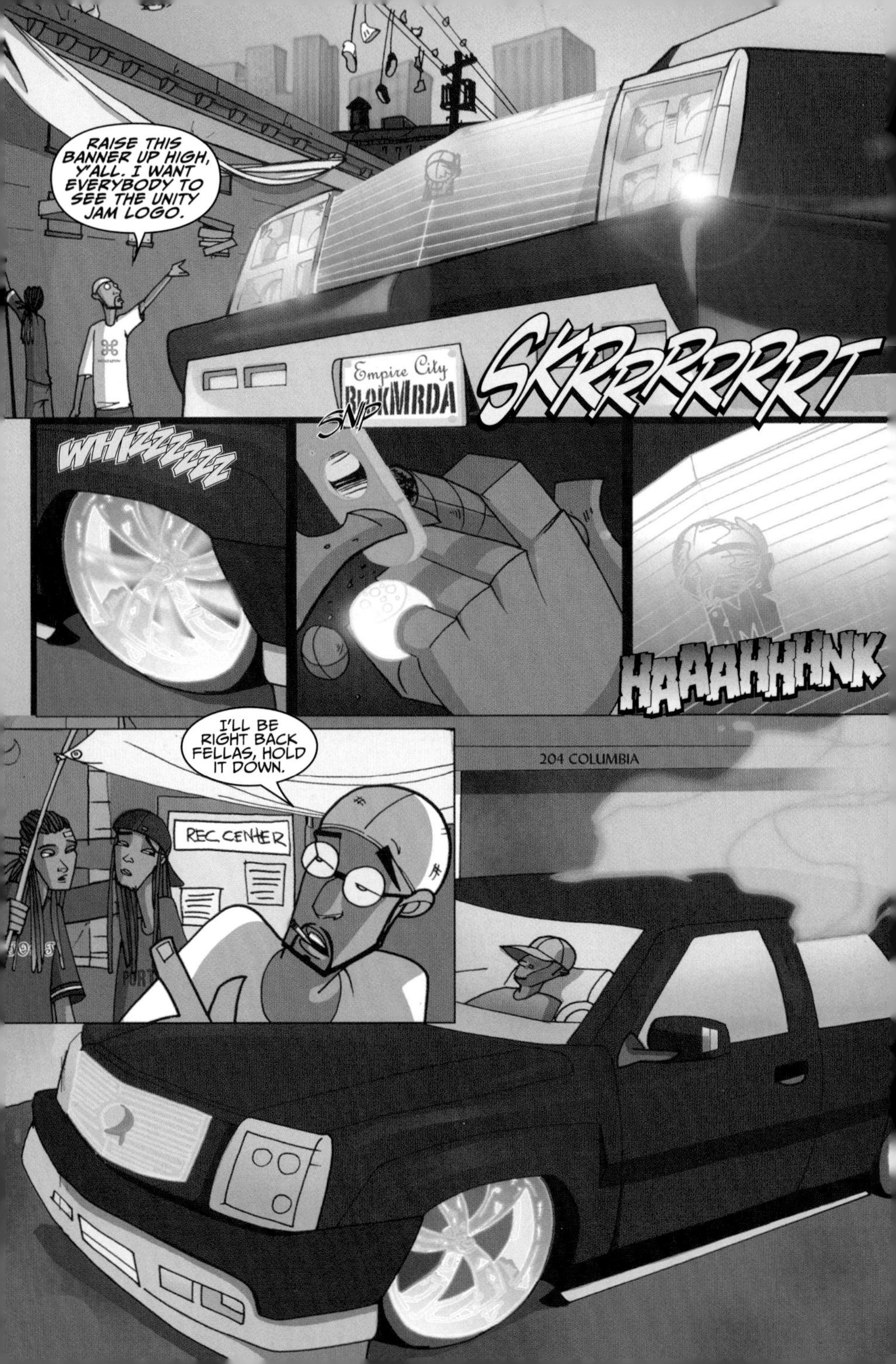
RAISE THIS BANNER UP HIGH, Y'ALL. I WANT EVERYBODY TO SEE THE UNITY JAM LOGO.
Empire City
BLOKMRDA
SKRRRRRRRT
SNIP
WHIZZZZZZZ
HAAAHHHNK
I'LL BE RIGHT BACK FELLAS, HOLD IT DOWN.
204 COLUMBIA
REC. CENTER

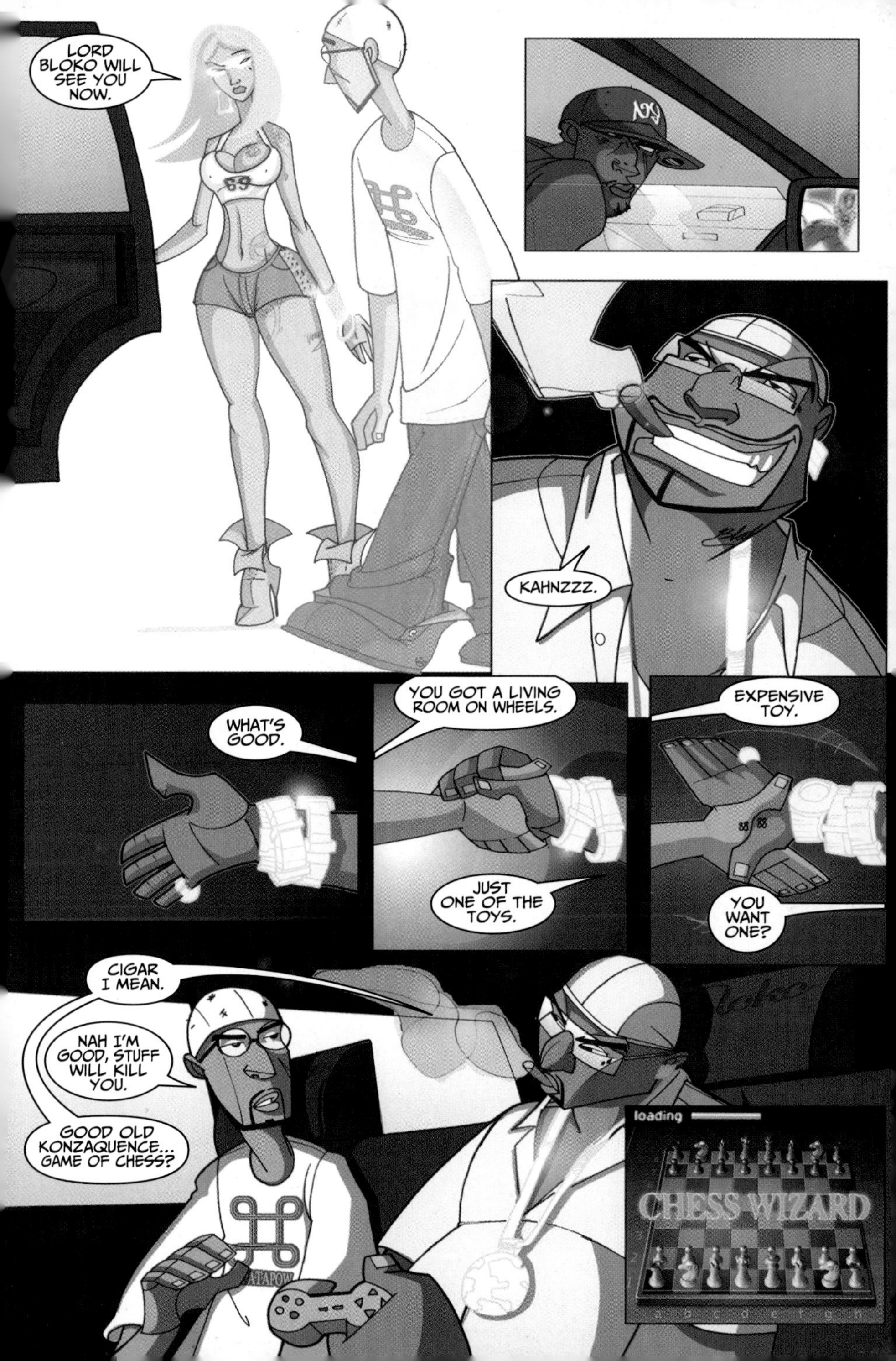
LORD BLOKO WILL SEE YOU NOW.
KAHNZZZ.
WHAT'S GOOD.
YOU GOT A LIVING ROOM ON WHEELS.
JUST ONE OF THE TOYS.
EXPENSIVE TOY.
YOU WANT ONE?
CIGAR I MEAN.
NAH I'M GOOD, STUFF WILL KILL YOU.
GOOD OLD KONZAQUENCE... GAME OF CHESS?
loading
CHESS WIZARD

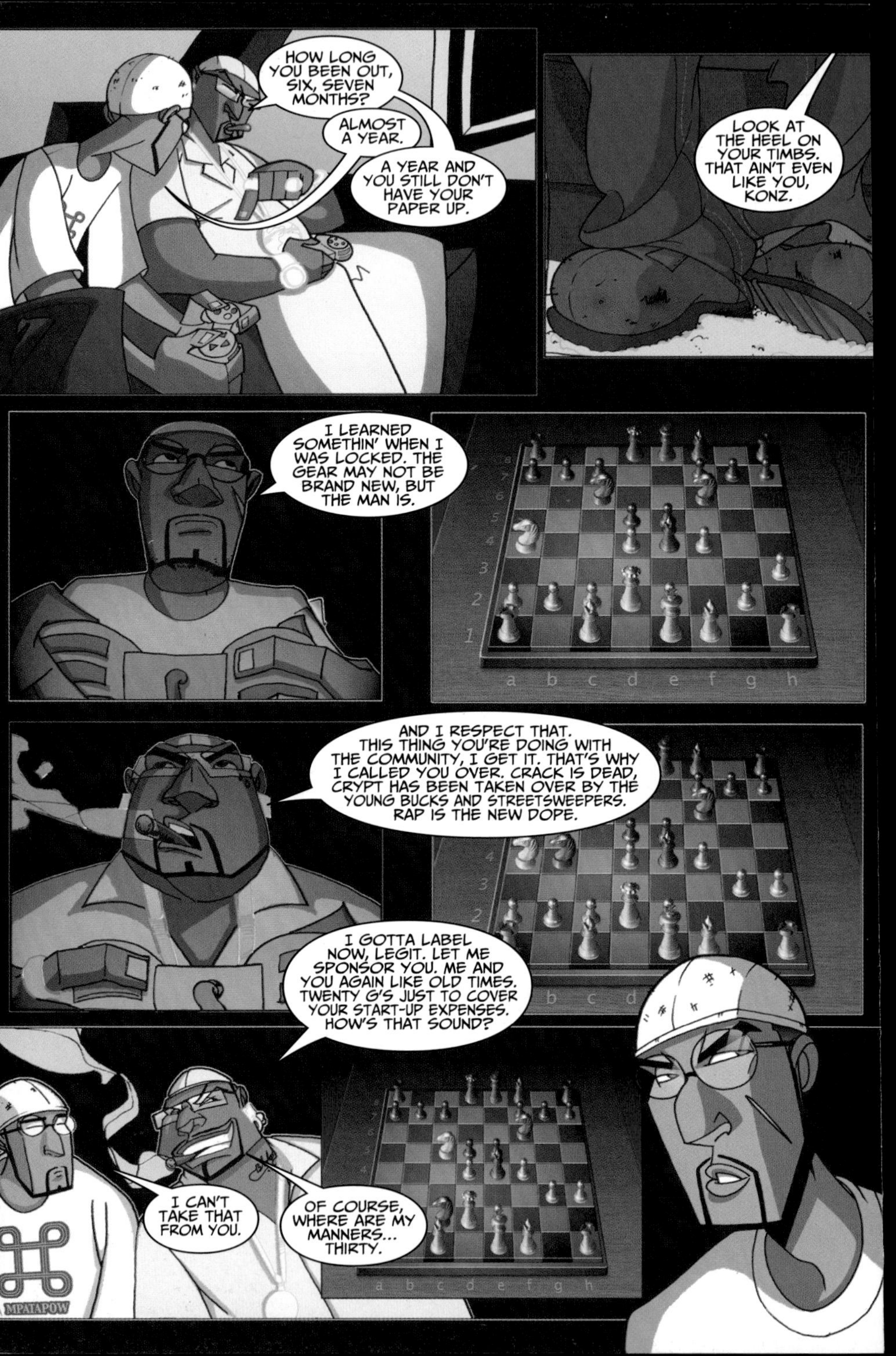
HOW LONG YOU BEEN OUT, SIX, SEVEN MONTHS?
ALMOST A YEAR.
A YEAR AND YOU STILL DON'T HAVE YOUR PAPER UP.
LOOK AT THE HEEL ON YOUR TIMBS. THAT AIN'T EVEN LIKE YOU, KONZ.
I LEARNED SOMETHIN' WHEN I WAS LOCKED. THE GEAR MAY NOT BE BRAND NEW, BUT THE MAN IS.
AND I RESPECT THAT. THIS THING YOU'RE DOING WITH THE COMMUNITY, I GET IT. THAT'S WHY I CALLED YOU OVER. CRACK IS DEAD, CRYPT HAS BEEN TAKEN OVER BY THE YOUNG BUCKS AND STREETSWEEPERS. RAP IS THE NEW DOPE.
I GOTTA LABEL NOW, LEGIT. LET ME SPONSOR YOU. ME AND YOU AGAIN LIKE OLD TIMES. TWENTY G'S JUST TO COVER YOUR START-UP EXPENSES. HOW'S THAT SOUND?
I CAN'T TAKE THAT FROM YOU.
OF COURSE, WHERE ARE MY MANNERS... THIRTY.
MPATAPOW

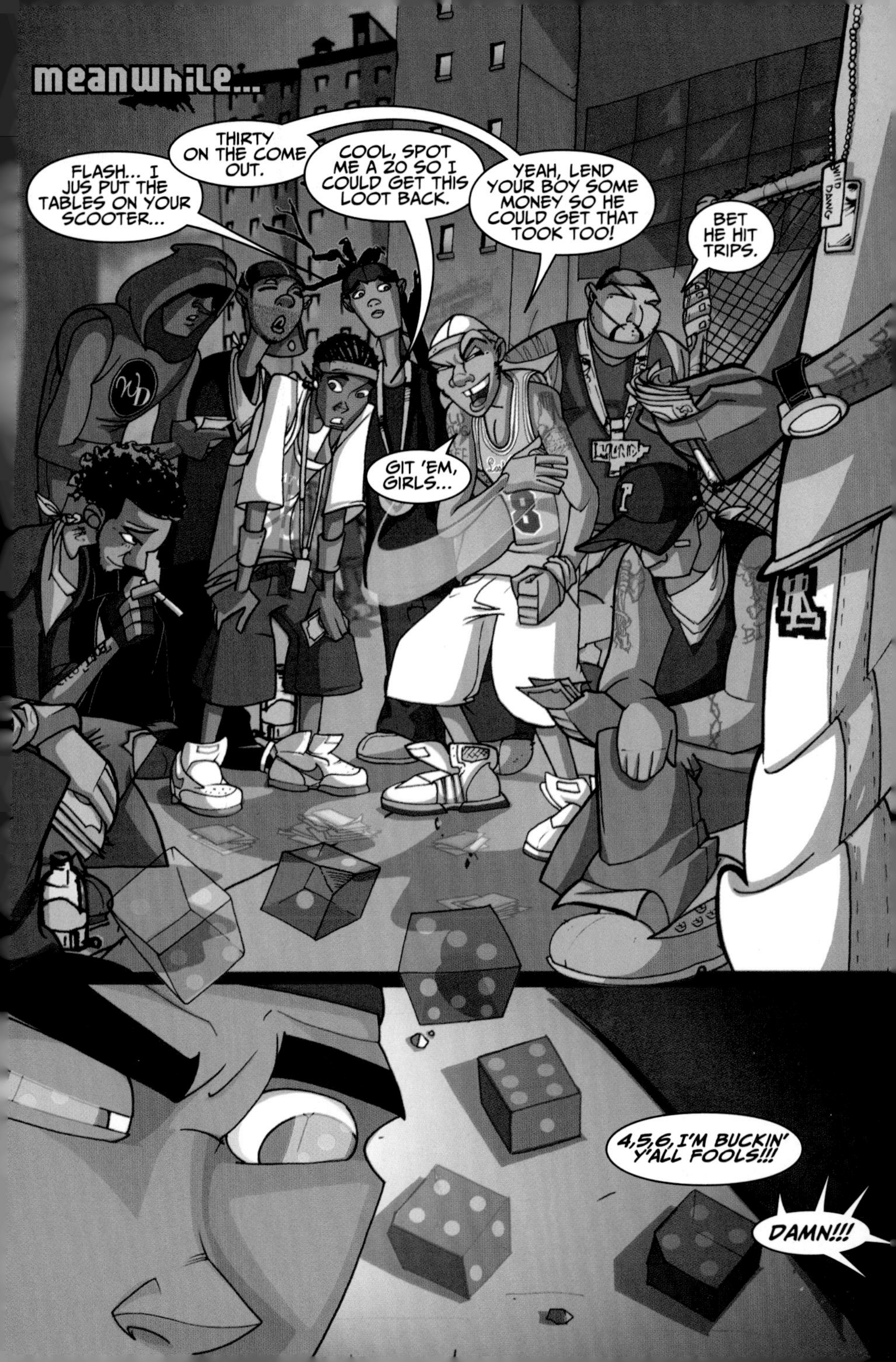
meanwhile...
FLASH... I JUS PUT THE TABLES ON YOUR SCOOTER...
THIRTY ON THE COME OUT.
COOL, SPOT ME A 20 SO I COULD GET THIS LOOT BACK.
YEAH, LEND YOUR BOY SOME MONEY SO HE COULD GET THAT TOOK TOO!
BET HE HIT TRIPS.
GIT 'EM, GIRLS...
4,5,6, I'M BUCKIN' Y'ALL FOOLS!!!
DAMN!!!

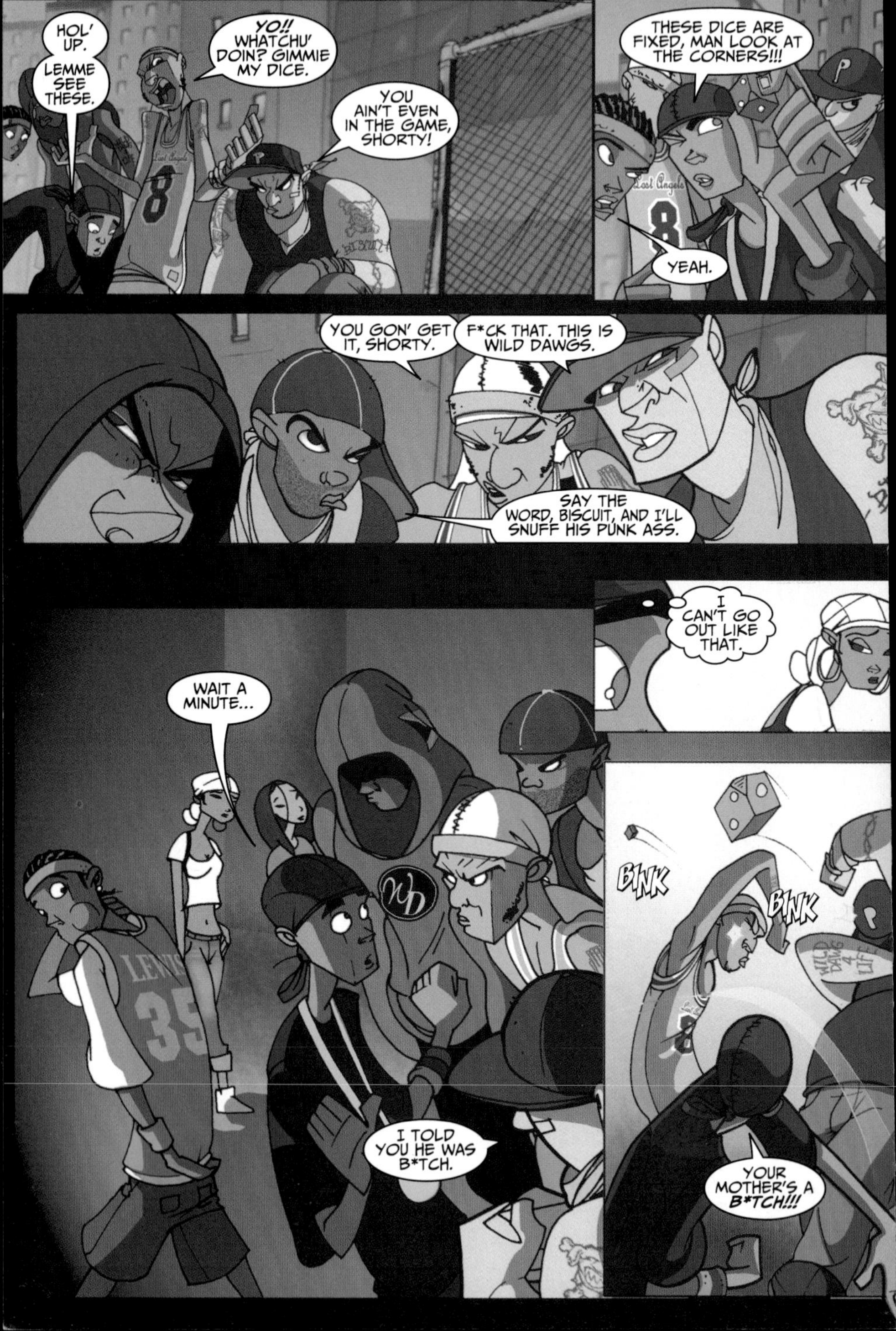

HOL' UP.
LEMME SEE THESE.
YO!! WHATCHU' DOIN? GIMMIE MY DICE.
YOU AIN'T EVEN IN THE GAME, SHORTY!
THESE DICE ARE FIXED, MAN LOOK AT THE CORNERS!!!
YEAH.
YOU GON' GET IT, SHORTY.
F*CK THAT. THIS IS WILD DAWGS.
SAY THE WORD, BISCUIT, AND I'LL SNUFF HIS PUNK ASS.
I CAN'T GO OUT LIKE THAT.
WAIT A MINUTE...
I TOLD YOU HE WAS B*TCH.
BINK
BINK
YOUR MOTHER'S A B*TCH!!!

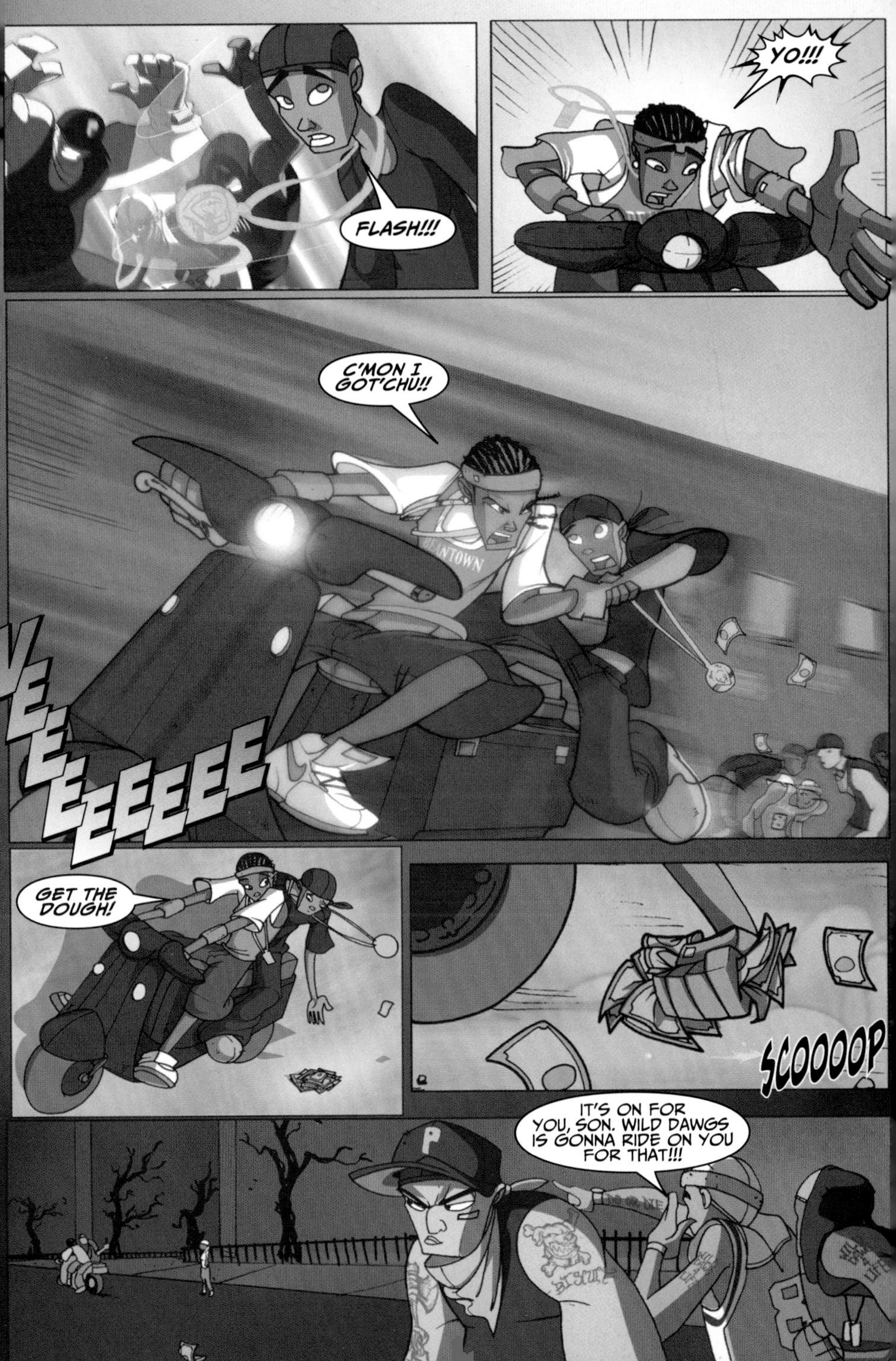
FLASH!!!
YO!!!
C'MON I GOT'CHU!!
VEEEEEEEEE
GET THE DOUGH!
SCOOOOP
IT'S ON FOR YOU, SON. WILD DAWGS IS GONNA RIDE ON YOU FOR THAT!!!

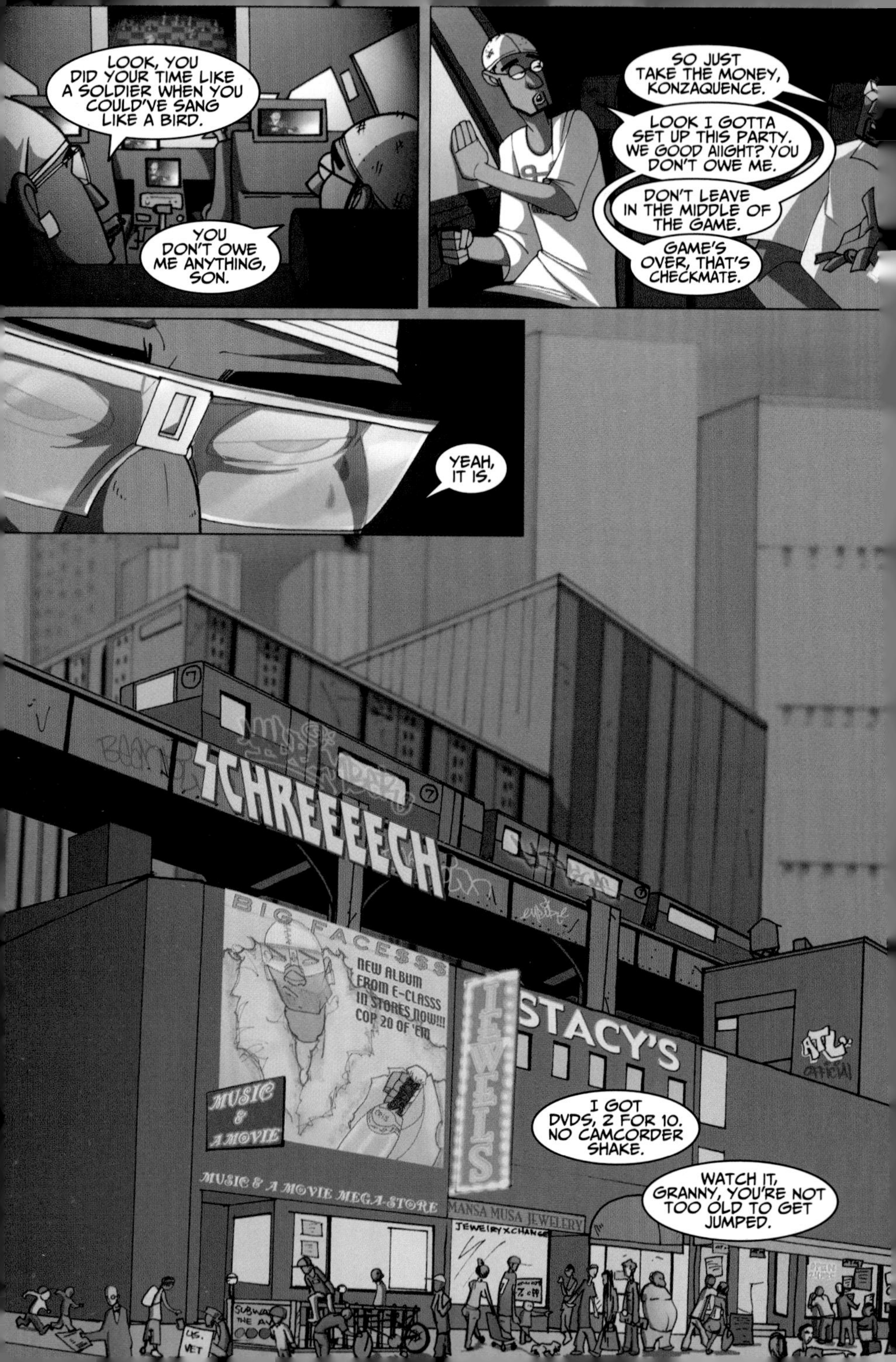

LOOK, YOU DID YOUR TIME LIKE A SOLDIER WHEN YOU COULD'VE SANG LIKE A BIRD.
YOU DON'T OWE ME ANYTHING, SON.
SO JUST TAKE THE MONEY, KONZAQUENCE.
LOOK I GOTTA SET UP THIS PARTY. WE GOOD AIIGHT? YOU DON'T OWE ME.
DON'T LEAVE IN THE MIDDLE OF THE GAME.
GAME'S OVER, THAT'S CHECKMATE.
YEAH, IT IS.
SCHREEEECH
BIG FACE$$$
NEW ALBUM FROM E-CLASSS IN STORES NOW!!! COP 20 OF 'EM
MUSIC & A MOVIE
MUSIC & A MOVIE MEGA-STORE
JEWELS
STACY'S
MANSA MUSA JEWELERY
JEWELRY XCHANGE
I GOT DVDS, 2 FOR 10. NO CAMCORDER SHAKE.
WATCH IT, GRANNY, YOU'RE NOT TOO OLD TO GET JUMPED.
U.S. VET

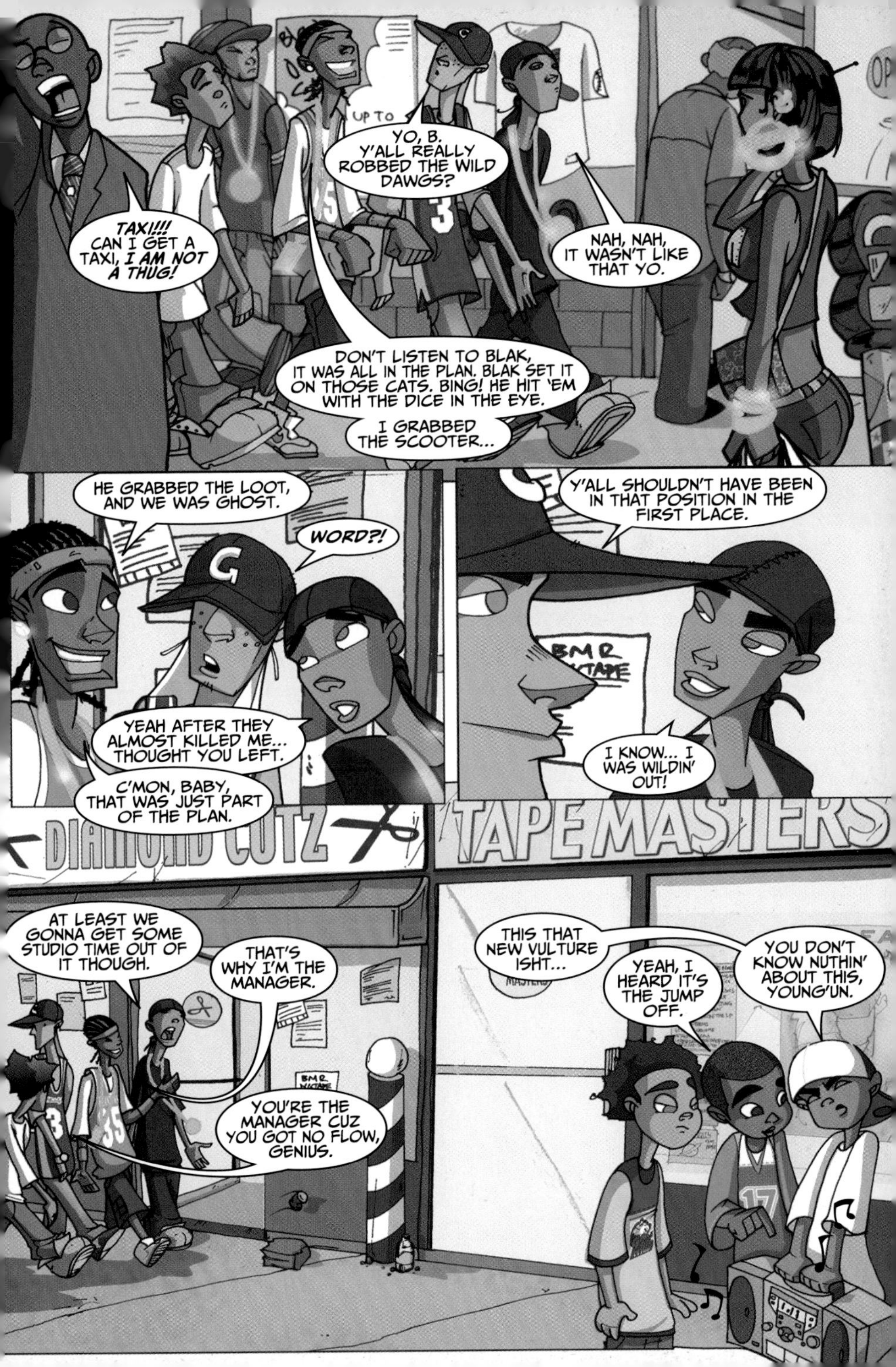
TAXI!!! CAN I GET A TAXI, I AM NOT A THUG!
UP TO
YO, B. Y'ALL REALLY ROBBED THE WILD DAWGS?
NAH, NAH, IT WASN'T LIKE THAT YO.
DON'T LISTEN TO BLAK, IT WAS ALL IN THE PLAN. BLAK SET IT ON THOSE CATS. BING! HE HIT 'EM WITH THE DICE IN THE EYE.
I GRABBED THE SCOOTER...
HE GRABBED THE LOOT, AND WE WAS GHOST.
WORD?!
YEAH AFTER THEY ALMOST KILLED ME... THOUGHT YOU LEFT.
C'MON, BABY, THAT WAS JUST PART OF THE PLAN.
Y'ALL SHOULDN'T HAVE BEEN IN THAT POSITION IN THE FIRST PLACE.
I KNOW... I WAS WILDIN' OUT!
DIAMOND CUTZ
TAPE MASTERS
AT LEAST WE GONNA GET SOME STUDIO TIME OUT OF IT THOUGH.
THAT'S WHY I'M THE MANAGER.
YOU'RE THE MANAGER CUZ YOU GOT NO FLOW, GENIUS.
THIS THAT NEW VULTURE ISHT...
YEAH, I HEARD IT'S THE JUMP OFF.
YOU DON'T KNOW NUTHIN' ABOUT THIS, YOUNG'UN.

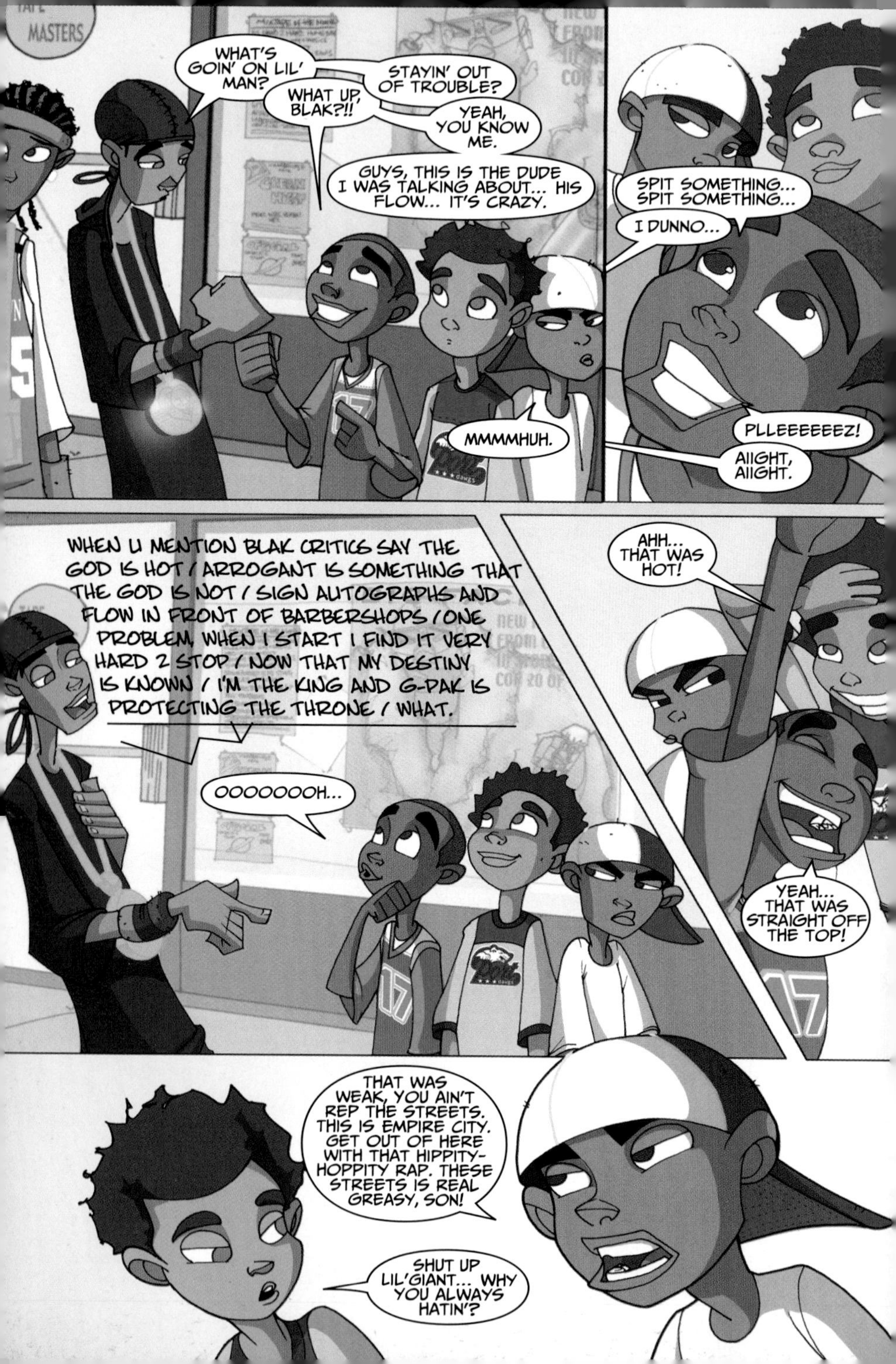

TAPE MASTERS
WHAT'S GOIN' ON LIL' MAN?
STAYIN' OUT OF TROUBLE?
WHAT UP, BLAK?!!
YEAH, YOU KNOW ME.
GUYS, THIS IS THE DUDE I WAS TALKING ABOUT... HIS FLOW... IT'S CRAZY.
MMMMHUH.
SPIT SOMETHING... SPIT SOMETHING...
I DUNNO...
PLLEEEEEEZ!
AIIGHT, AIIGHT.
WHEN U MENTION BLAK CRITICS SAY THE GOD IS HOT / ARROGANT IS SOMETHING THAT THE GOD IS NOT / SIGN AUTOGRAPHS AND FLOW IN FRONT OF BARBERSHOPS / ONE PROBLEM, WHEN I START I FIND IT VERY HARD 2 STOP / NOW THAT MY DESTINY IS KNOWN / I'M THE KING AND G-PAK IS PROTECTING THE THRONE / WHAT.
OOOOOOOH...
AHH... THAT WAS HOT!
YEAH... THAT WAS STRAIGHT OFF THE TOP!
THAT WAS WEAK, YOU AIN'T REP THE STREETS. THIS IS EMPIRE CITY. GET OUT OF HERE WITH THAT HIPPITY-HOPPITY RAP. THESE STREETS IS REAL GREASY, SON!
SHUT UP LIL'GIANT... WHY YOU ALWAYS HATIN'?

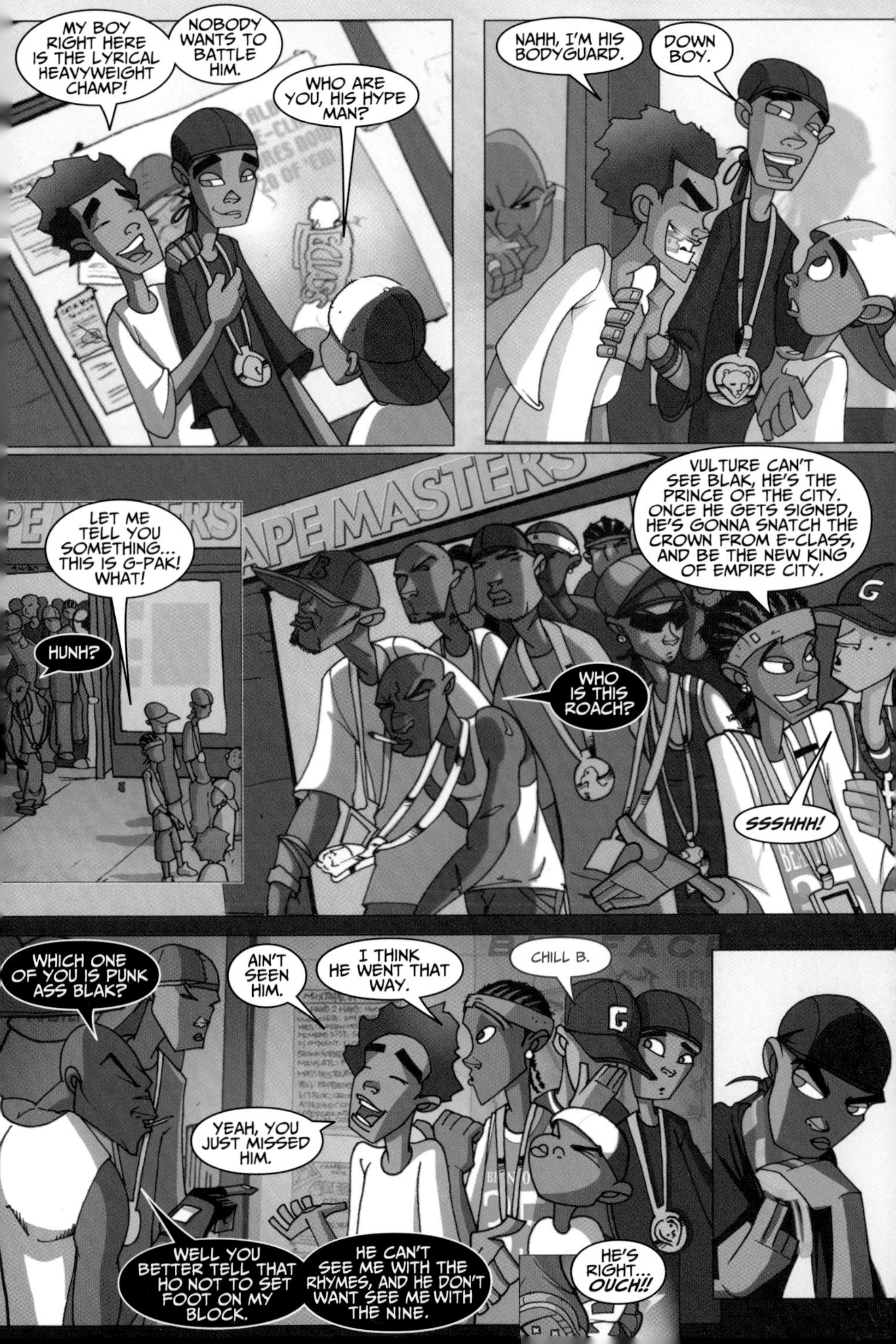
MY BOY RIGHT HERE IS THE LYRICAL HEAVYWEIGHT CHAMP!
NOBODY WANTS TO BATTLE HIM.
WHO ARE YOU, HIS HYPE MAN?
NAHH, I'M HIS BODYGUARD.
DOWN BOY.
APE MASTERS
LET ME TELL YOU SOMETHING... THIS IS G-PAK! WHAT!
HUNH?
VULTURE CAN'T SEE BLAK, HE'S THE PRINCE OF THE CITY. ONCE HE GETS SIGNED, HE'S GONNA SNATCH THE CROWN FROM E-CLASS, AND BE THE NEW KING OF EMPIRE CITY.
WHO IS THIS ROACH?
SSSHHH!
WHICH ONE OF YOU IS PUNK ASS BLAK?
AIN'T SEEN HIM.
I THINK HE WENT THAT WAY.
CHILL B.
YEAH, YOU JUST MISSED HIM.
WELL YOU BETTER TELL THAT HO NOT TO SET FOOT ON MY BLOCK.
HE CAN'T SEE ME WITH THE RHYMES, AND HE DON'T WANT SEE ME WITH THE NINE.
HE'S RIGHT... OUCH!!

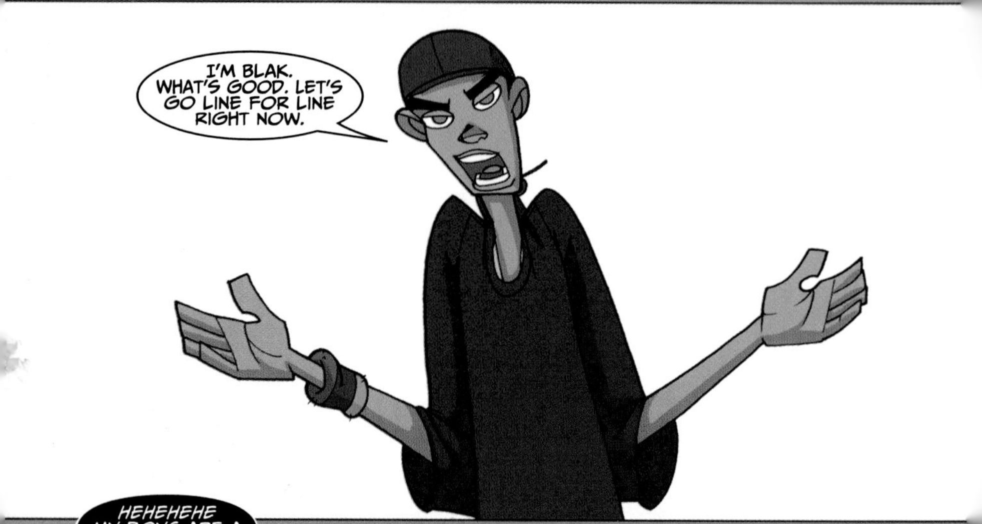
I'M BLAK. WHAT'S GOOD. LET'S GO LINE FOR LINE RIGHT NOW.

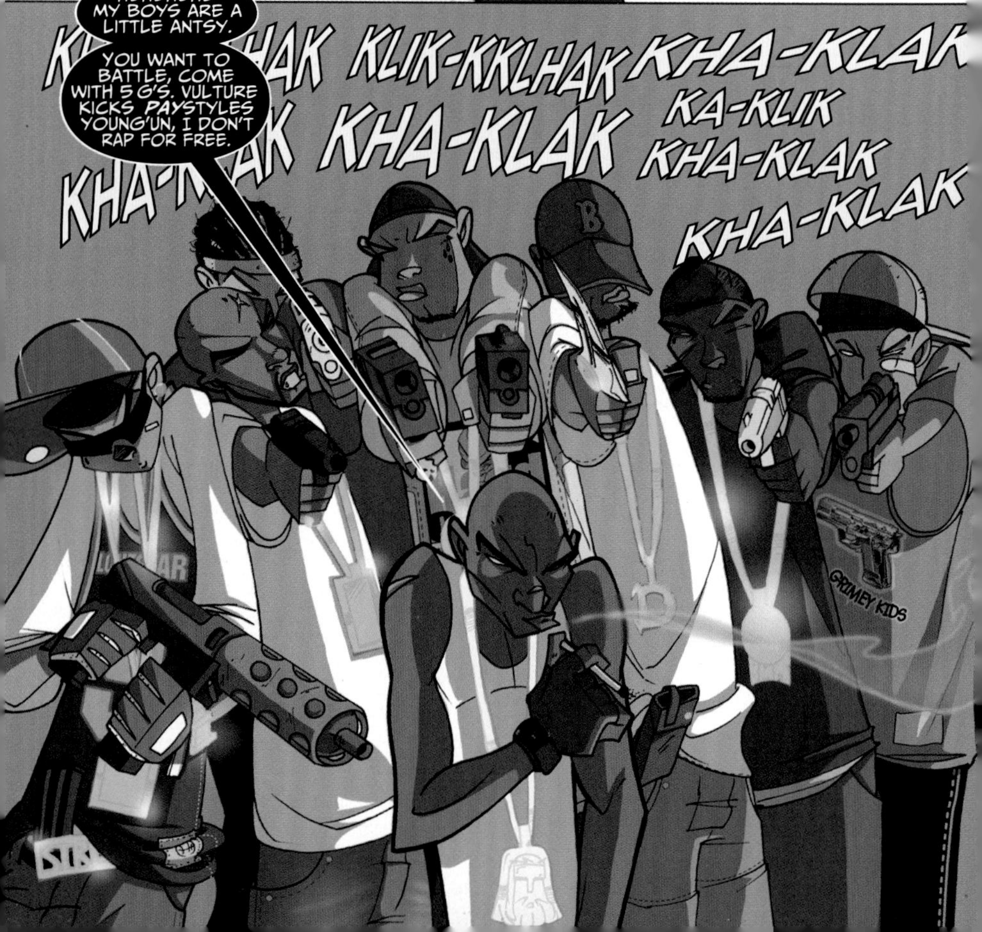
HEHEHEHE MY BOYS ARE A LITTLE ANTSY.
YOU WANT TO BATTLE, COME WITH 5 G'S. VULTURE KICKS *PAY*STYLES YOUNG'UN, I DON'T RAP FOR FREE.
KLIK-KKLHAK
KHA-KLAK
KA-KLIK
KHA-KLAK
KHA-KLAK
KHA-KLAK
GRIMEY KIDS

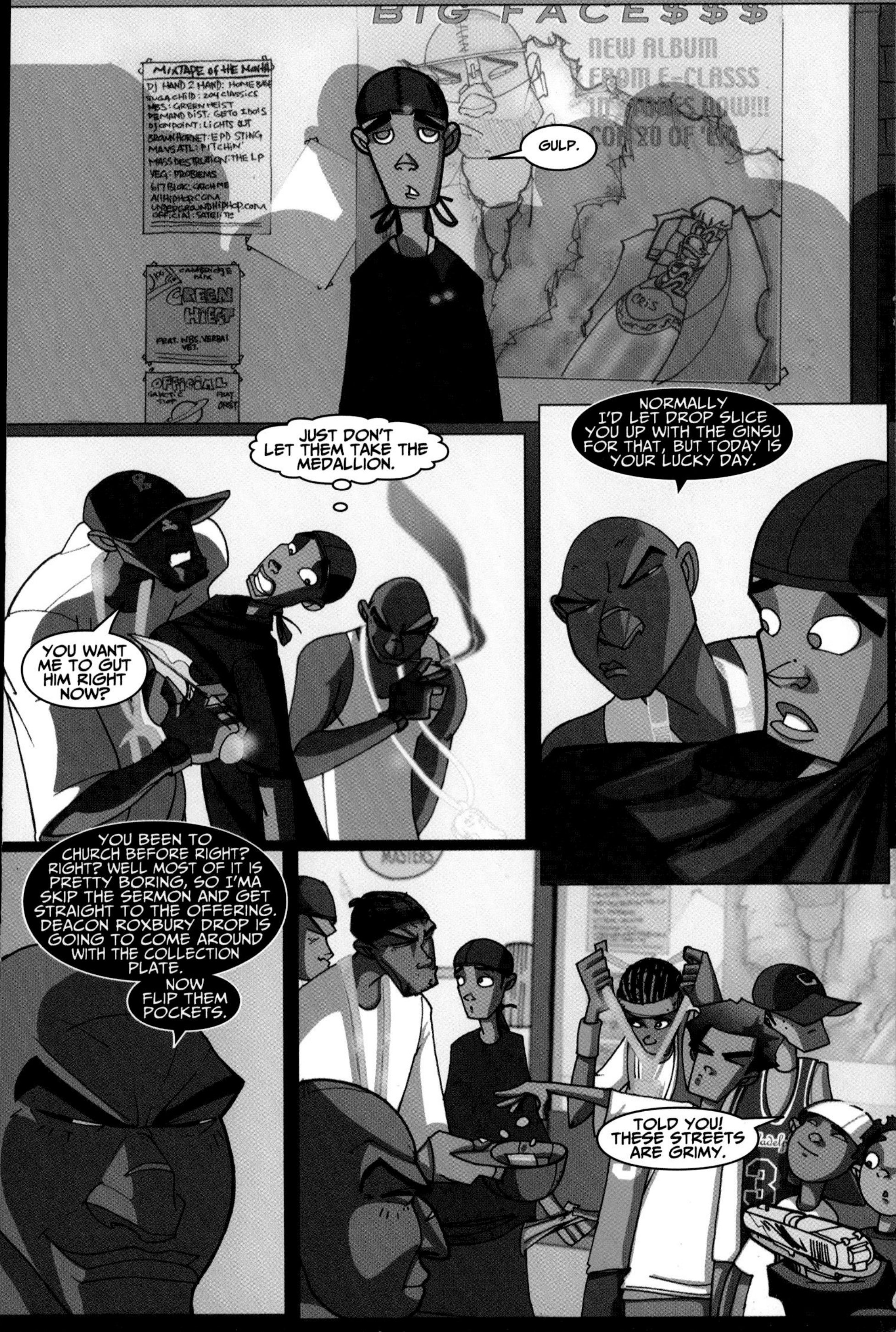

BIG FACE$$$
NEW ALBUM
MIXTAPE of the MONTH
GULP.
JUST DON'T LET THEM TAKE THE MEDALLION.
YOU WANT ME TO GUT HIM RIGHT NOW?
NORMALLY I'D LET DROP SLICE YOU UP WITH THE GINSU FOR THAT, BUT TODAY IS YOUR LUCKY DAY.
YOU BEEN TO CHURCH BEFORE RIGHT? RIGHT? WELL MOST OF IT IS PRETTY BORING, SO I'MA SKIP THE SERMON AND GET STRAIGHT TO THE OFFERING. DEACON ROXBURY DROP IS GOING TO COME AROUND WITH THE COLLECTION PLATE.
NOW FLIP THEM POCKETS.
TOLD YOU! THESE STREETS ARE GRIMY.

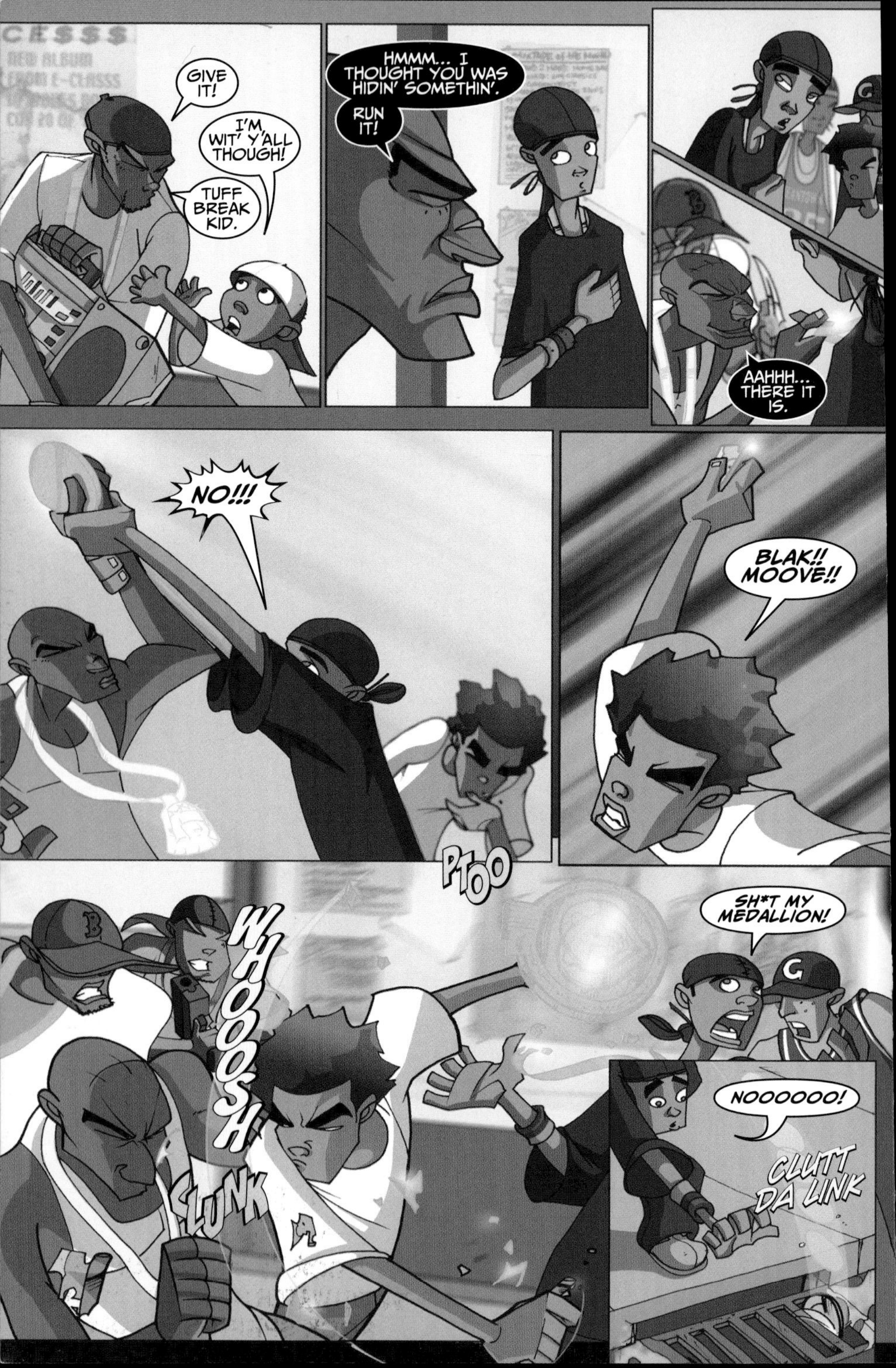
GIVE IT!
I'M WIT' Y'ALL THOUGH!
TUFF BREAK KID.
HMMM... I THOUGHT YOU WAS HIDIN' SOMETHIN'.
RUN IT!
AAHHH... THERE IT IS.
NO!!!
BLAK!! MOOVE!!
PTOO
WHOOOOSH
CLUNK
SH*T MY MEDALLION!
NOOOOOO!
CLUTT DA LINK

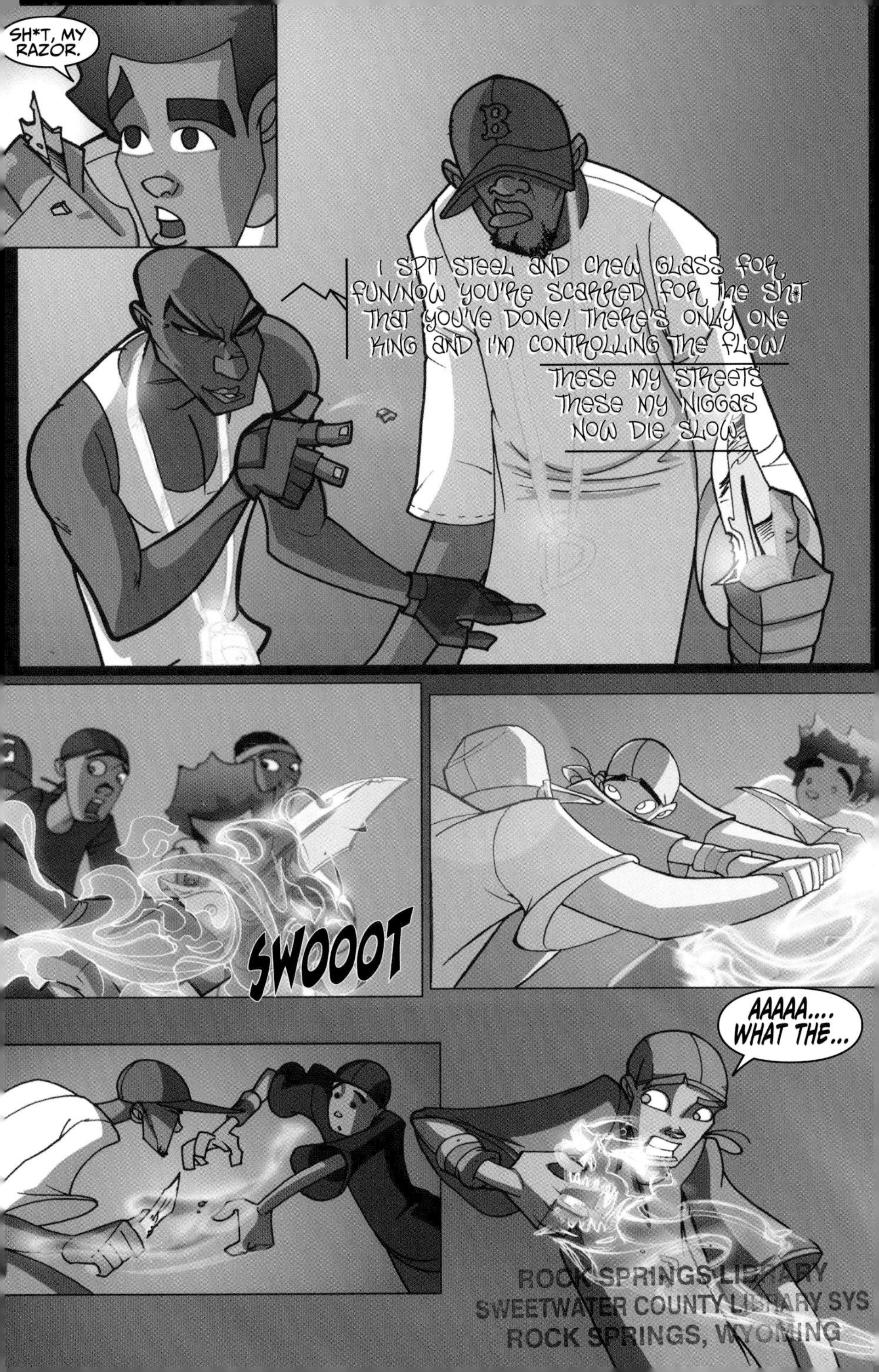
SH*T, MY RAZOR.
I SPIT STEEL AND CHEW GLASS FOR FUN/NOW YOU'RE SCARRED FOR THE SH*T THAT YOU'VE DONE/ THERE'S ONLY ONE KING AND I'M CONTROLLING THE FLOW/
THESE MY STREETS THESE MY NIGGAS NOW DIE SLOW.
SWOOOT
AAAAA.... WHAT THE...

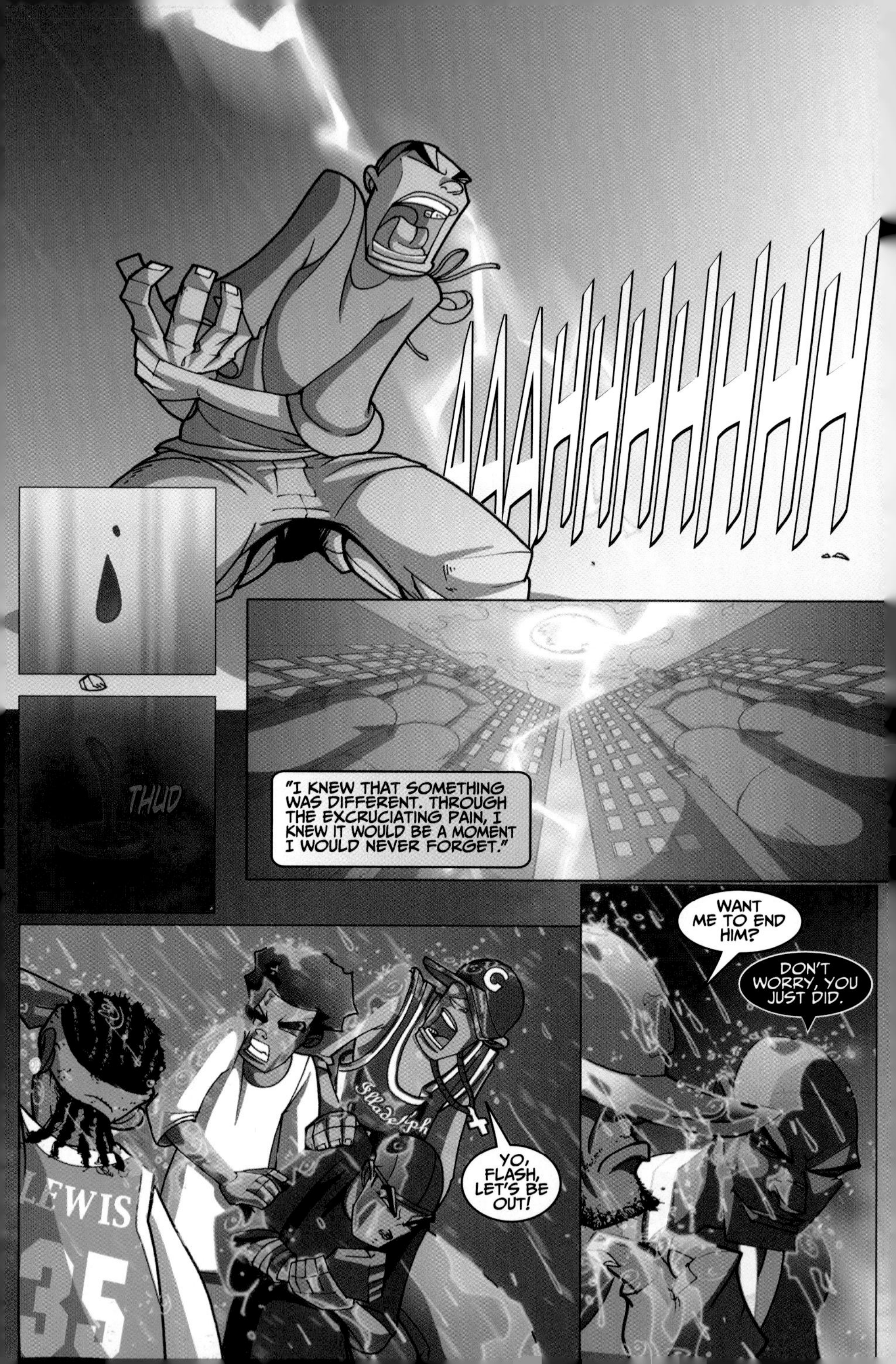

AAAHHHHHHHHHH
THUD
"I KNEW THAT SOMETHING WAS DIFFERENT. THROUGH THE EXCRUCIATING PAIN, I KNEW IT WOULD BE A MOMENT I WOULD NEVER FORGET."
YO, FLASH, LET'S BE OUT!
WANT ME TO END HIM?
DON'T WORRY, YOU JUST DID.

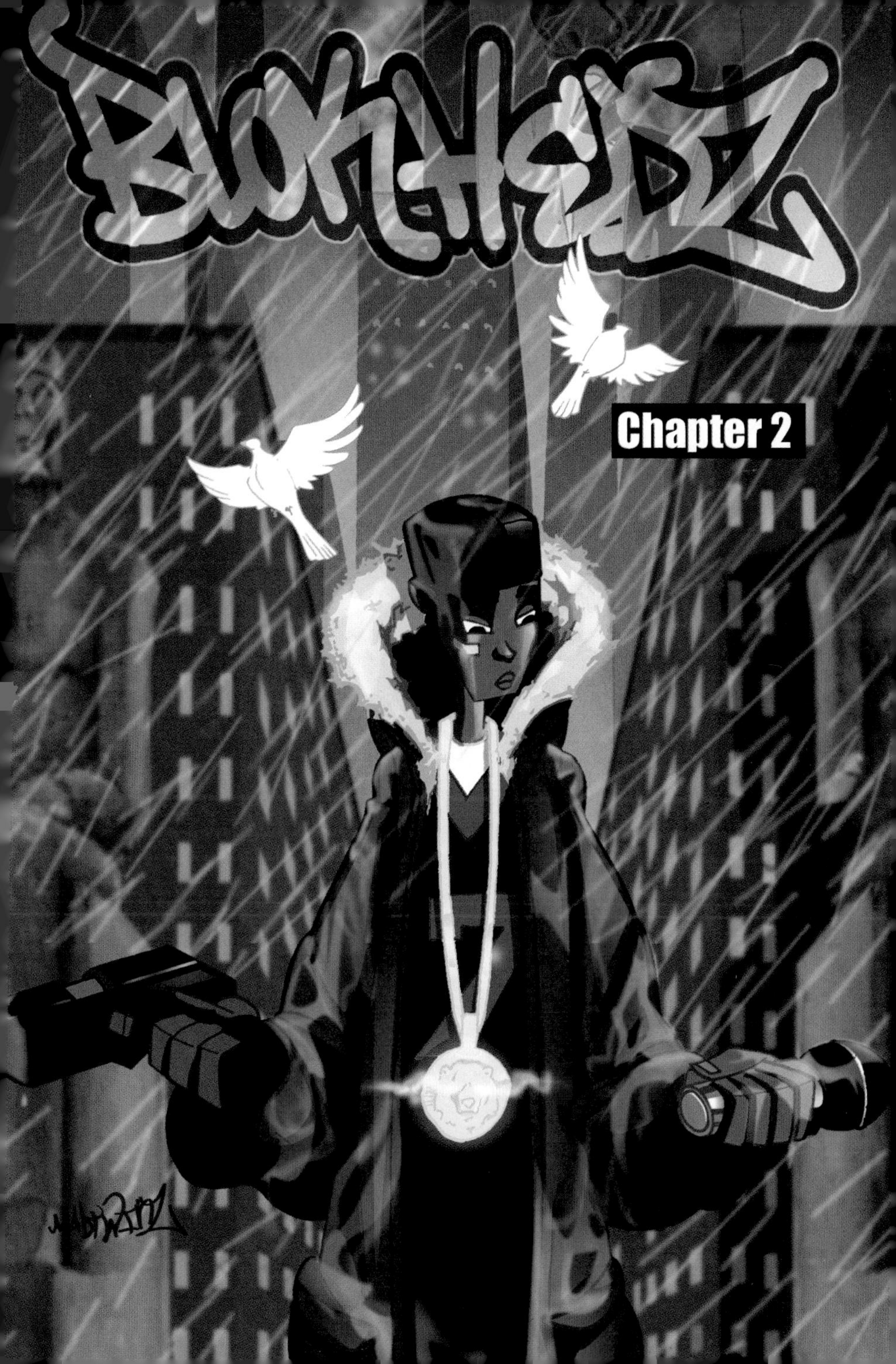
BLOKHEDZ
Chapter 2

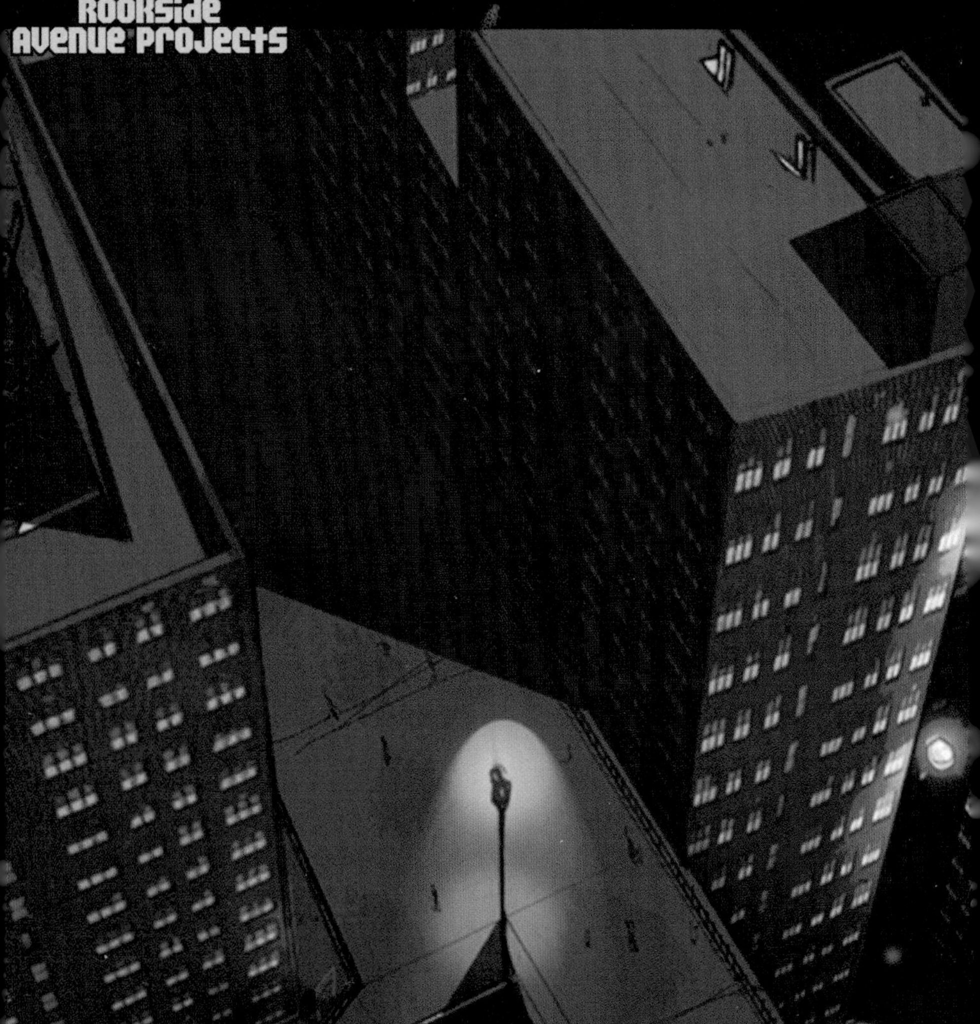
ROOKSIDE
AVENUE PROJECTS

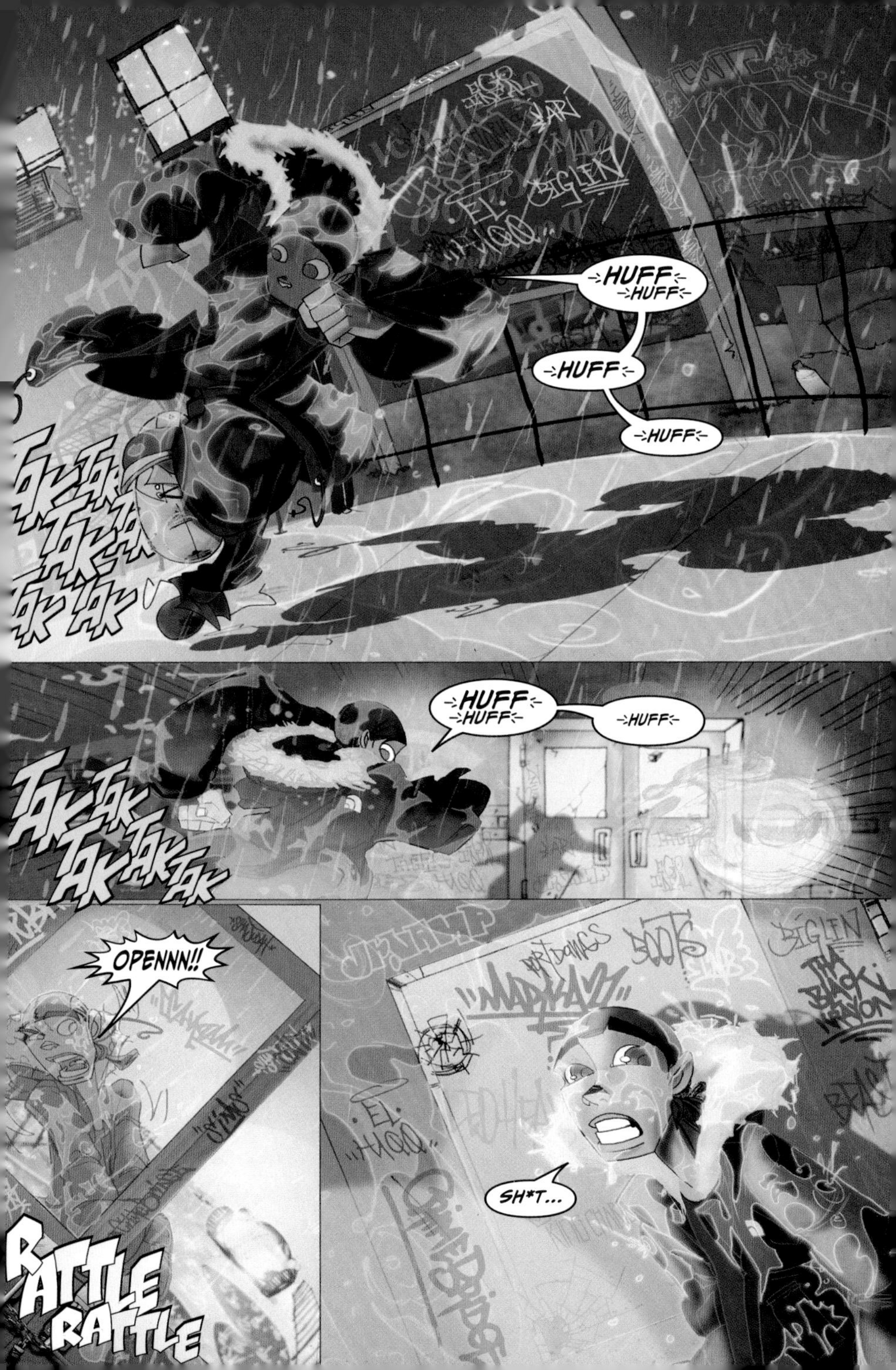
HUFF HUFF
HUFF
HUFF
TAK TAK TAK TAK TAK TAK
HUFF HUFF
HUFF
TAK TAK TAK TAK TAK TAK
OPENNN!!
RATTLE RATTLE
SH*T...

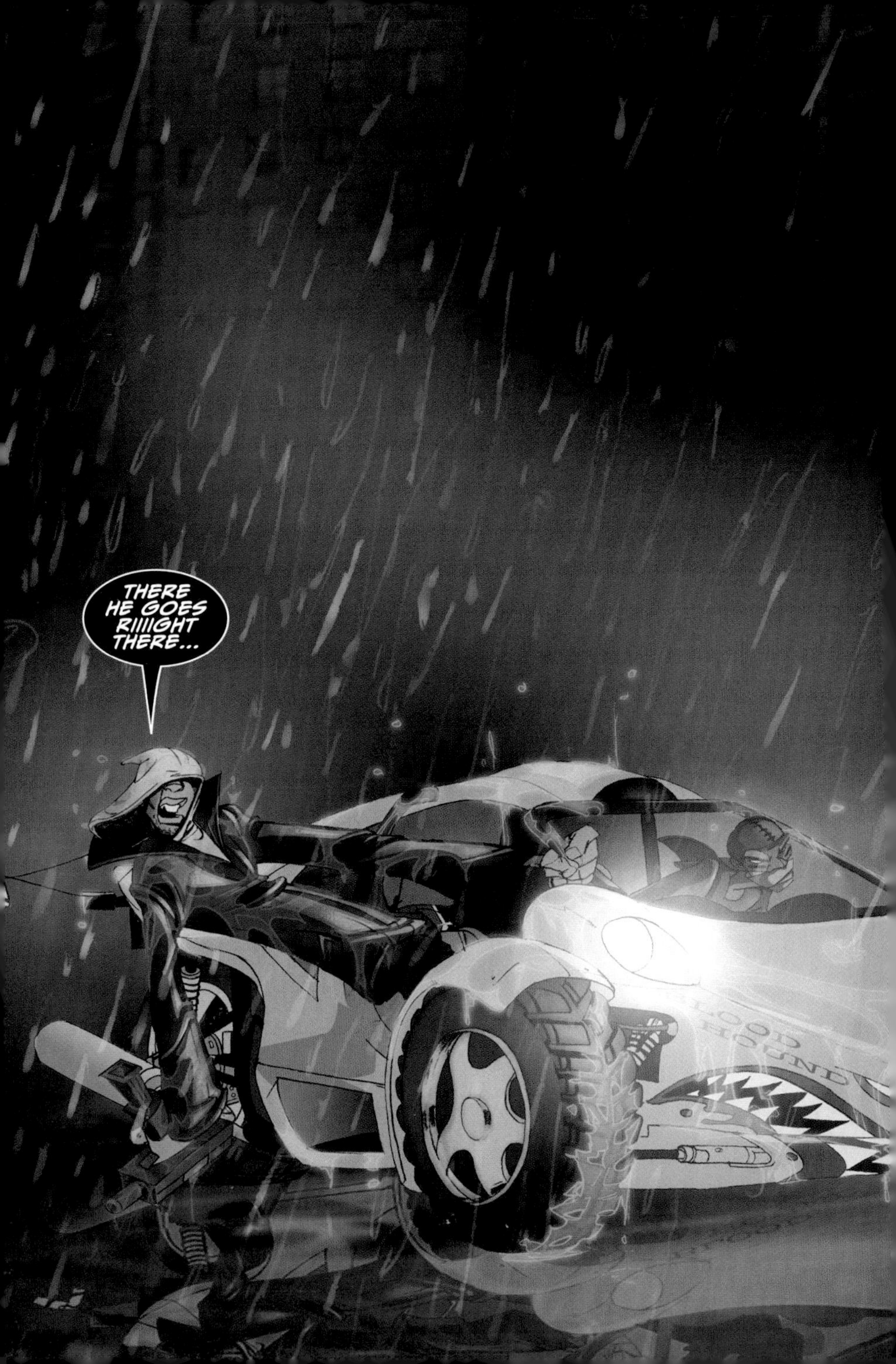
THERE HE GOES RIIIIGHT THERE...

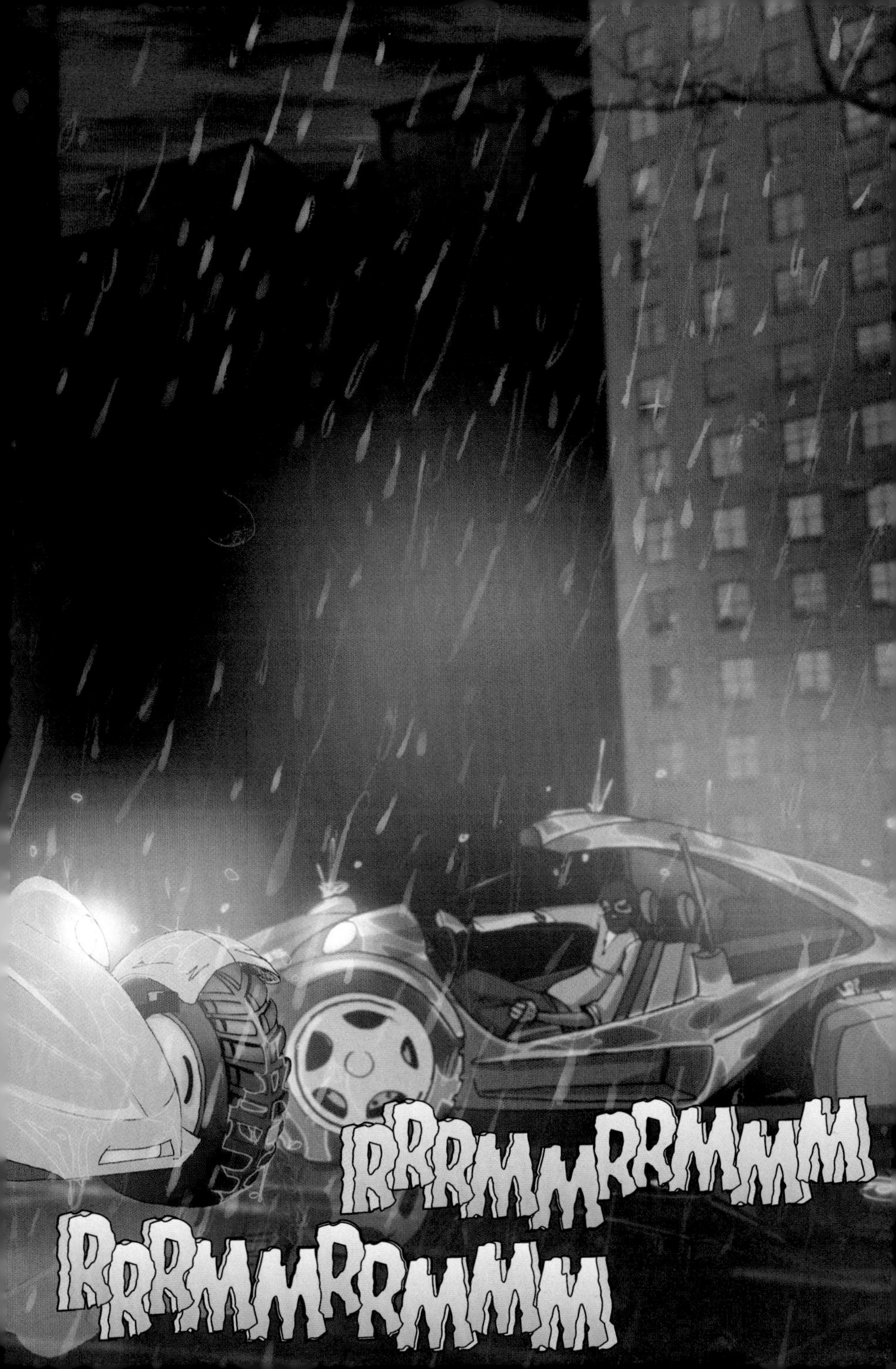
RRRMMMRRRMMMM
RRRMMMRRRMMMM

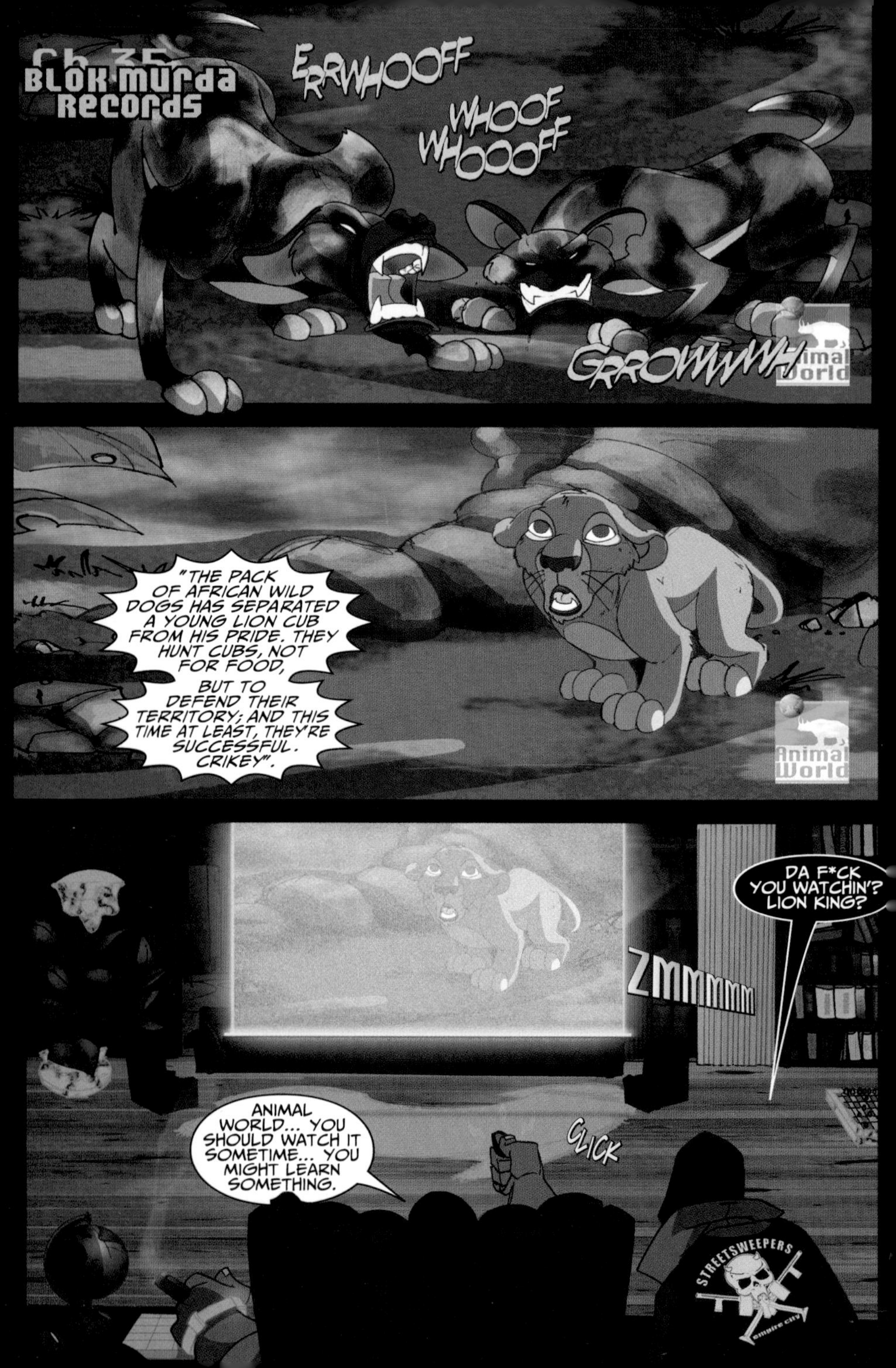
Ch 35
BLOK MURDA RECORDS
ERRWHOOFF
WHOOF WHOOOFF
GRROWWWH
Animal World
"THE PACK OF AFRICAN WILD DOGS HAS SEPARATED A YOUNG LION CUB FROM HIS PRIDE. THEY HUNT CUBS, NOT FOR FOOD,
BUT TO DEFEND THEIR TERRITORY; AND THIS TIME AT LEAST, THEY'RE SUCCESSFUL. CRIKEY".
Animal World
DA F*CK YOU WATCHIN'? LION KING?
ZMMMMMM
ANIMAL WORLD... YOU SHOULD WATCH IT SOMETIME... YOU MIGHT LEARN SOMETHING.
CLICK
STREETSWEEPERS

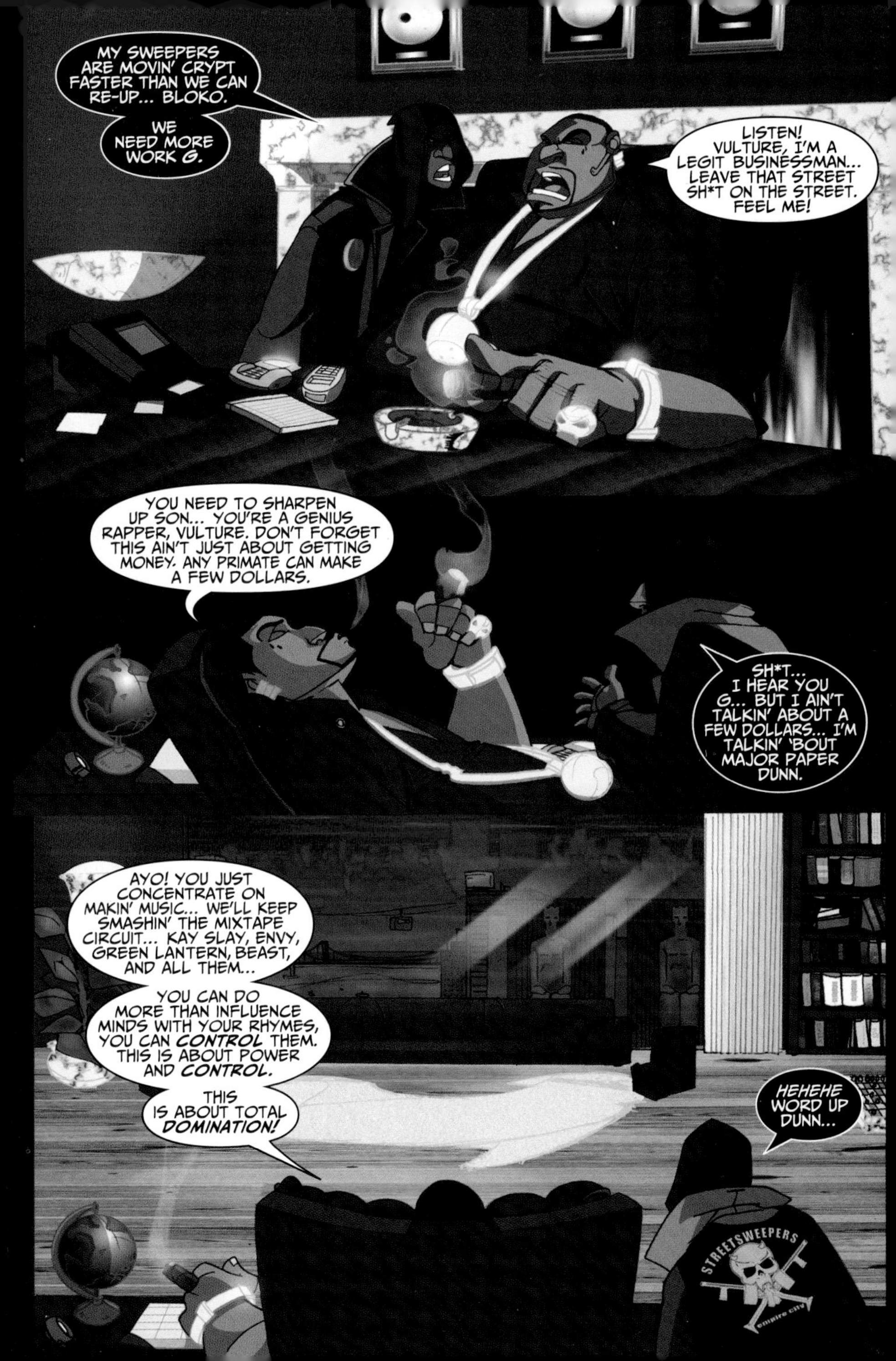
MY SWEEPERS ARE MOVIN' CRYPT FASTER THAN WE CAN RE-UP... BLOKO.
WE NEED MORE WORK G.
LISTEN! VULTURE, I'M A LEGIT BUSINESSMAN... LEAVE THAT STREET SH*T ON THE STREET. FEEL ME!
YOU NEED TO SHARPEN UP SON... YOU'RE A GENIUS RAPPER, VULTURE. DON'T FORGET THIS AIN'T JUST ABOUT GETTING MONEY. ANY PRIMATE CAN MAKE A FEW DOLLARS.
SH*T... I HEAR YOU G... BUT I AIN'T TALKIN' ABOUT A FEW DOLLARS... I'M TALKIN' 'BOUT MAJOR PAPER DUNN.
AYO! YOU JUST CONCENTRATE ON MAKIN' MUSIC... WE'LL KEEP SMASHIN' THE MIXTAPE CIRCUIT... KAY SLAY, ENVY, GREEN LANTERN, BEAST, AND ALL THEM...
YOU CAN DO MORE THAN INFLUENCE MINDS WITH YOUR RHYMES, YOU CAN *CONTROL* THEM. THIS IS ABOUT POWER AND *CONTROL.*
THIS IS ABOUT TOTAL *DOMINATION!*
HEHEHE WORD UP DUNN...
STREETSWEEPERS
empire city

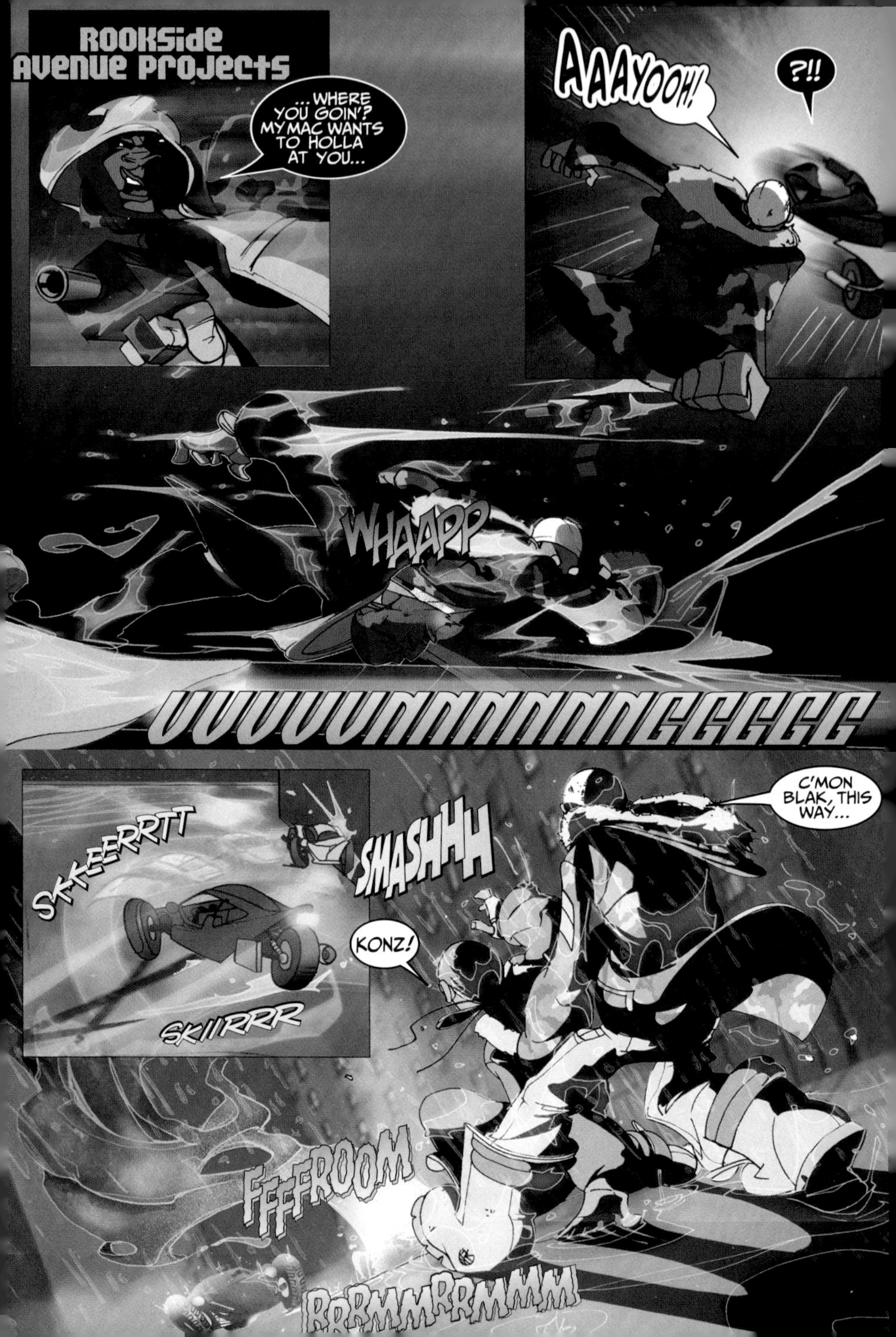

ROOKSIDE AVENUE PROJECTS
...WHERE YOU GOIN'? MY MAC WANTS TO HOLLA AT YOU...
AAAYOOH!
?!!
WHAAPP
VVVVVVNNNNNNNNGGGGG
SKKEERRTT
SMASHHH
SKIIRRR
KONZ!
C'MON BLAK, THIS WAY...
FFFFROOM
RRRMMMRRMMM

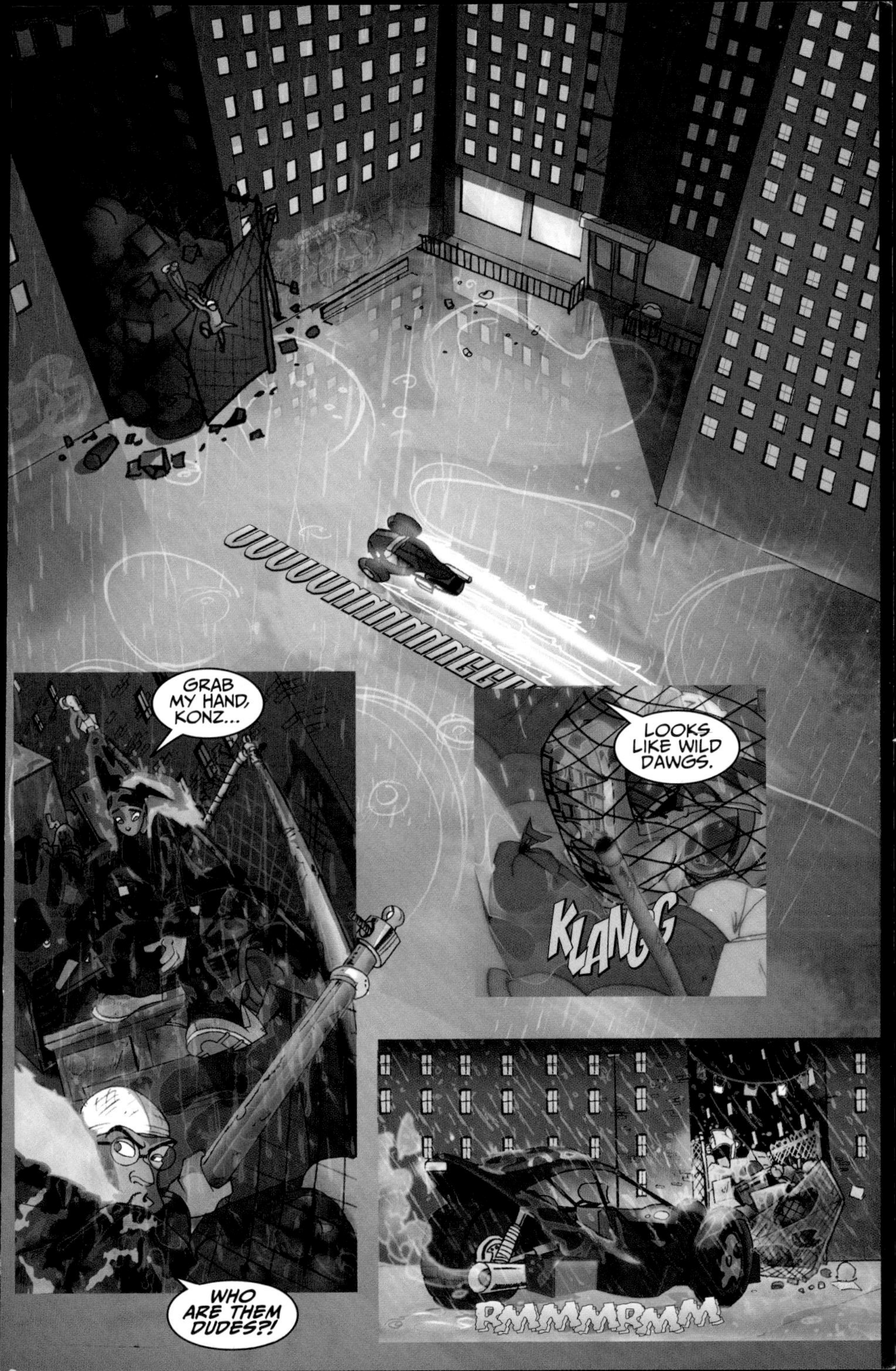
GRAB MY HAND, KONZ...
LOOKS LIKE WILD DAWGS.
KLANGG
WHO ARE THEM DUDES?!
RMMMRMM

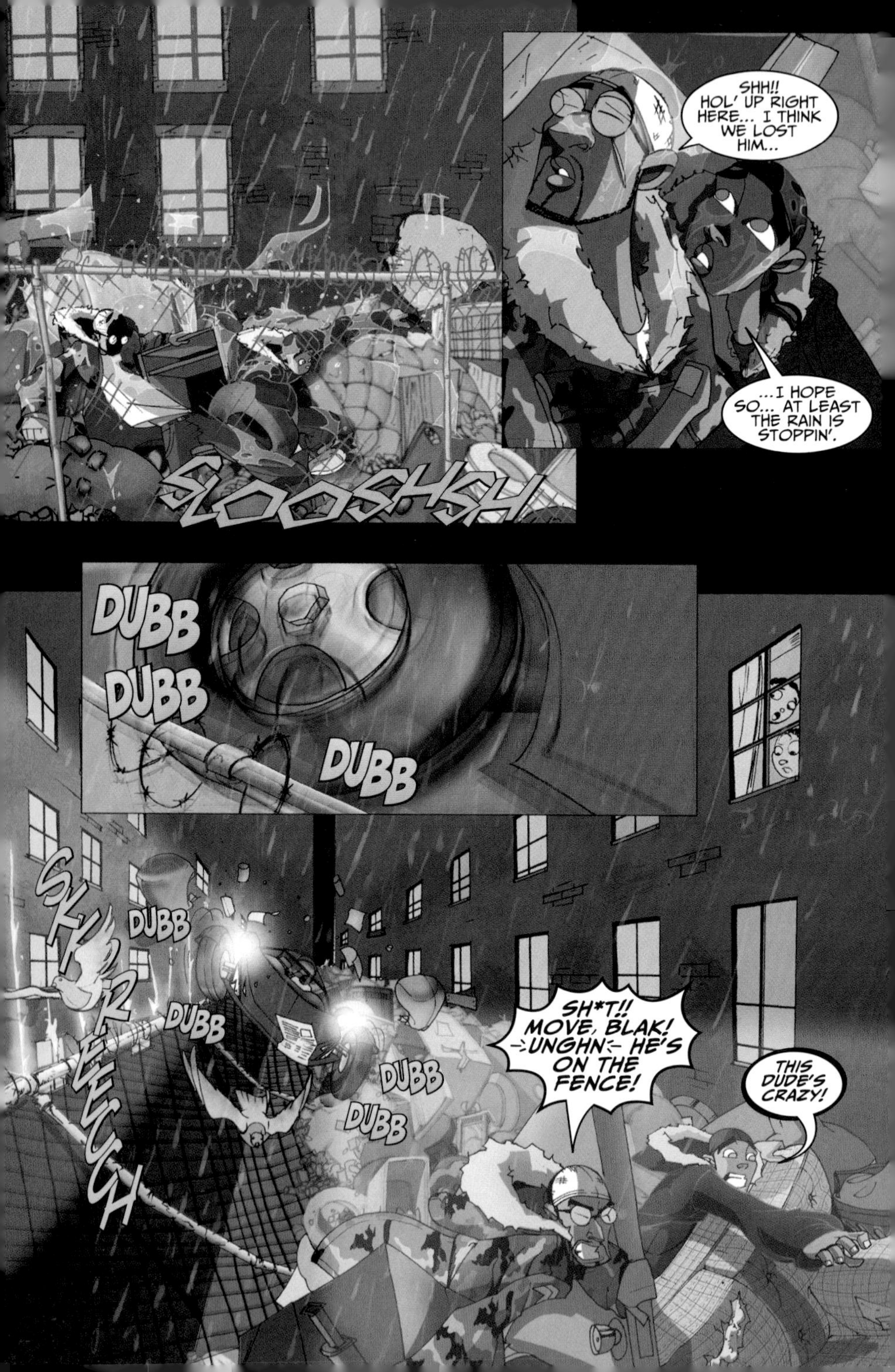
SHH!! HOL' UP RIGHT HERE... I THINK WE LOST HIM...
...I HOPE SO... AT LEAST THE RAIN IS STOPPIN'.
SLOOSHSH
DUBB
DUBB
DUBB
SKKREEEUCH
DUBB
DUBB
DUBB
DUBB
SH*T!! MOVE, BLAK! UNGHN HE'S ON THE FENCE!
THIS DUDE'S CRAZY!

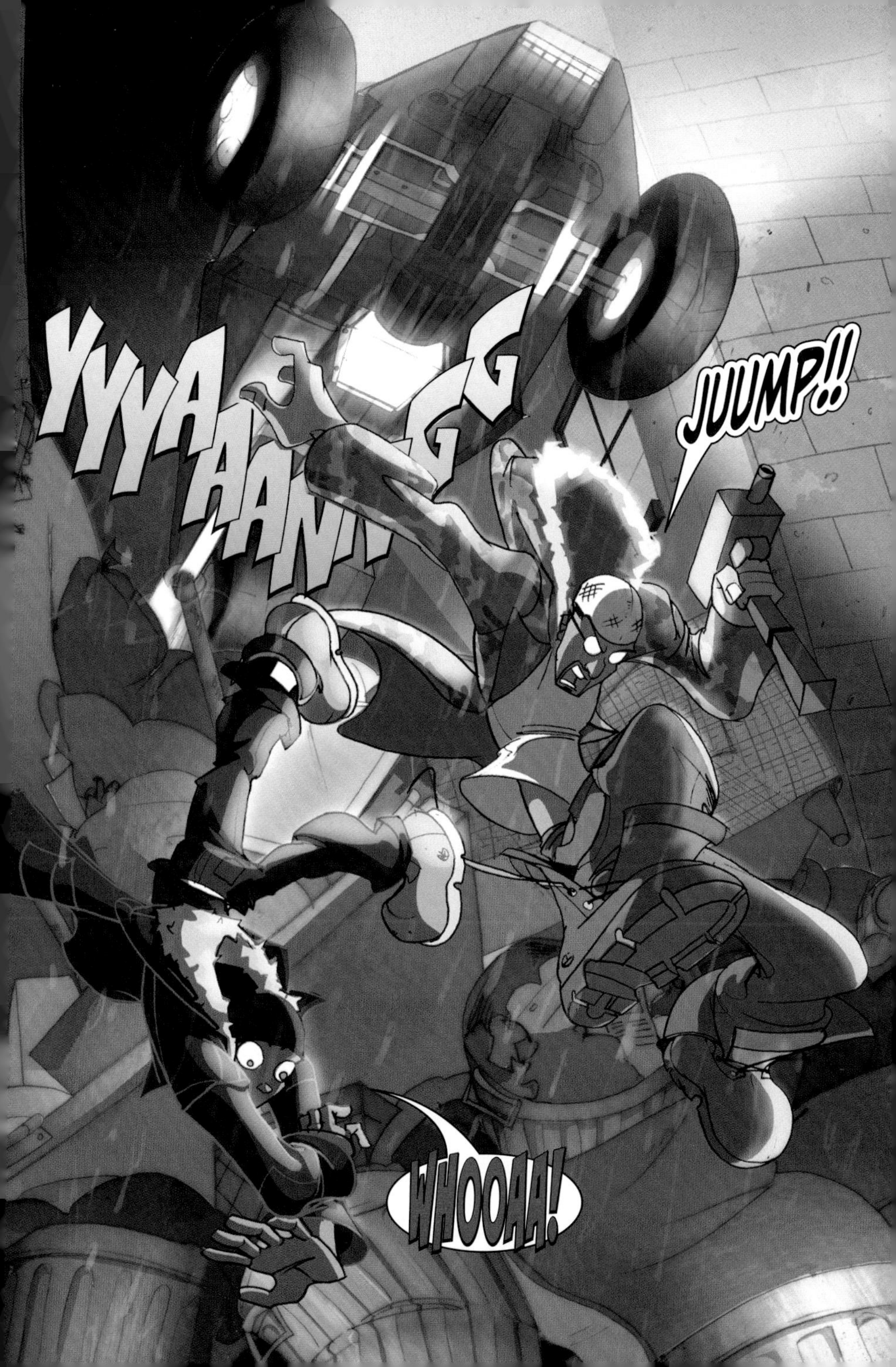
JUUMP!!
WHOOAA!

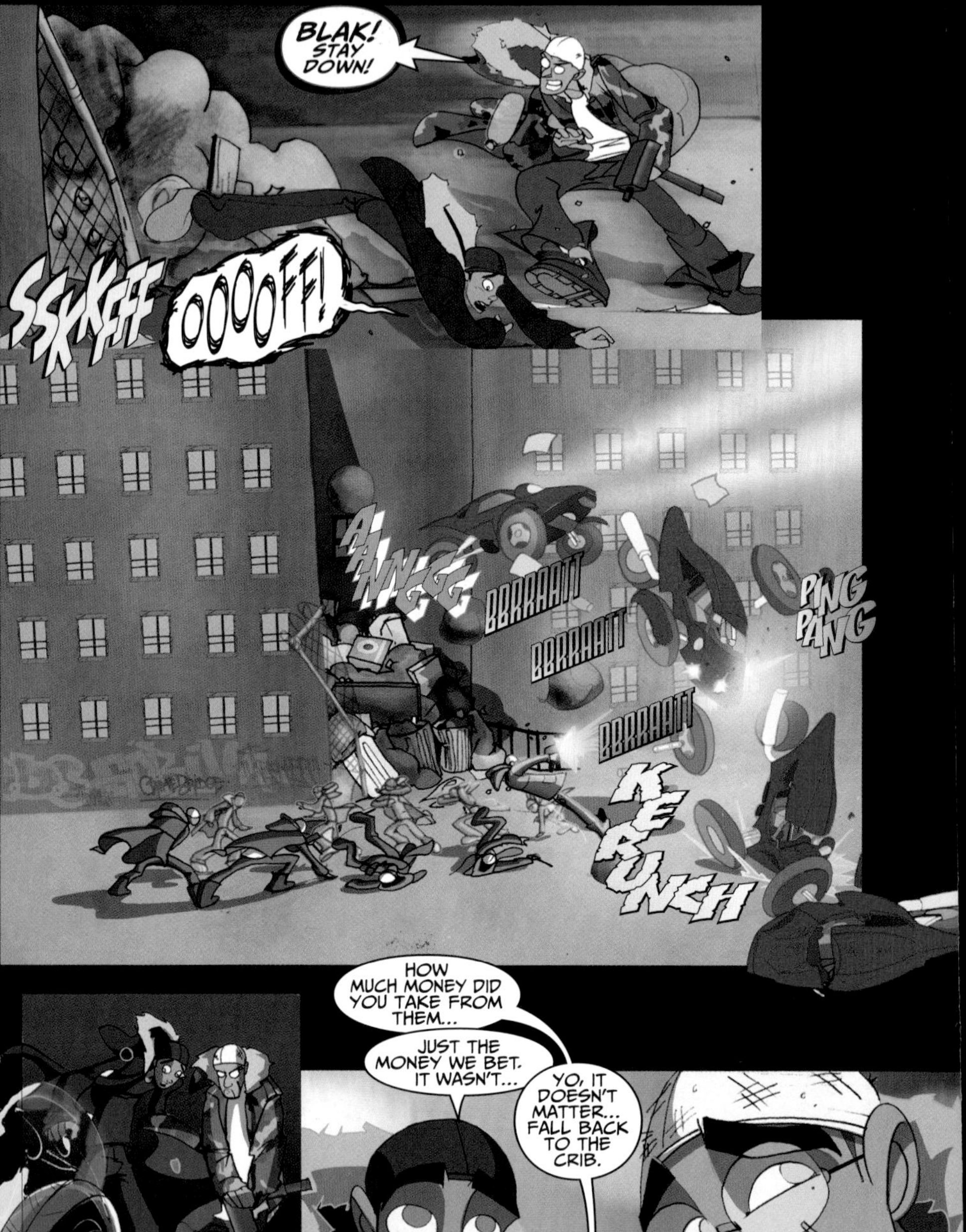
BLAK! STAY DOWN!
SSKKFFF
OOOOFF!
AANNGGG
BBRRAATT
BBRRAATT
BBRRAATT
PING PANG
KERUNCH
HOW MUCH MONEY DID YOU TAKE FROM THEM...
JUST THE MONEY WE BET. IT WASN'T...
YO, IT DOESN'T MATTER... FALL BACK TO THE CRIB.
...I'M GONNA MAKE SURE EVERYTHING'S COOL HERE...
WOOBBLLE WOOBBLLE

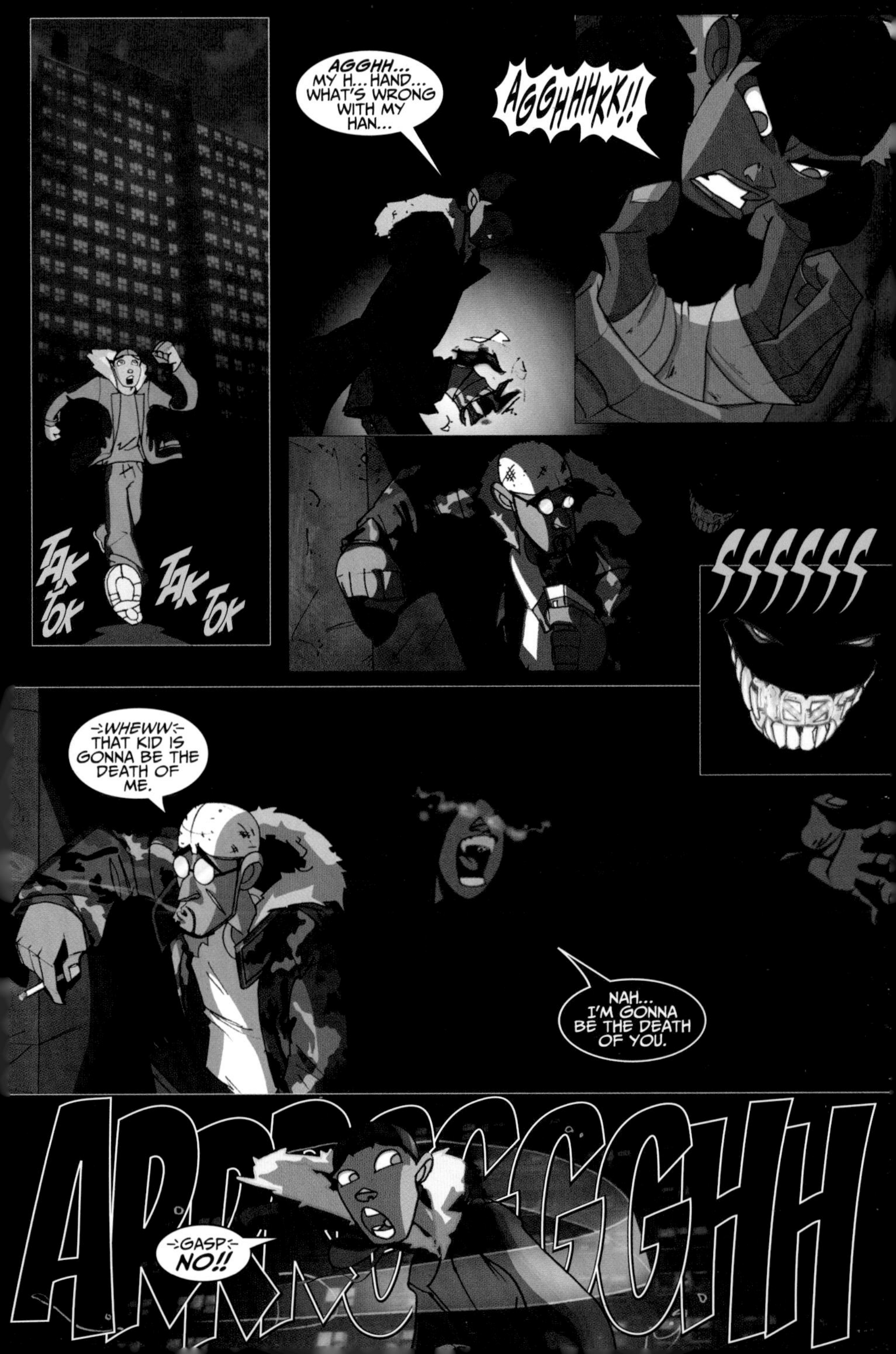
AGGHH...
MY H...HAND...
WHAT'S WRONG
WITH MY
HAN...
AGGHHHKK!!
TAK TOK
TAK TOK
SSSSSS
WHEWW
THAT KID IS
GONNA BE THE
DEATH OF
ME.
NAH...
I'M GONNA
BE THE DEATH
OF YOU.
GASP
NO!!

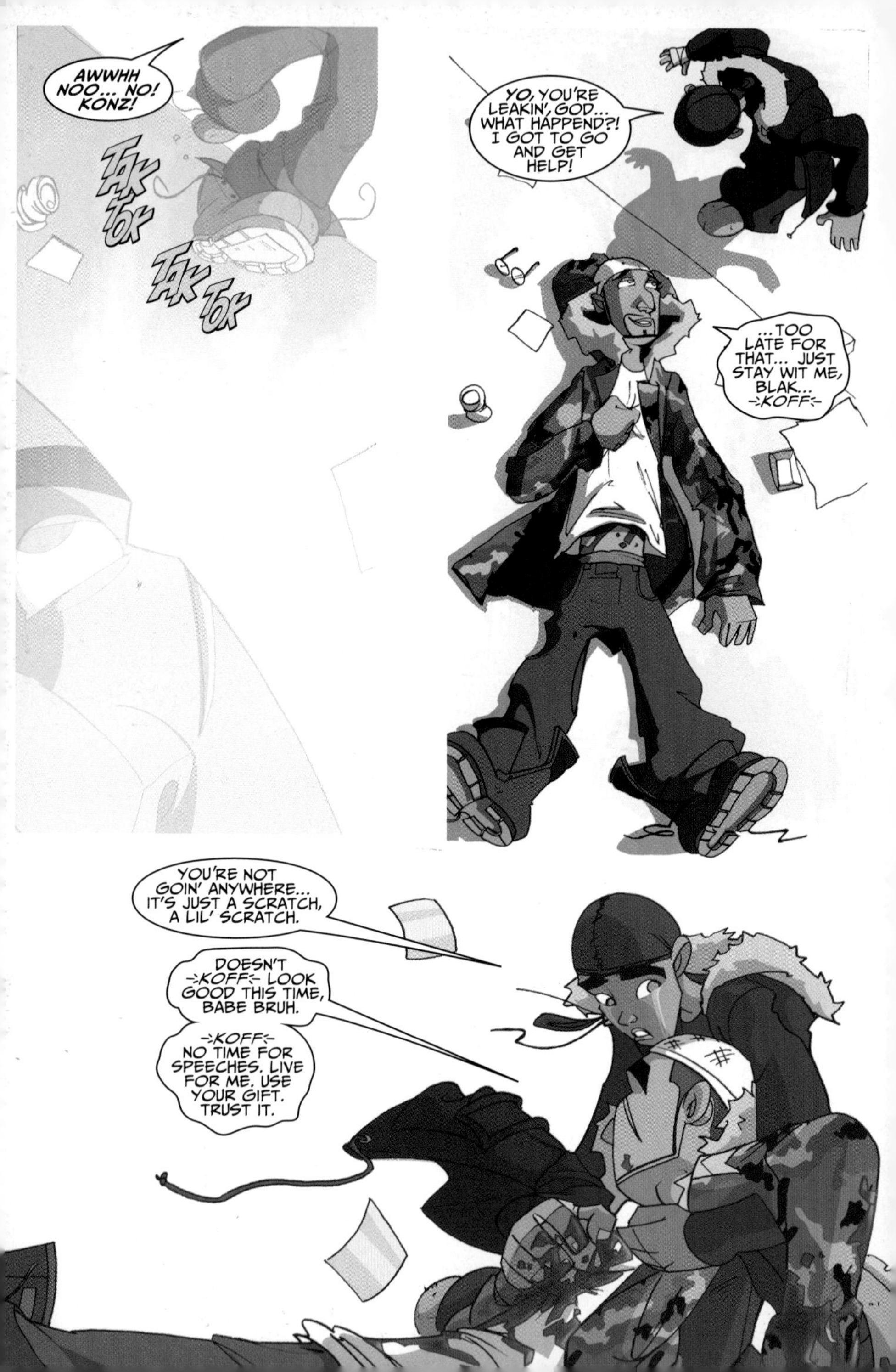
AWWHH NOO... NO! KONZ!
TAK TOK
TAK TOK
YO, YOU'RE LEAKIN', GOD... WHAT HAPPEND?! I GOT TO GO AND GET HELP!
...TOO LATE FOR THAT... JUST STAY WIT ME, BLAK... -KOFF-
YOU'RE NOT GOIN' ANYWHERE... IT'S JUST A SCRATCH, A LIL' SCRATCH.
DOESN'T -KOFF- LOOK GOOD THIS TIME, BABE BRUH.
-KOFF- NO TIME FOR SPEECHES. LIVE FOR ME. USE YOUR GIFT. TRUST IT.

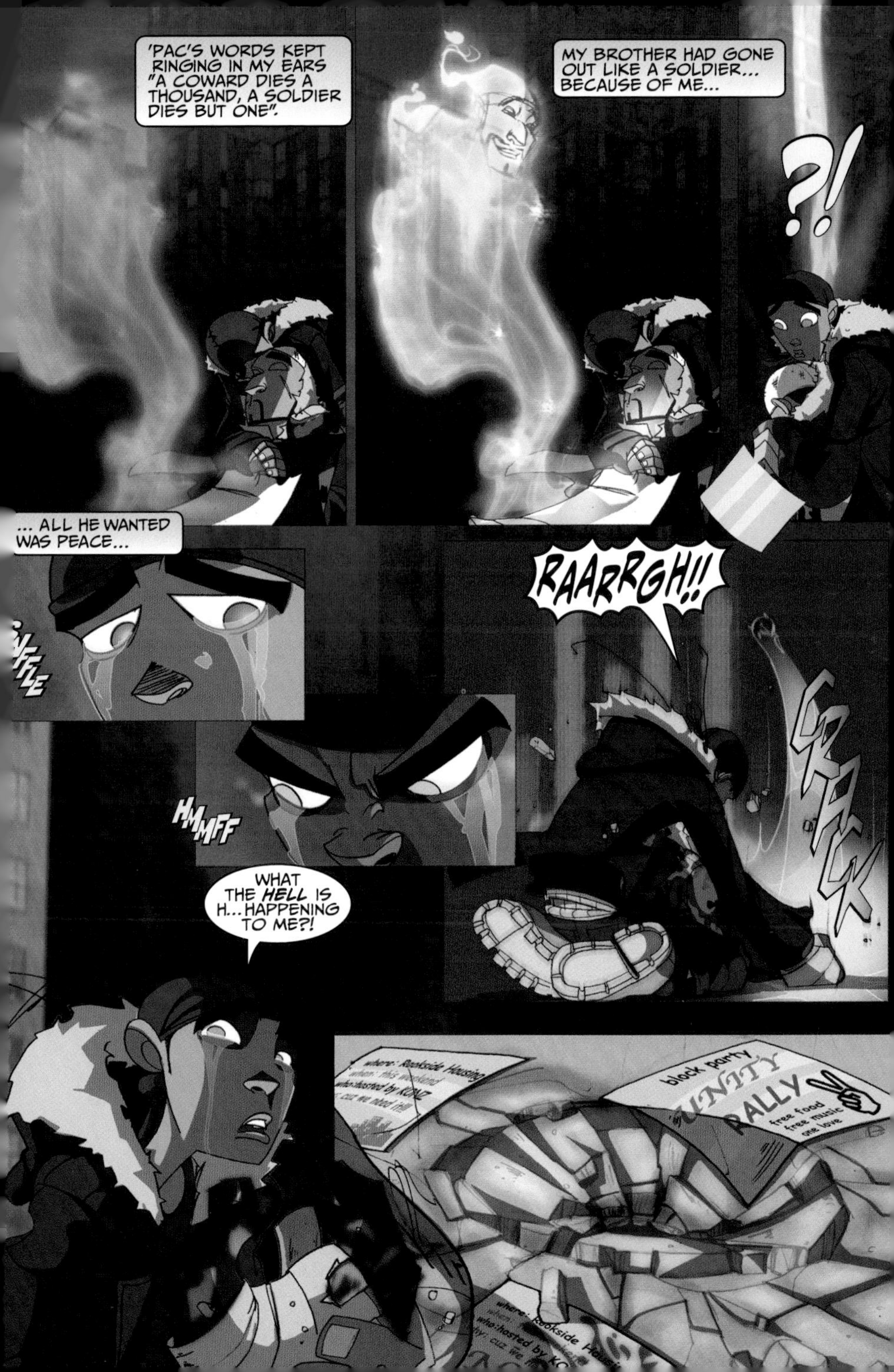

'PAC'S WORDS KEPT RINGING IN MY EARS "A COWARD DIES A THOUSAND, A SOLDIER DIES BUT ONE".
MY BROTHER HAD GONE OUT LIKE A SOLDIER... BECAUSE OF ME...
?!
... ALL HE WANTED WAS PEACE...
HMMFF
RAARRGH!!
CRACK
WHAT THE HELL IS H...HAPPENING TO ME?!
black party
UNITY RALLY
free food
free music
one love
where: Rookside Housing

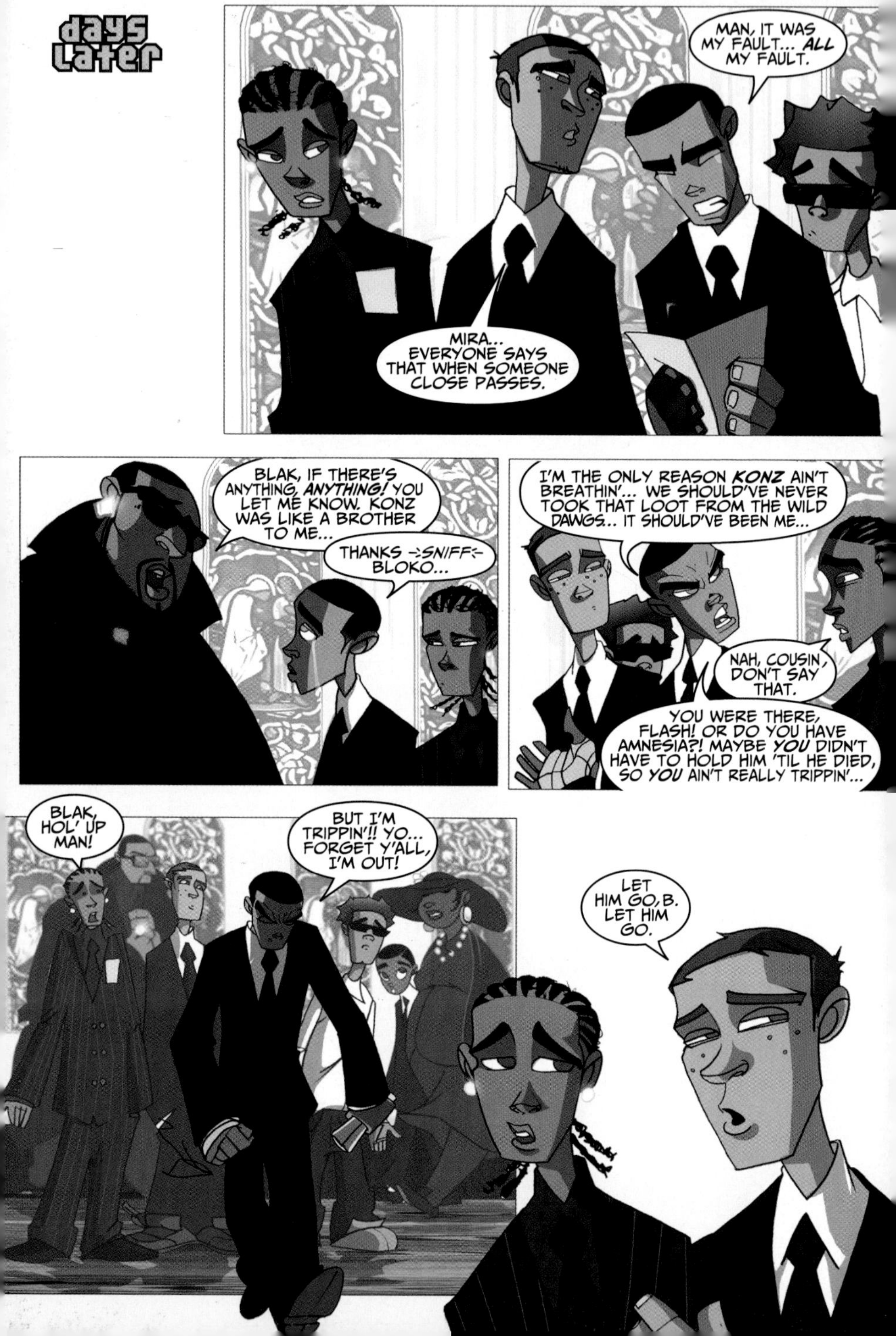
days later
MAN, IT WAS MY FAULT... ALL MY FAULT.
MIRA... EVERYONE SAYS THAT WHEN SOMEONE CLOSE PASSES.
BLAK, IF THERE'S ANYTHING, ANYTHING! YOU LET ME KNOW. KONZ WAS LIKE A BROTHER TO ME...
THANKS -SNIFF- BLOKO...
I'M THE ONLY REASON KONZ AIN'T BREATHIN'... WE SHOULD'VE NEVER TOOK THAT LOOT FROM THE WILD DAWGS... IT SHOULD'VE BEEN ME...
NAH, COUSIN, DON'T SAY THAT.
YOU WERE THERE, FLASH! OR DO YOU HAVE AMNESIA?! MAYBE YOU DIDN'T HAVE TO HOLD HIM 'TIL HE DIED, SO YOU AIN'T REALLY TRIPPIN'...
BLAK, HOL' UP MAN!
BUT I'M TRIPPIN'!! YO... FORGET Y'ALL, I'M OUT!
LET HIM GO, B. LET HIM GO.

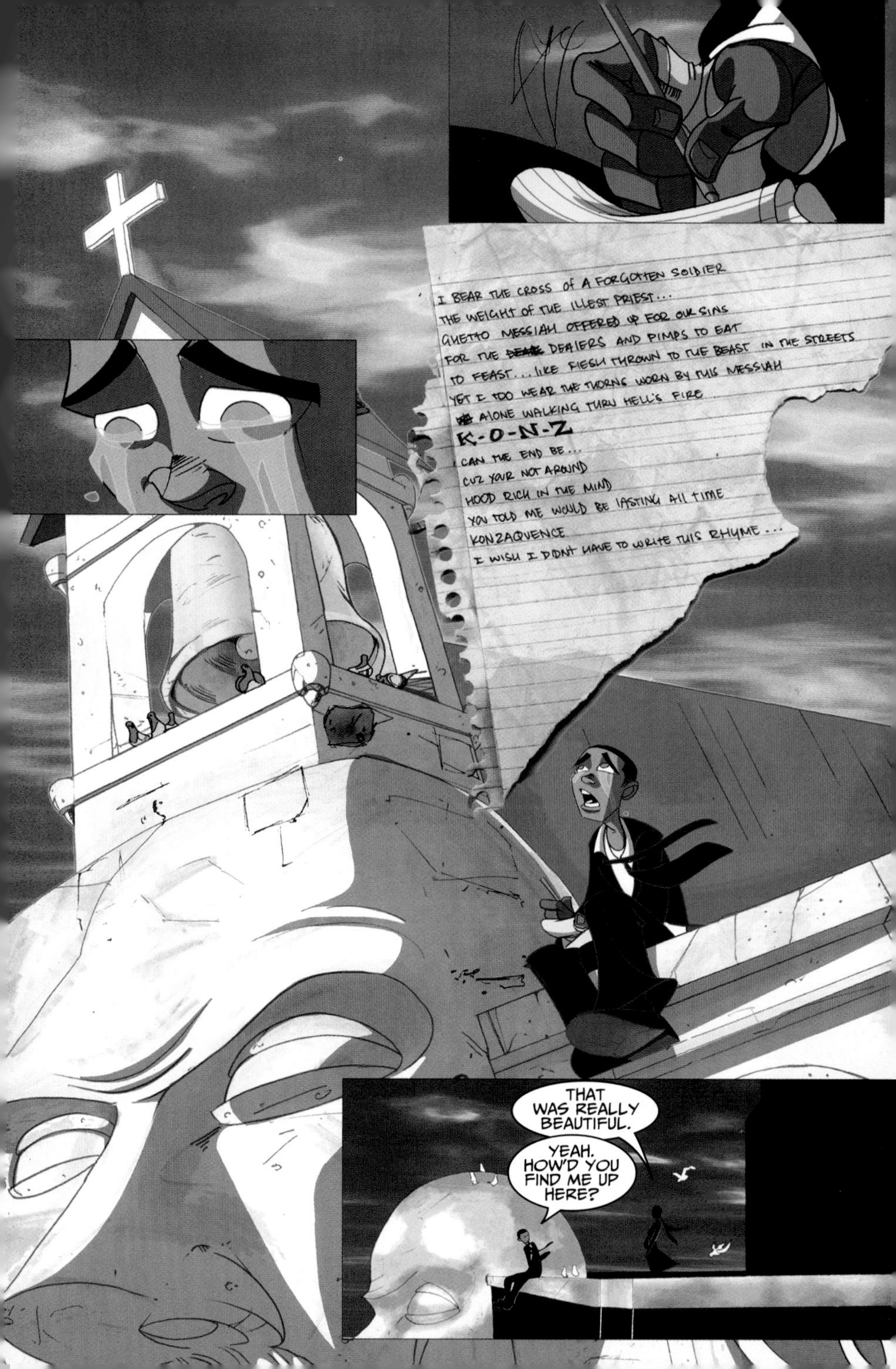
I BEAR THE CROSS OF A FORGOTTEN SOLDIER
THE WEIGHT OF THE ILLEST PRIEST...
GHETTO MESSIAH OFFERED UP FOR OUR SINS
FOR THE DEALERS AND PIMPS TO EAT
TO FEAST... LIKE FLESH THROWN TO THE BEAST IN THE STREETS
YET I TOO WEAR THE THORNS WORN BY THIS MESSIAH
ALONE WALKING THRU HELL'S FIRE
K-O-N-Z
CAN THE END BE...
CUZ YOUR NOT AROUND
HOOD RICH IN THE MIND
YOU TOLD ME WOULD BE LASTING ALL TIME
KONZAQUENCE
I WISH I DIDNT HAVE TO WRITE THIS RHYME...
THAT WAS REALLY BEAUTIFUL.
YEAH. HOW'D YOU FIND ME UP HERE?

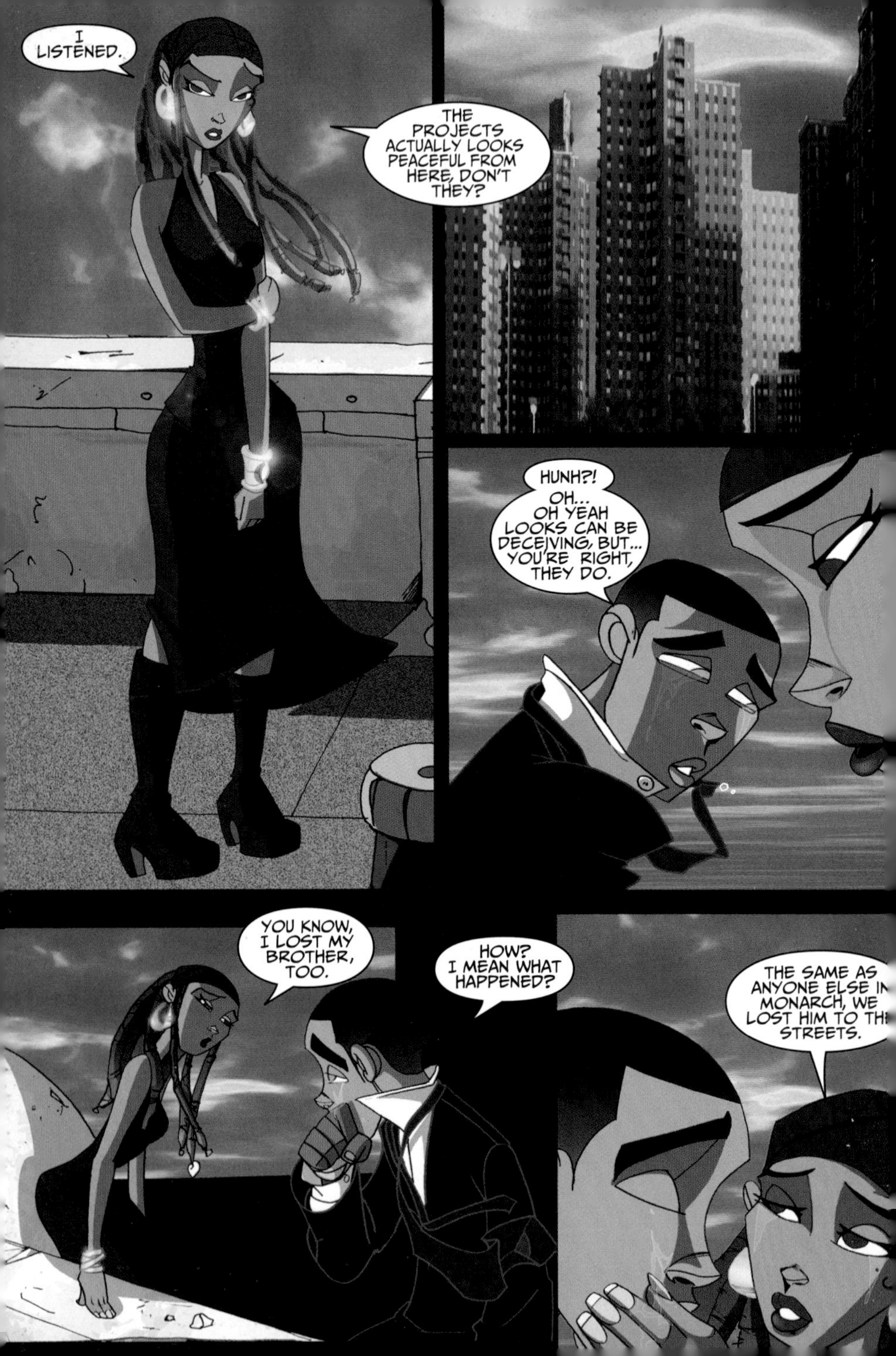
I LISTENED.
THE PROJECTS ACTUALLY LOOKS PEACEFUL FROM HERE, DON'T THEY?
HUNH?! OH... OH YEAH LOOKS CAN BE DECEIVING, BUT... YOU'RE RIGHT, THEY DO.
YOU KNOW, I LOST MY BROTHER, TOO.
HOW? I MEAN WHAT HAPPENED?
THE SAME AS ANYONE ELSE IN MONARCH, WE LOST HIM TO THE STREETS.

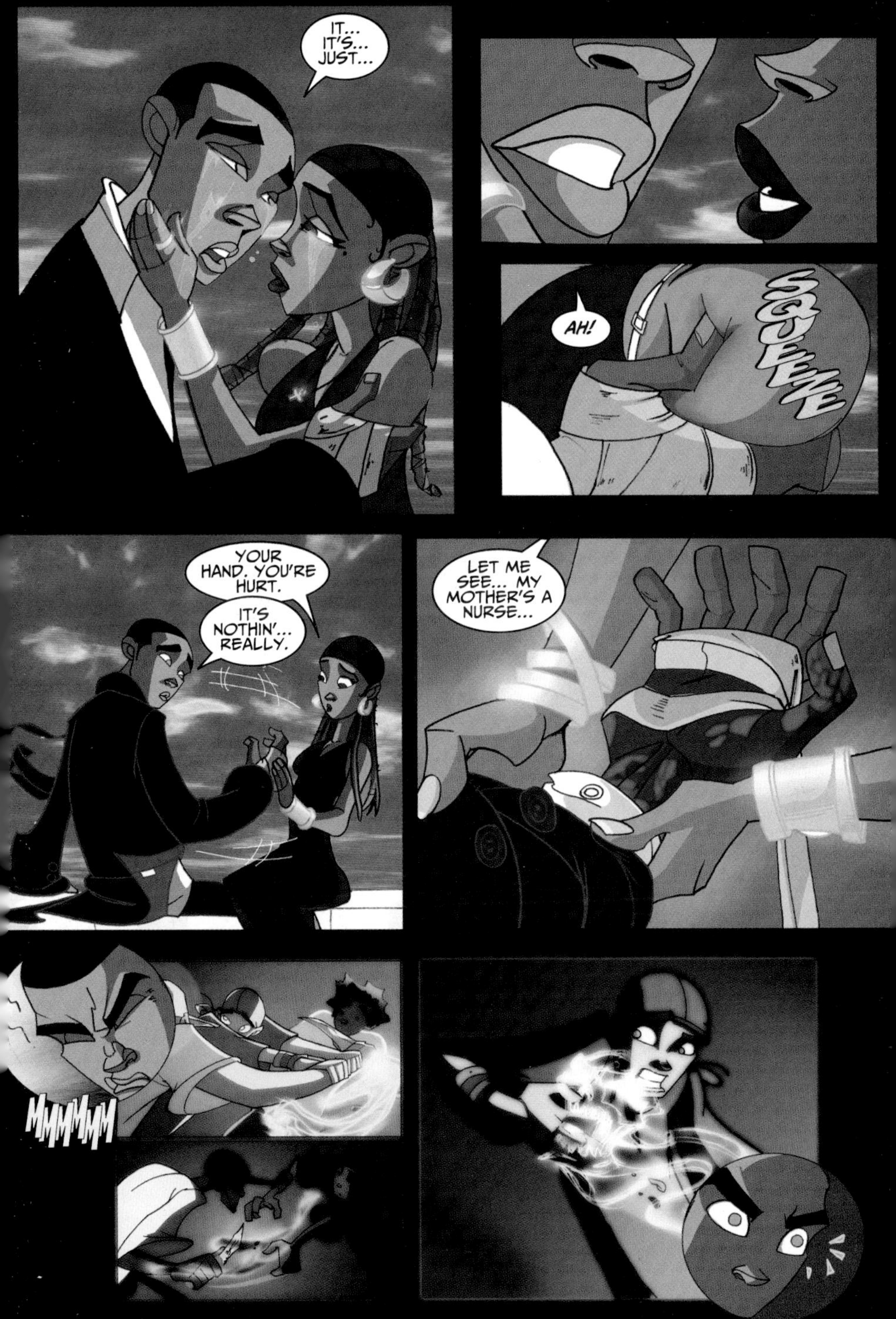
IT... IT'S... JUST...
AH!
SQUEEZE
YOUR HAND. YOU'RE HURT.
IT'S NOTHIN'... REALLY.
LET ME SEE... MY MOTHER'S A NURSE...
MMMMMM

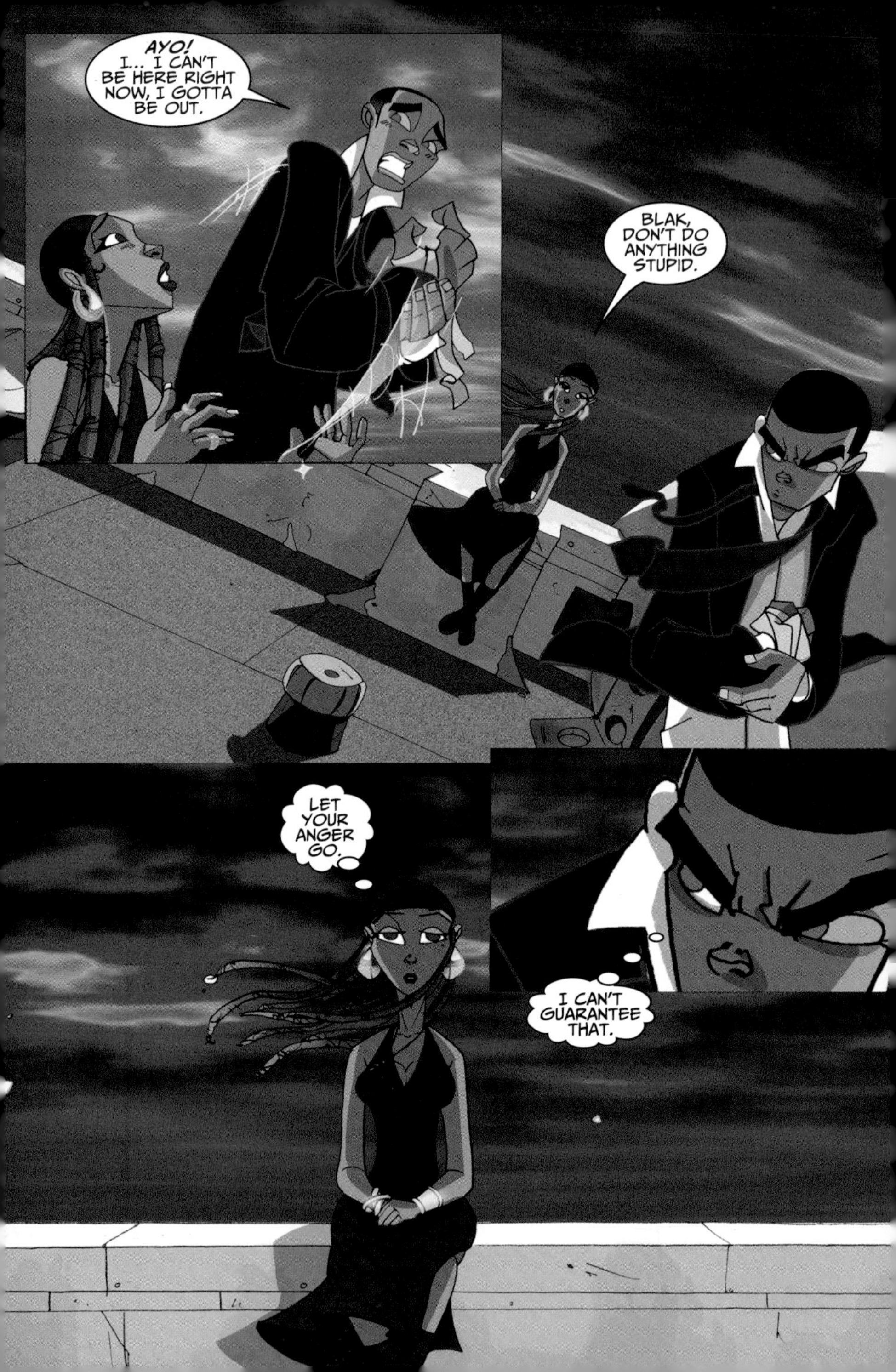
AYO! I... I CAN'T BE HERE RIGHT NOW, I GOTTA BE OUT.
BLAK, DON'T DO ANYTHING STUPID.
LET YOUR ANGER GO.
I CAN'T GUARANTEE THAT.

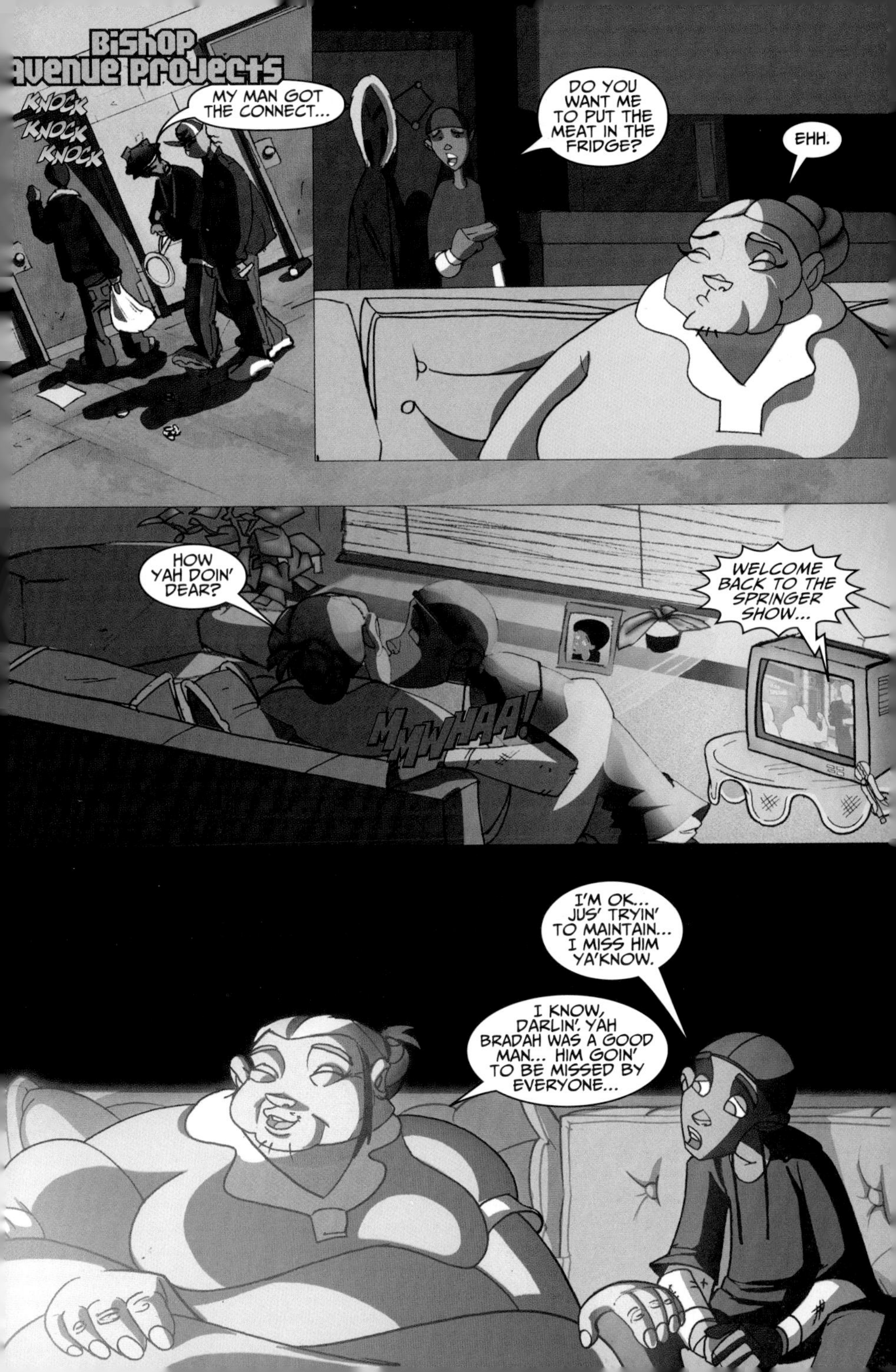
BISHOP AVENUE PROJECTS
KNOCK KNOCK KNOCK
MY MAN GOT THE CONNECT...
DO YOU WANT ME TO PUT THE MEAT IN THE FRIDGE?
EHH.
HOW YAH DOIN' DEAR?
WELCOME BACK TO THE SPRINGER SHOW...
MMWHAA!
I'M OK... JUS' TRYIN' TO MAINTAIN... I MISS HIM YA'KNOW.
I KNOW, DARLIN'. YAH BRADAH WAS A GOOD MAN... HIM GOIN' TO BE MISSED BY EVERYONE...

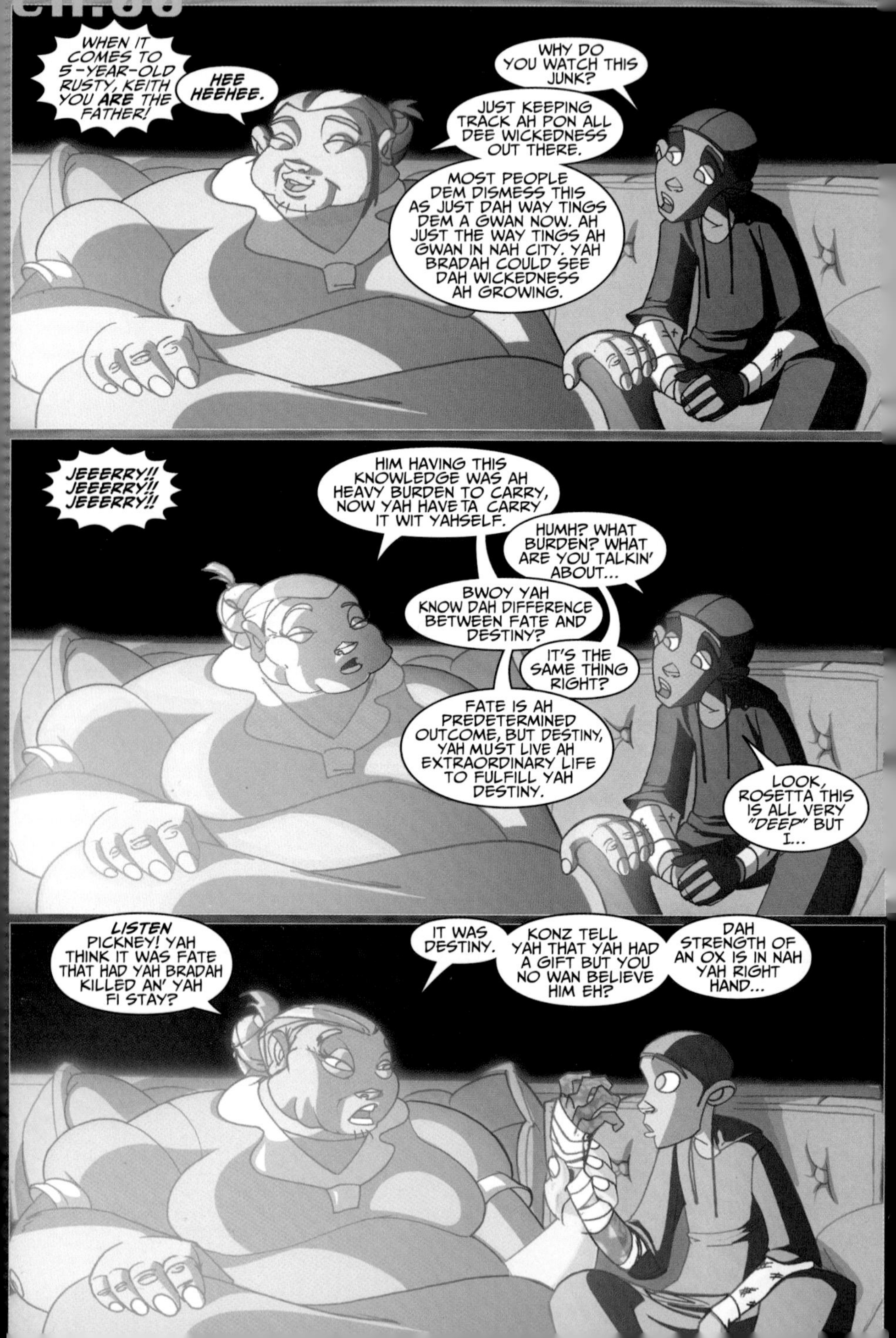
WHEN IT COMES TO 5-YEAR-OLD RUSTY, KEITH YOU ARE THE FATHER!
HEE HEEHEE.
WHY DO YOU WATCH THIS JUNK?
JUST KEEPING TRACK AH PON ALL DEE WICKEDNESS OUT THERE.
MOST PEOPLE DEM DISMESS THIS AS JUST DAH WAY TINGS DEM A GWAN NOW. AH JUST THE WAY TINGS AH GWAN IN NAH CITY. YAH BRADAH COULD SEE DAH WICKEDNESS AH GROWING.
JEEERRY!! JEEERRY!! JEEERRY!!
HIM HAVING THIS KNOWLEDGE WAS AH HEAVY BURDEN TO CARRY, NOW YAH HAVE TA CARRY IT WIT YAHSELF.
HUMH? WHAT BURDEN? WHAT ARE YOU TALKIN' ABOUT...
BWOY YAH KNOW DAH DIFFERENCE BETWEEN FATE AND DESTINY?
IT'S THE SAME THING RIGHT?
FATE IS AH PREDETERMINED OUTCOME, BUT DESTINY, YAH MUST LIVE AH EXTRAORDINARY LIFE TO FULFILL YAH DESTINY.
LOOK, ROSETTA THIS IS ALL VERY "DEEP" BUT I...
LISTEN PICKNEY! YAH THINK IT WAS FATE THAT HAD YAH BRADAH KILLED AN' YAH FI STAY?
IT WAS DESTINY.
KONZ TELL YAH THAT YAH HAD A GIFT BUT YOU NO WAN BELIEVE HIM EH?
DAH STRENGTH OF AN OX IS IN NAH YAH RIGHT HAND...

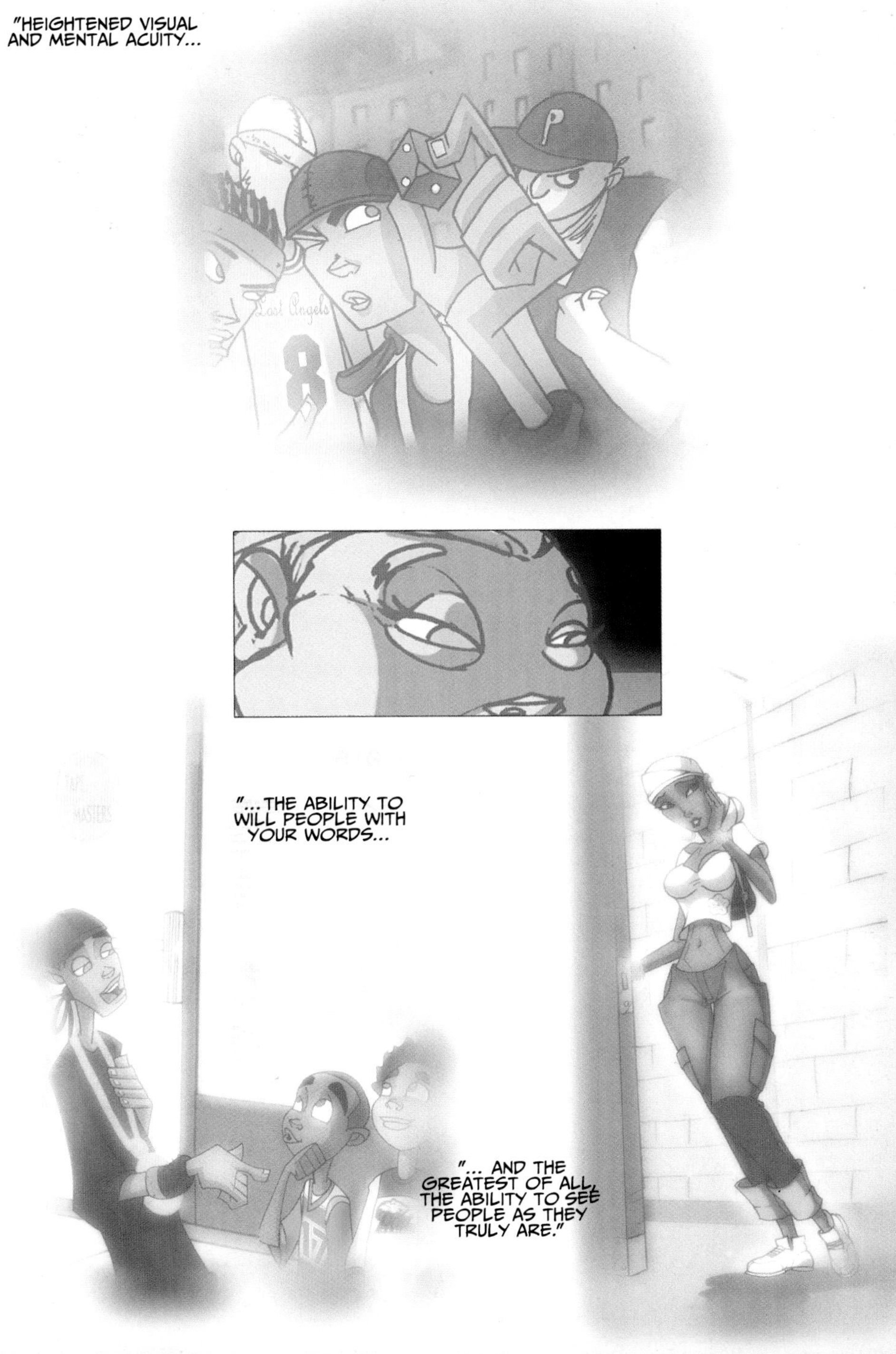
"HEIGHTENED VISUAL AND MENTAL ACUITY...
Last Angels
"...THE ABILITY TO WILL PEOPLE WITH YOUR WORDS...
"... AND THE GREATEST OF ALL, THE ABILITY TO SEE PEOPLE AS THEY TRULY ARE."

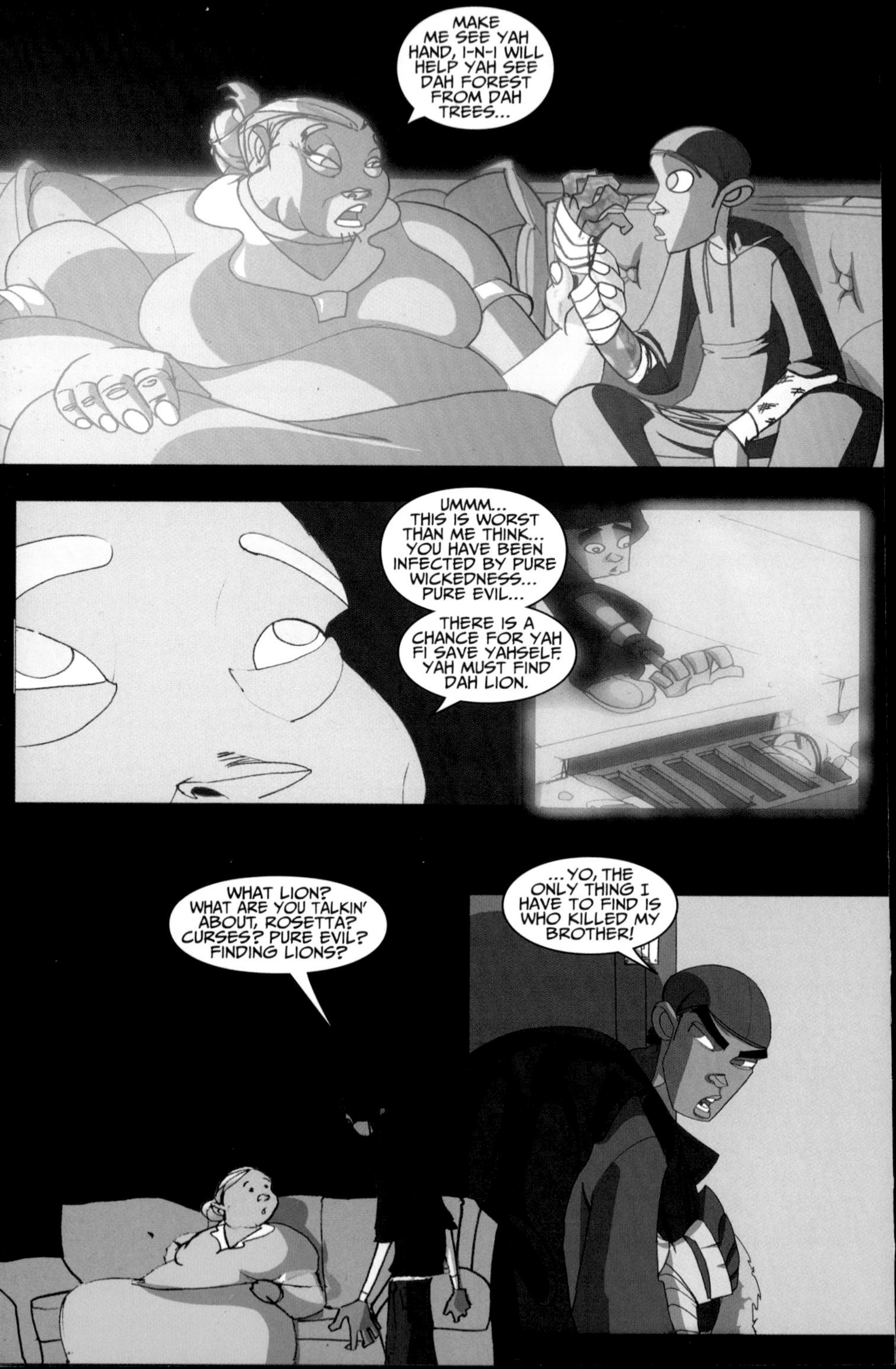
MAKE ME SEE YAH HAND, I-N-I WILL HELP YAH SEE DAH FOREST FROM DAH TREES...
UMMM... THIS IS WORST THAN ME THINK... YOU HAVE BEEN INFECTED BY PURE WICKEDNESS... PURE EVIL...
THERE IS A CHANCE FOR YAH FI SAVE YAHSELF. YAH MUST FIND DAH LION.
WHAT LION? WHAT ARE YOU TALKIN' ABOUT, ROSETTA? CURSES? PURE EVIL? FINDING LIONS?
...YO, THE ONLY THING I HAVE TO FIND IS WHO KILLED MY BROTHER!

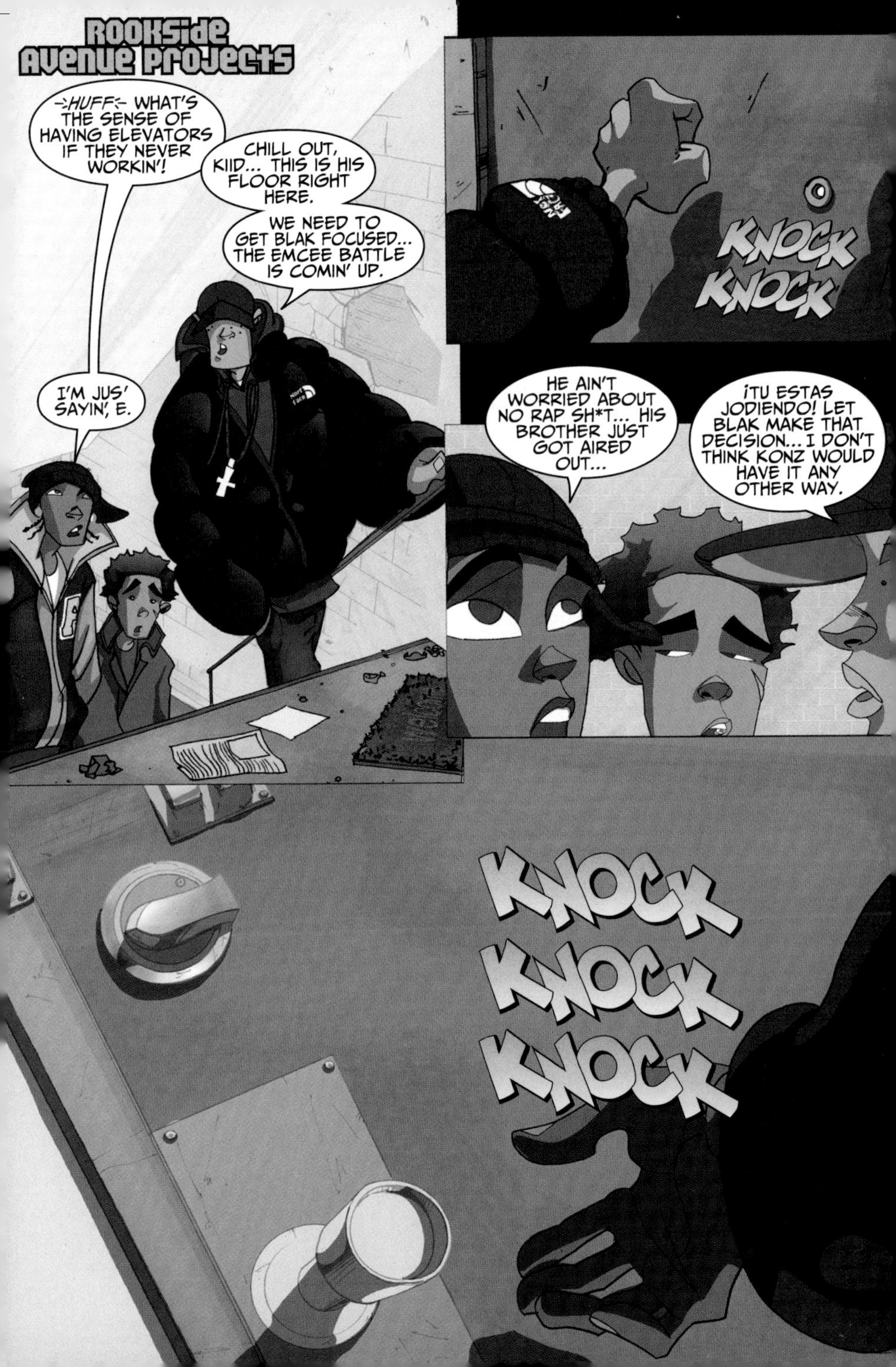
ROOKSIDE AVENUE PROJECTS
-HUFF- WHAT'S THE SENSE OF HAVING ELEVATORS IF THEY NEVER WORKIN'!
CHILL OUT, KIID... THIS IS HIS FLOOR RIGHT HERE.
WE NEED TO GET BLAK FOCUSED... THE EMCEE BATTLE IS COMIN' UP.
I'M JUS' SAYIN', E.
KNOCK KNOCK
HE AIN'T WORRIED ABOUT NO RAP SH*T... HIS BROTHER JUST GOT AIRED OUT...
¡TU ESTAS JODIENDO! LET BLAK MAKE THAT DECISION... I DON'T THINK KONZ WOULD HAVE IT ANY OTHER WAY.
KNOCK KNOCK KNOCK

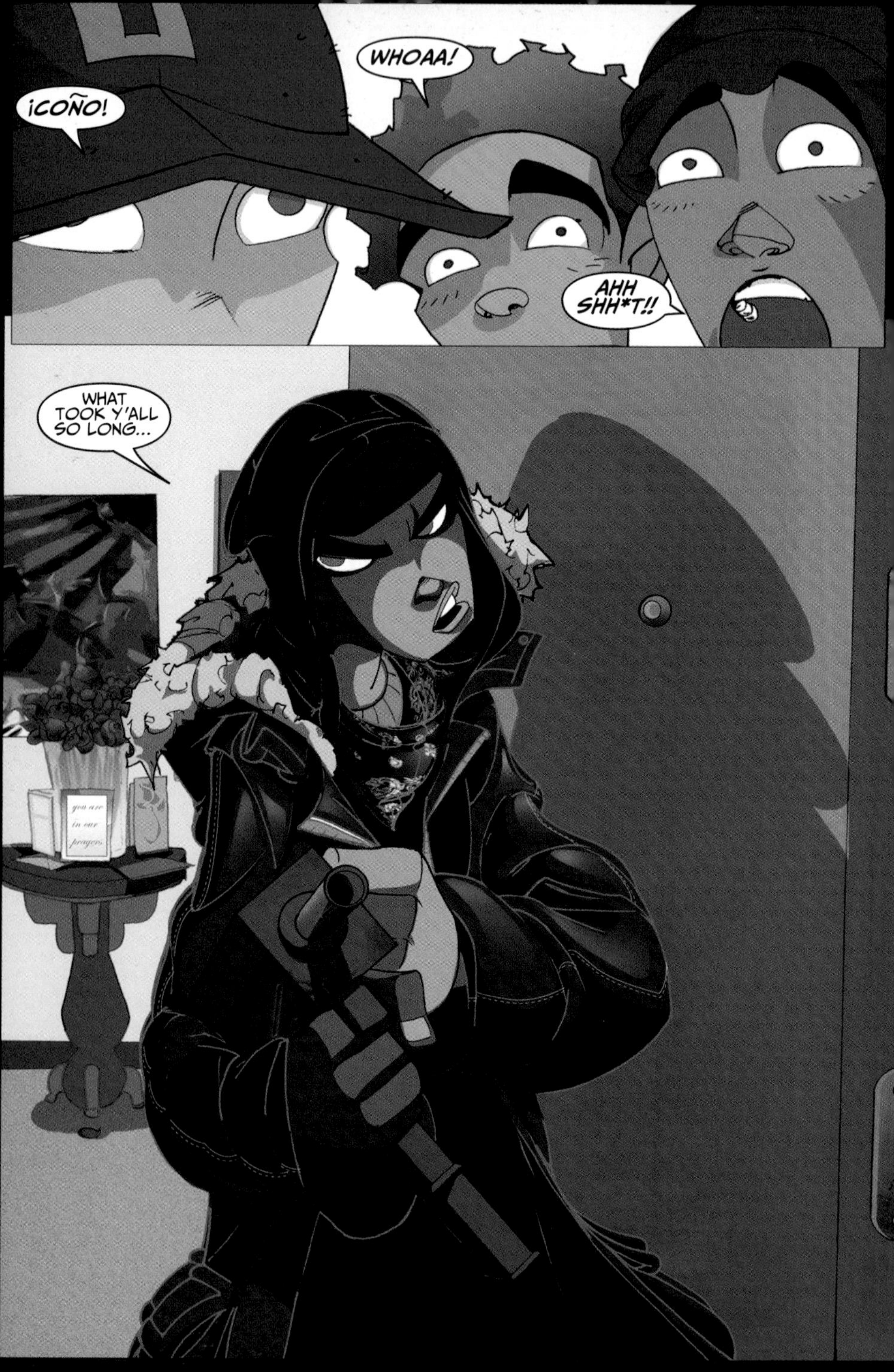
¡COÑO!
WHOAA!
AHH SHH*T!!
WHAT TOOK Y'ALL SO LONG...
you are in our prayers

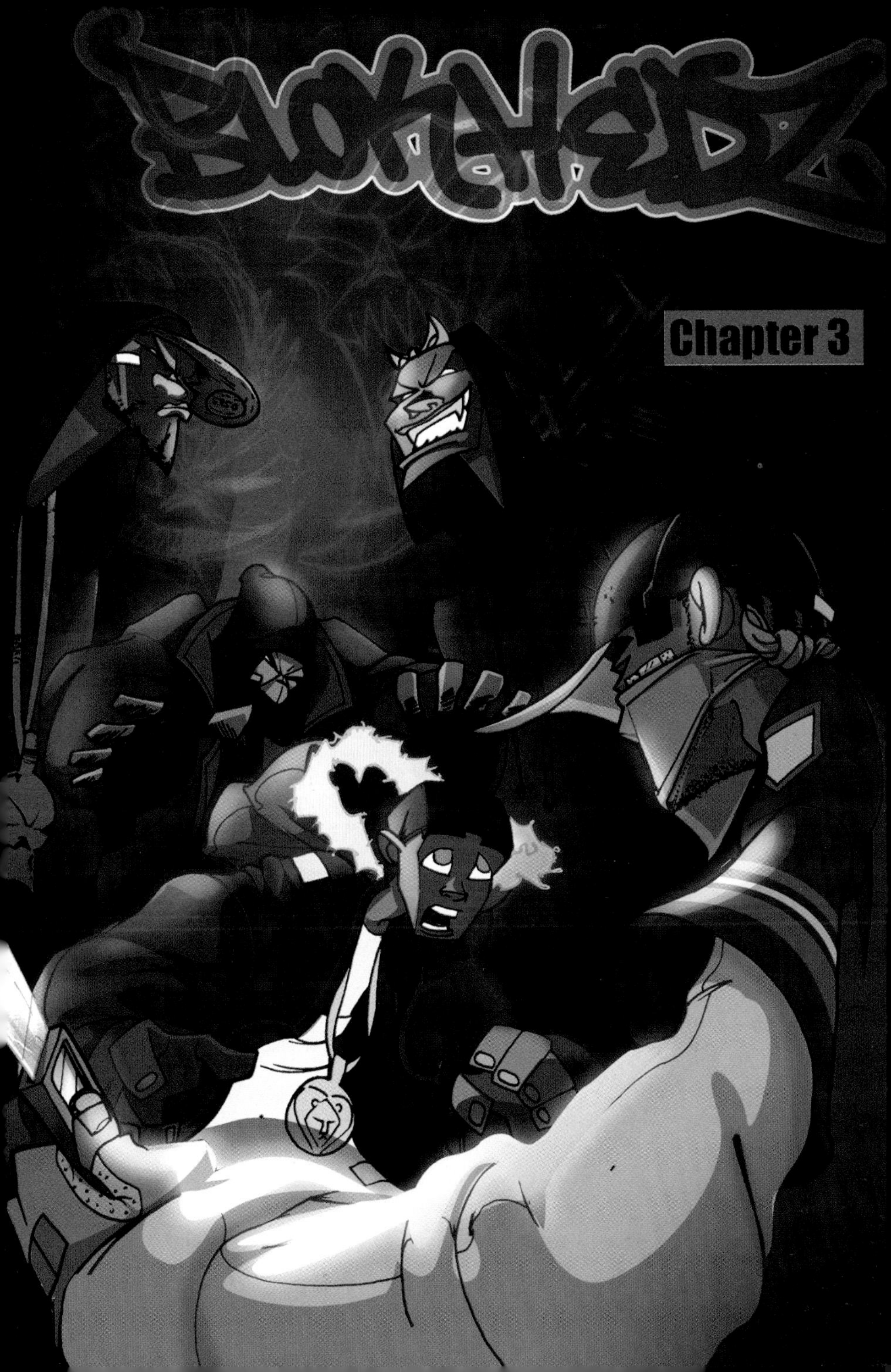
Chapter 3

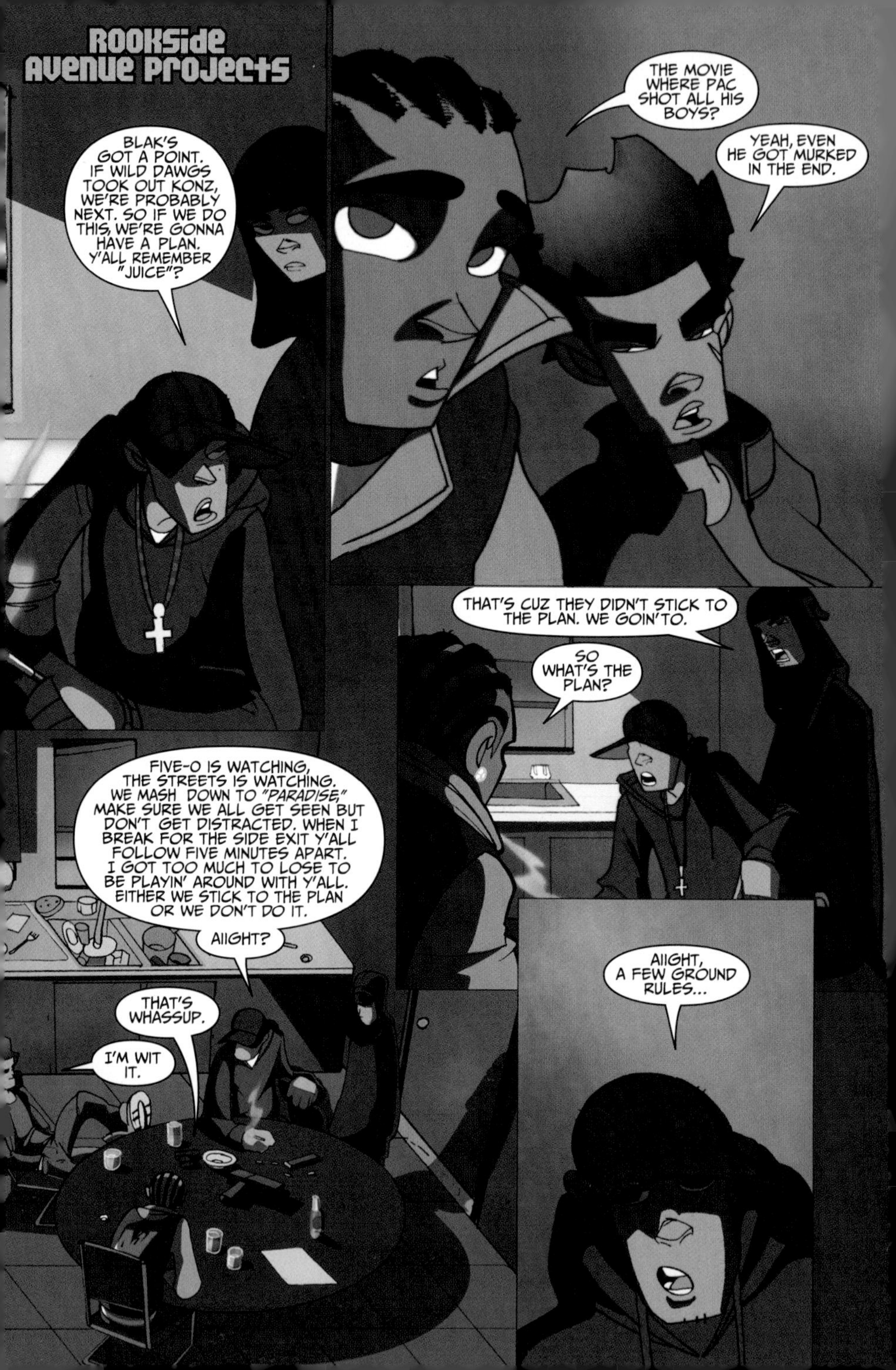
ROOKSIDE AVENUE PROJECTS
BLAK'S GOT A POINT. IF WILD DAWGS TOOK OUT KONZ, WE'RE PROBABLY NEXT. SO IF WE DO THIS, WE'RE GONNA HAVE A PLAN. Y'ALL REMEMBER "JUICE"?
THE MOVIE WHERE PAC SHOT ALL HIS BOYS?
YEAH, EVEN HE GOT MURKED IN THE END.
THAT'S CUZ THEY DIDN'T STICK TO THE PLAN. WE GOIN' TO.
SO WHAT'S THE PLAN?
FIVE-O IS WATCHING, THE STREETS IS WATCHING. WE MASH DOWN TO *"PARADISE,"* MAKE SURE WE ALL GET SEEN BUT DON'T GET DISTRACTED. WHEN I BREAK FOR THE SIDE EXIT Y'ALL FOLLOW FIVE MINUTES APART. I GOT TOO MUCH TO LOSE TO BE PLAYIN' AROUND WITH Y'ALL. EITHER WE STICK TO THE PLAN OR WE DON'T DO IT.
AIIGHT?
THAT'S WHASSUP.
I'M WIT IT.
AIIGHT, A FEW GROUND RULES...

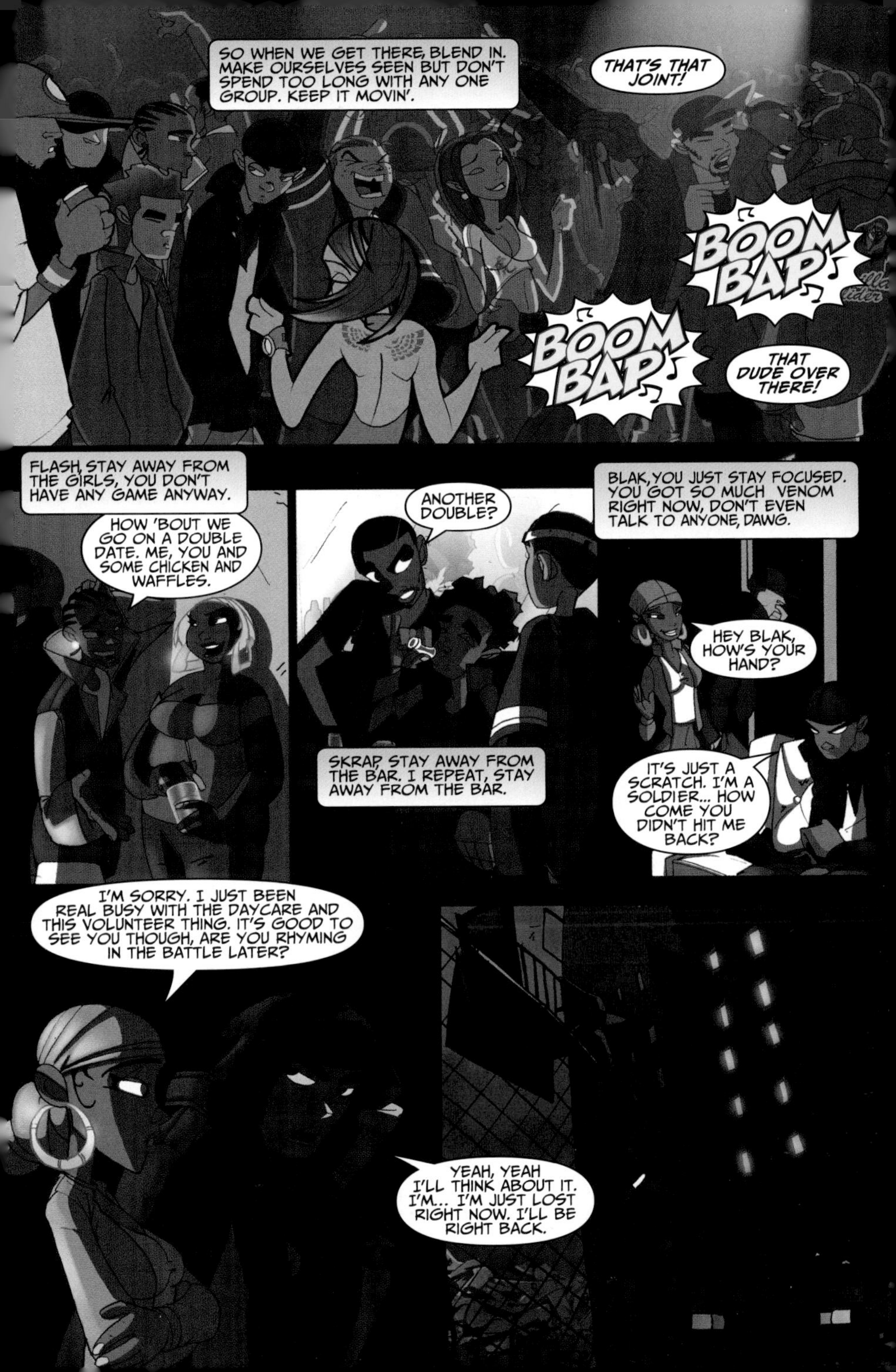
SO WHEN WE GET THERE, BLEND IN. MAKE OURSELVES SEEN BUT DON'T SPEND TOO LONG WITH ANY ONE GROUP. KEEP IT MOVIN'.
THAT'S THAT JOINT!
BOOM BAP
BOOM BAP
THAT DUDE OVER THERE!
FLASH, STAY AWAY FROM THE GIRLS, YOU DON'T HAVE ANY GAME ANYWAY.
HOW 'BOUT WE GO ON A DOUBLE DATE. ME, YOU AND SOME CHICKEN AND WAFFLES.
ANOTHER DOUBLE?
SKRAP, STAY AWAY FROM THE BAR. I REPEAT, STAY AWAY FROM THE BAR.
BLAK, YOU JUST STAY FOCUSED. YOU GOT SO MUCH VENOM RIGHT NOW, DON'T EVEN TALK TO ANYONE, DAWG.
HEY BLAK, HOW'S YOUR HAND?
IT'S JUST A SCRATCH. I'M A SOLDIER... HOW COME YOU DIDN'T HIT ME BACK?
I'M SORRY. I JUST BEEN REAL BUSY WITH THE DAYCARE AND THIS VOLUNTEER THING. IT'S GOOD TO SEE YOU THOUGH, ARE YOU RHYMING IN THE BATTLE LATER?
YEAH, YEAH I'LL THINK ABOUT IT. I'M... I'M JUST LOST RIGHT NOW. I'LL BE RIGHT BACK.

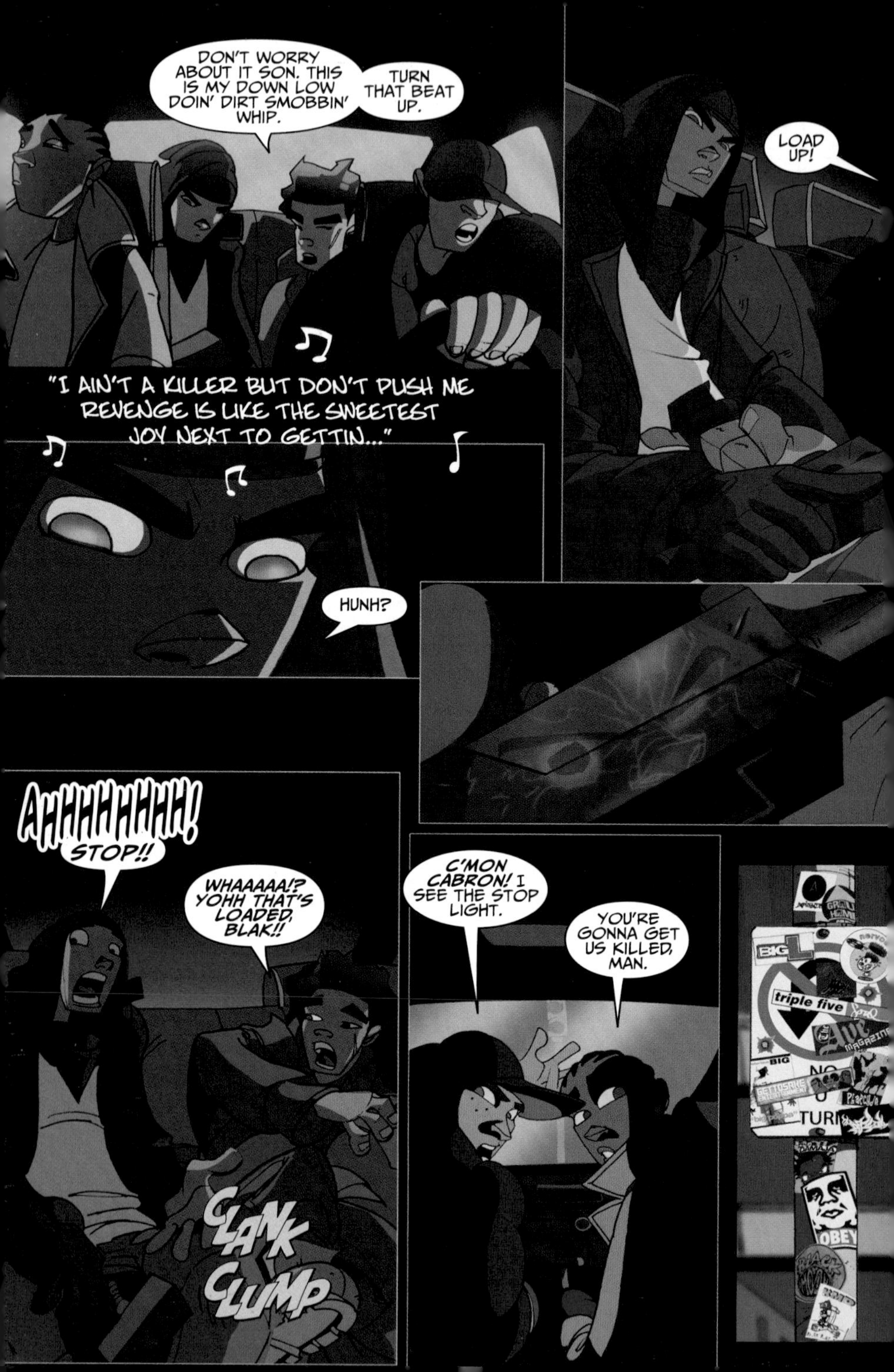
DON'T WORRY ABOUT IT SON. THIS IS MY DOWN LOW DOIN' DIRT SMOBBIN' WHIP.
TURN THAT BEAT UP.
LOAD UP!
"I AIN'T A KILLER BUT DON'T PUSH ME REVENGE IS LIKE THE SWEETEST JOY NEXT TO GETTIN..."
HUNH?
AHHHHHHHH!
STOP!!
WHAAAAA!? YOHH THAT'S LOADED, BLAK!!
CLANK
CLUMP
C'MON CABRON! I SEE THE STOP LIGHT.
YOU'RE GONNA GET US KILLED, MAN.
triple five
OBEY

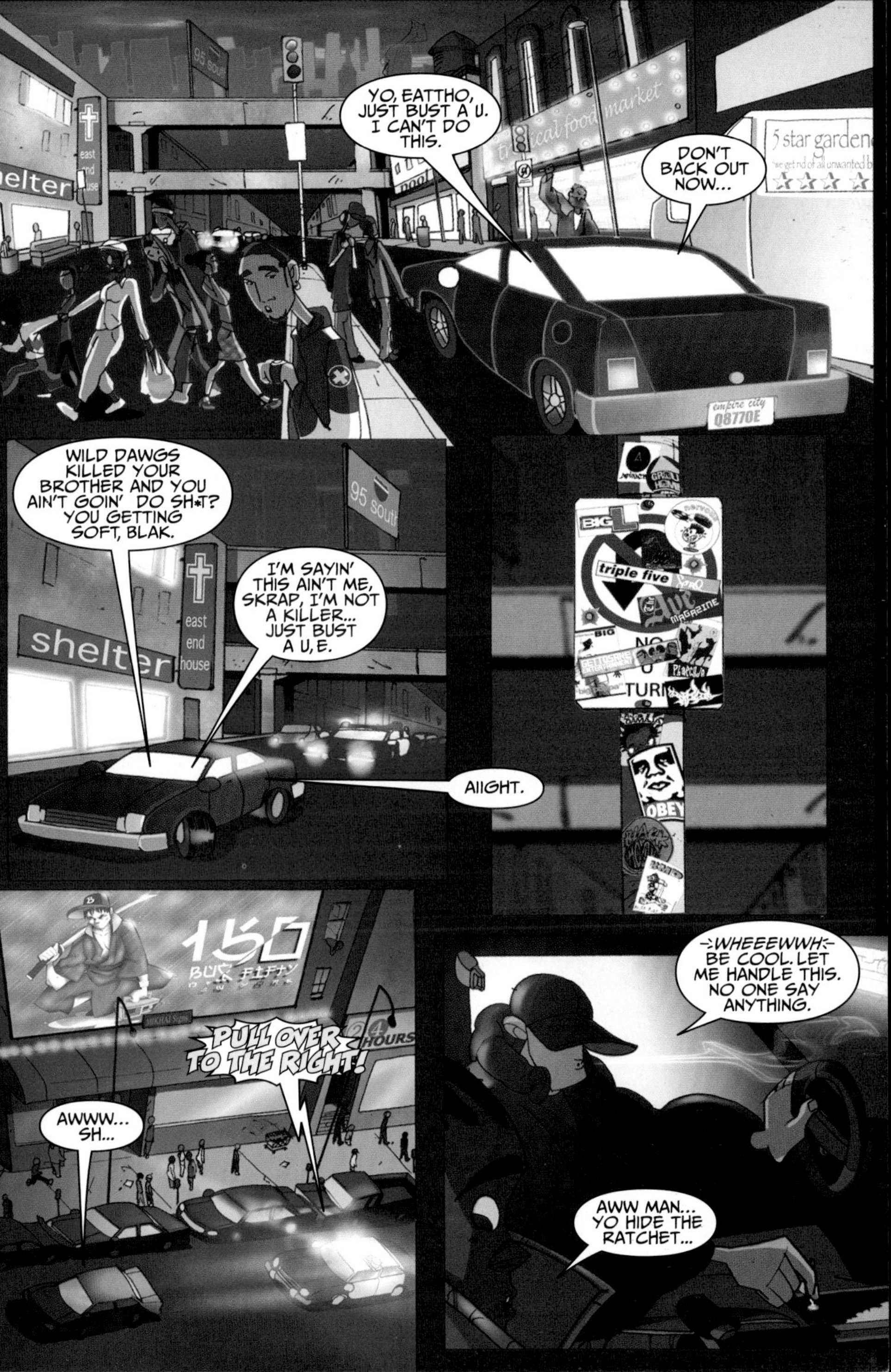
YO, EATTHO, JUST BUST A U. I CAN'T DO THIS.
DON'T BACK OUT NOW...
empire city
Q8770E
WILD DAWGS KILLED YOUR BROTHER AND YOU AIN'T GOIN' DO SH*T? YOU GETTING SOFT, BLAK.
I'M SAYIN' THIS AIN'T ME, SKRAP, I'M NOT A KILLER... JUST BUST A U, E.
AIIGHT.
shelter
east end house
triple five
NO U TURN
OBEY
150
HOURS
PULL OVER TO THE RIGHT!
AWWW... SH...
WHEEEWWH BE COOL. LET ME HANDLE THIS. NO ONE SAY ANYTHING.
AWW MAN... YO HIDE THE RATCHET...

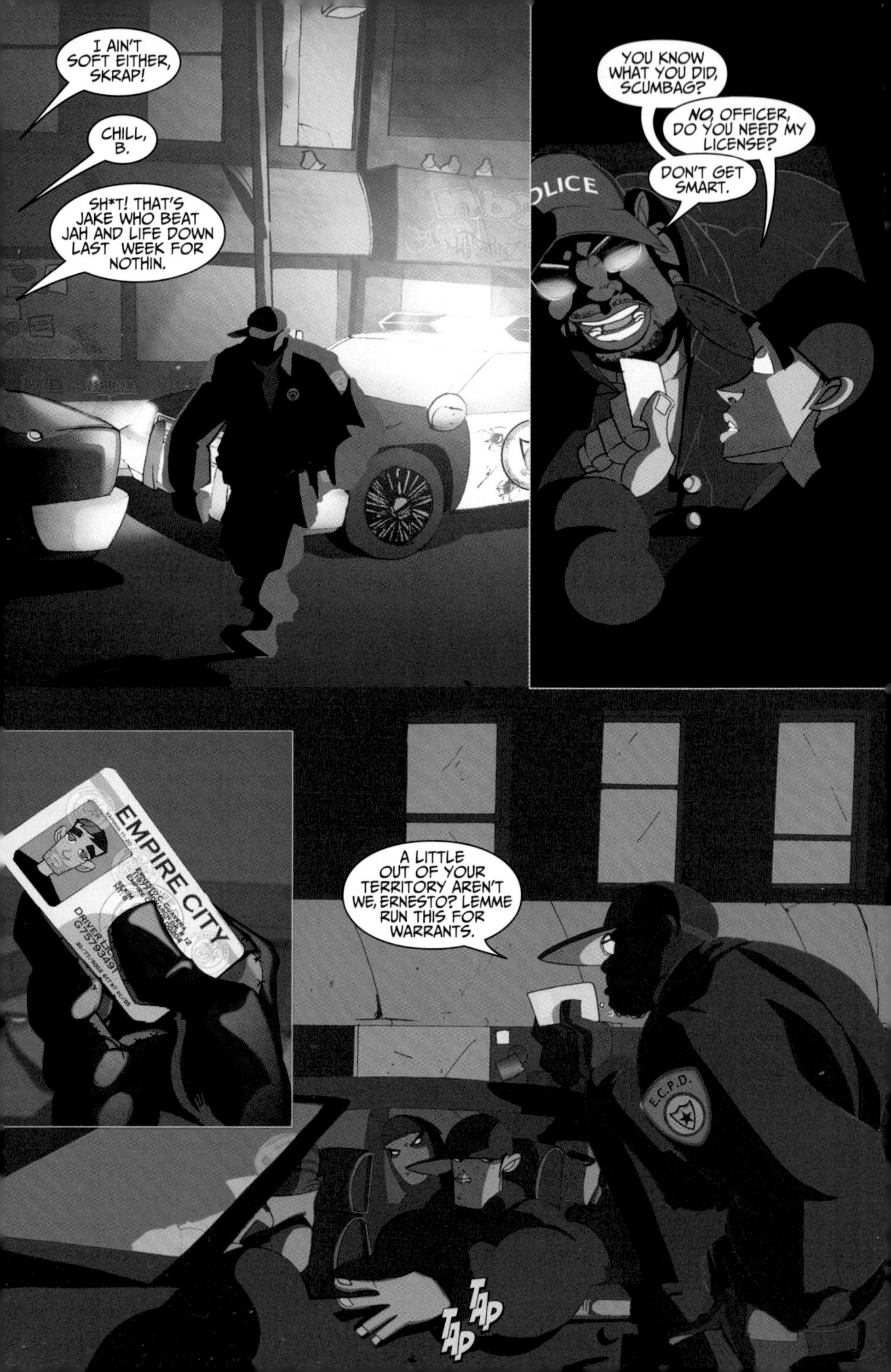
I AIN'T SOFT EITHER, SKRAP!
CHILL, B.
SH*T! THAT'S JAKE WHO BEAT JAH AND LIFE DOWN LAST WEEK FOR NOTHIN.
YOU KNOW WHAT YOU DID, SCUMBAG?
NO, OFFICER, DO YOU NEED MY LICENSE?
DON'T GET SMART.
EMPIRE CITY
A LITTLE OUT OF YOUR TERRITORY AREN'T WE, ERNESTO? LEMME RUN THIS FOR WARRANTS.
E.C.P.D.
TAP
TAP

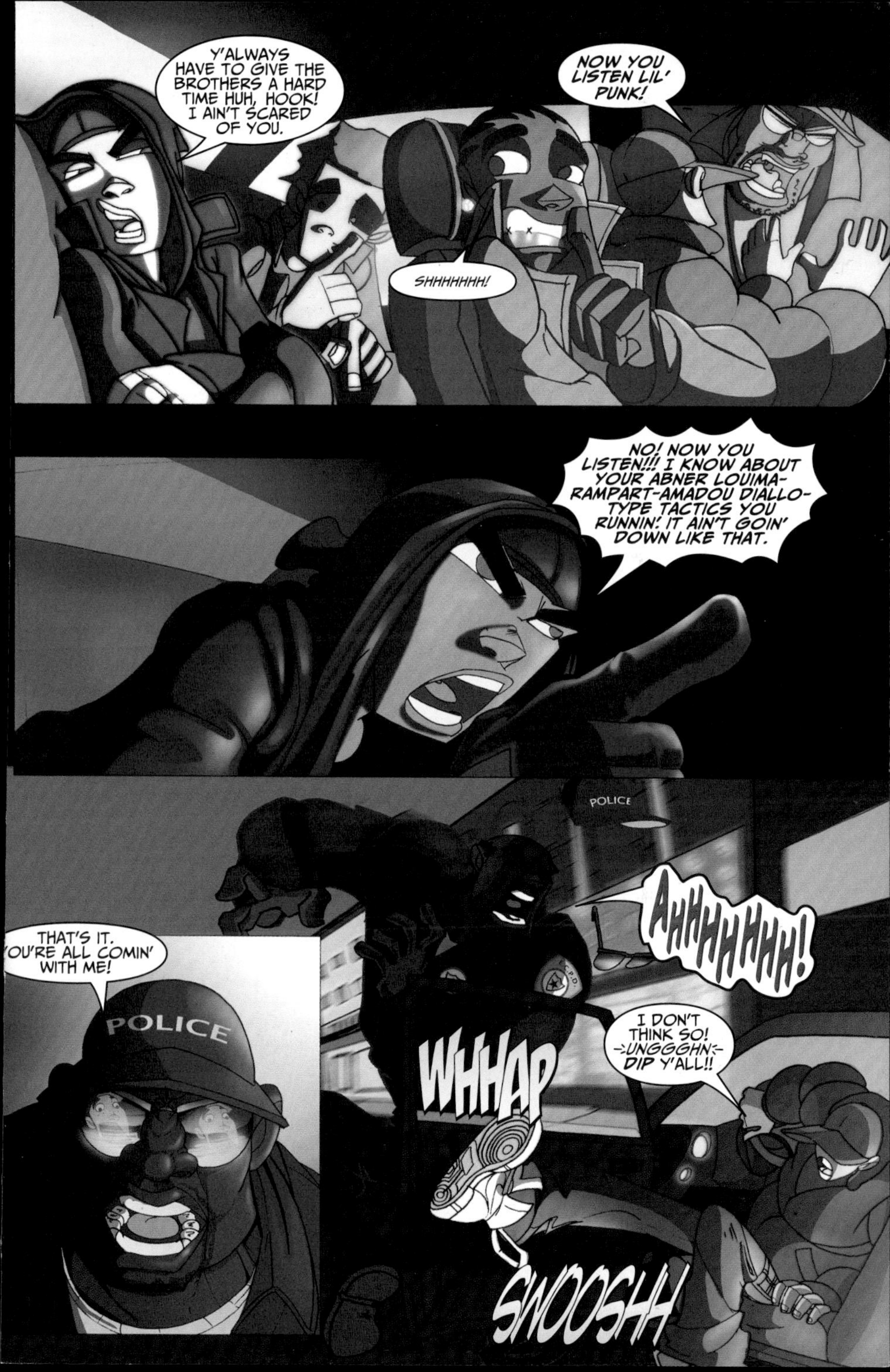
Y'ALWAYS HAVE TO GIVE THE BROTHERS A HARD TIME HUH, HOOK! I AIN'T SCARED OF YOU.
NOW YOU LISTEN LIL' PUNK!
SHHHHHHH!
NO! NOW YOU LISTEN!!! I KNOW ABOUT YOUR ABNER LOUIMA-RAMPART-AMADOU DIALLO-TYPE TACTICS YOU RUNNIN'. IT AIN'T GOIN' DOWN LIKE THAT.
POLICE
THAT'S IT. YOU'RE ALL COMIN' WITH ME!
POLICE
AHHHHHHHH!
I DON'T THINK SO! -UNGGGHN- DIP Y'ALL!!
WHHAP
SWOOSHH

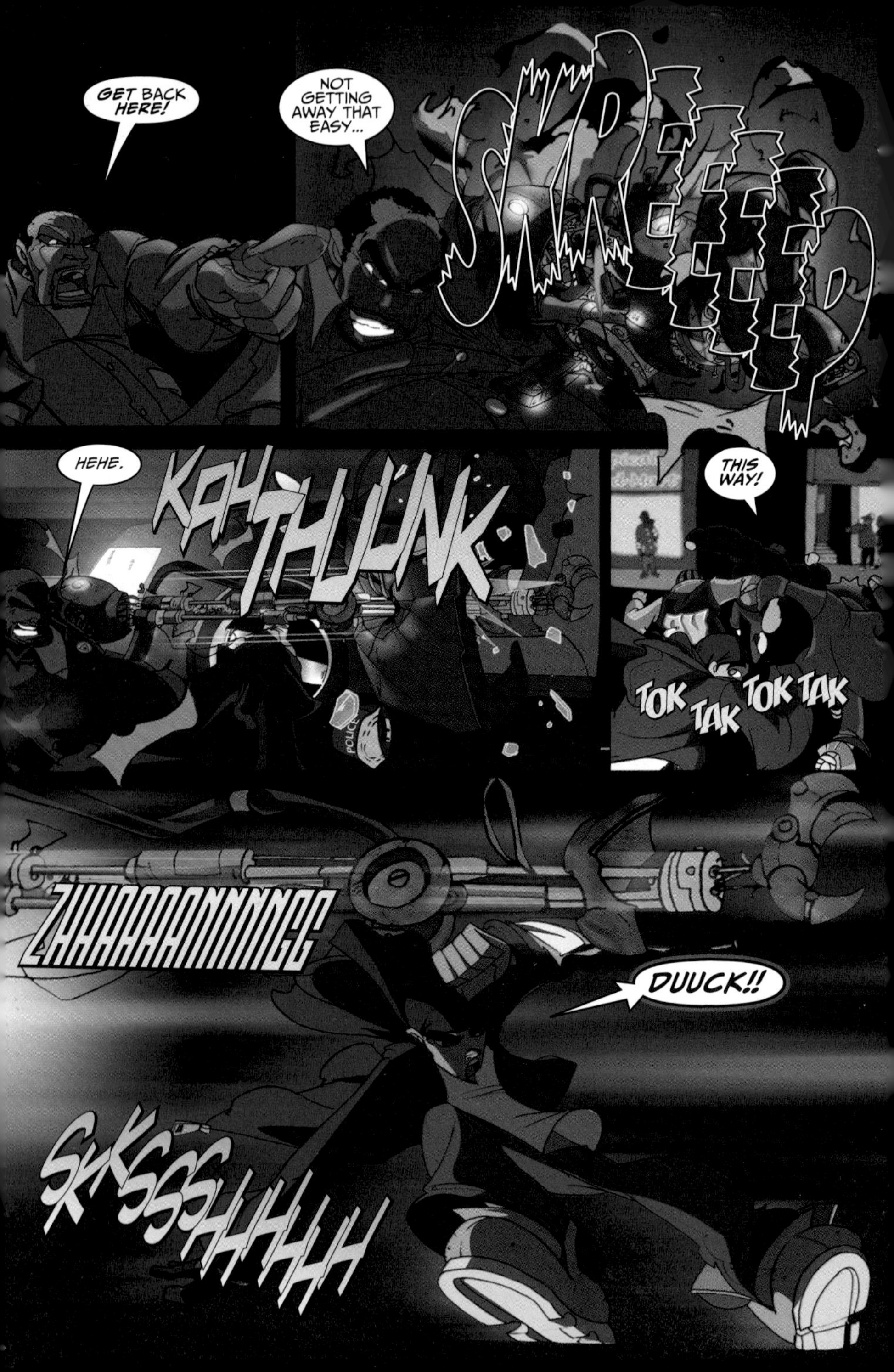
GET BACK HERE!
NOT GETTING AWAY THAT EASY...
SWREEEED
HEHE.
KAH THUNK
THIS WAY!
TOK TAK TOK TAK
ZHAAAAANNNGG
DUUCK!!
SKSSSHHHHH

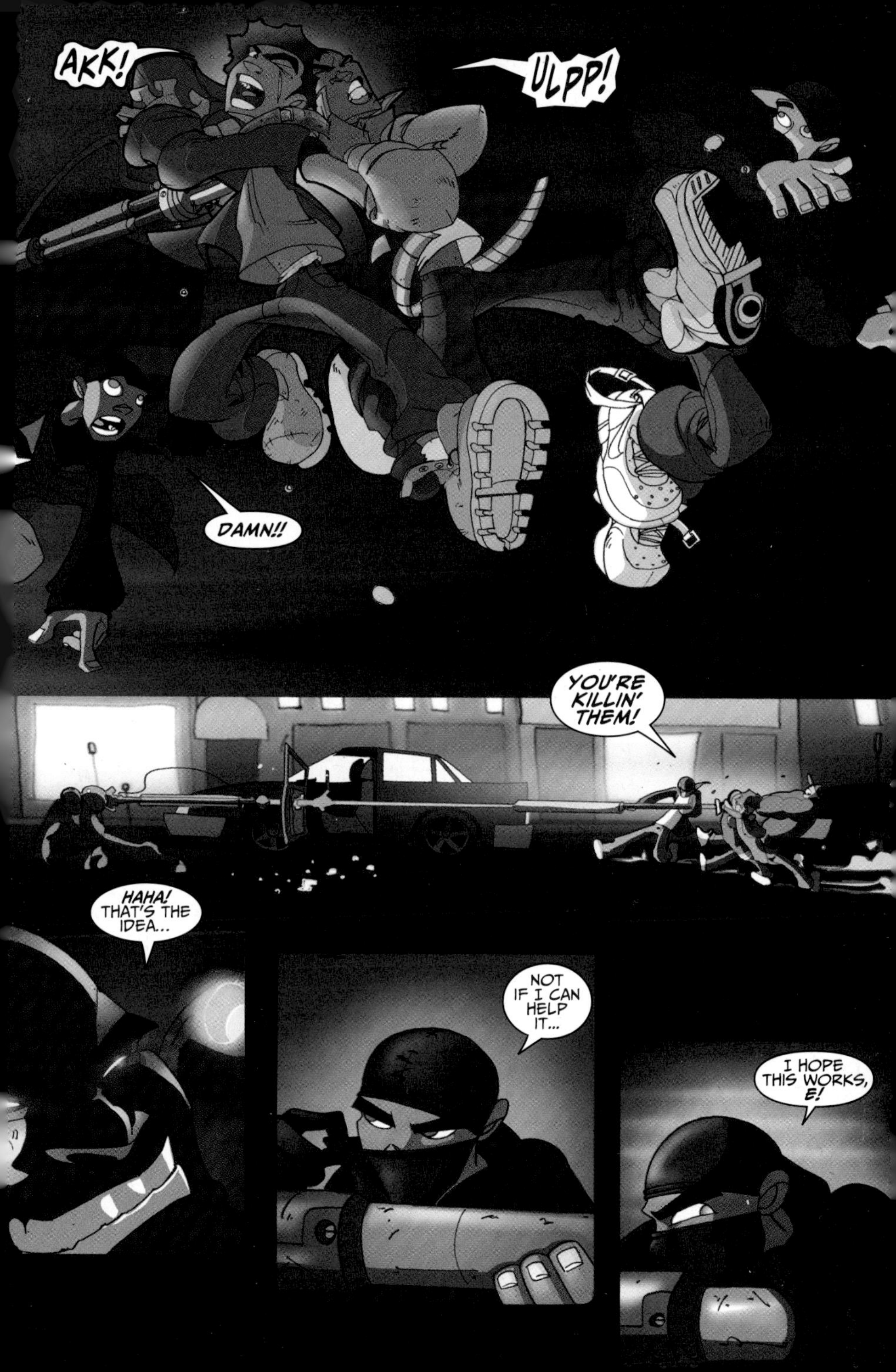
AKK!
ULPP!
DAMN!!
YOU'RE KILLIN' THEM!
HAHA! THAT'S THE IDEA...
NOT IF I CAN HELP IT...
I HOPE THIS WORKS, E!

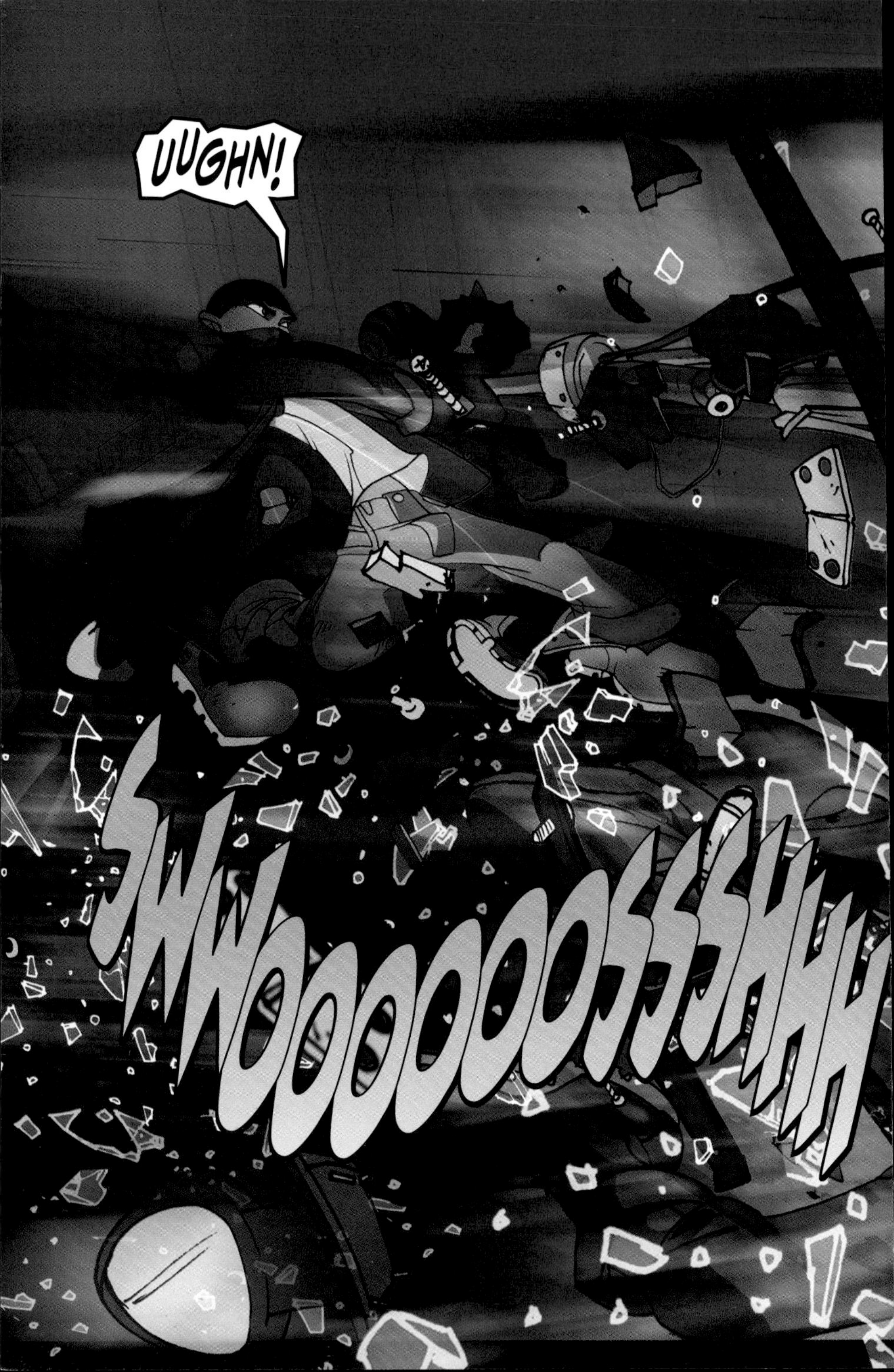
UUGHN!
SWHOOOOOSSHHH

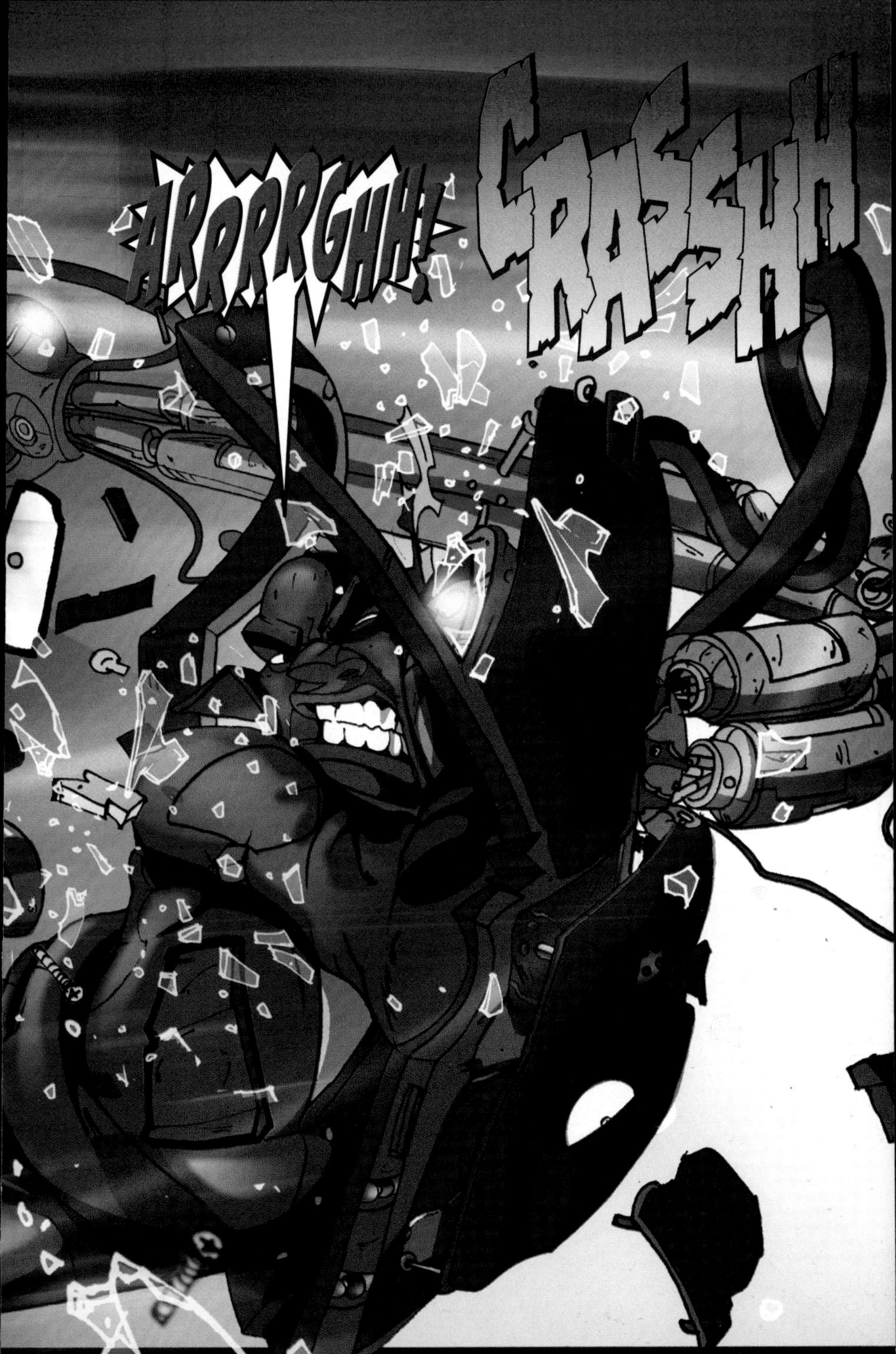
ARRRRGHH!
CRASSHH

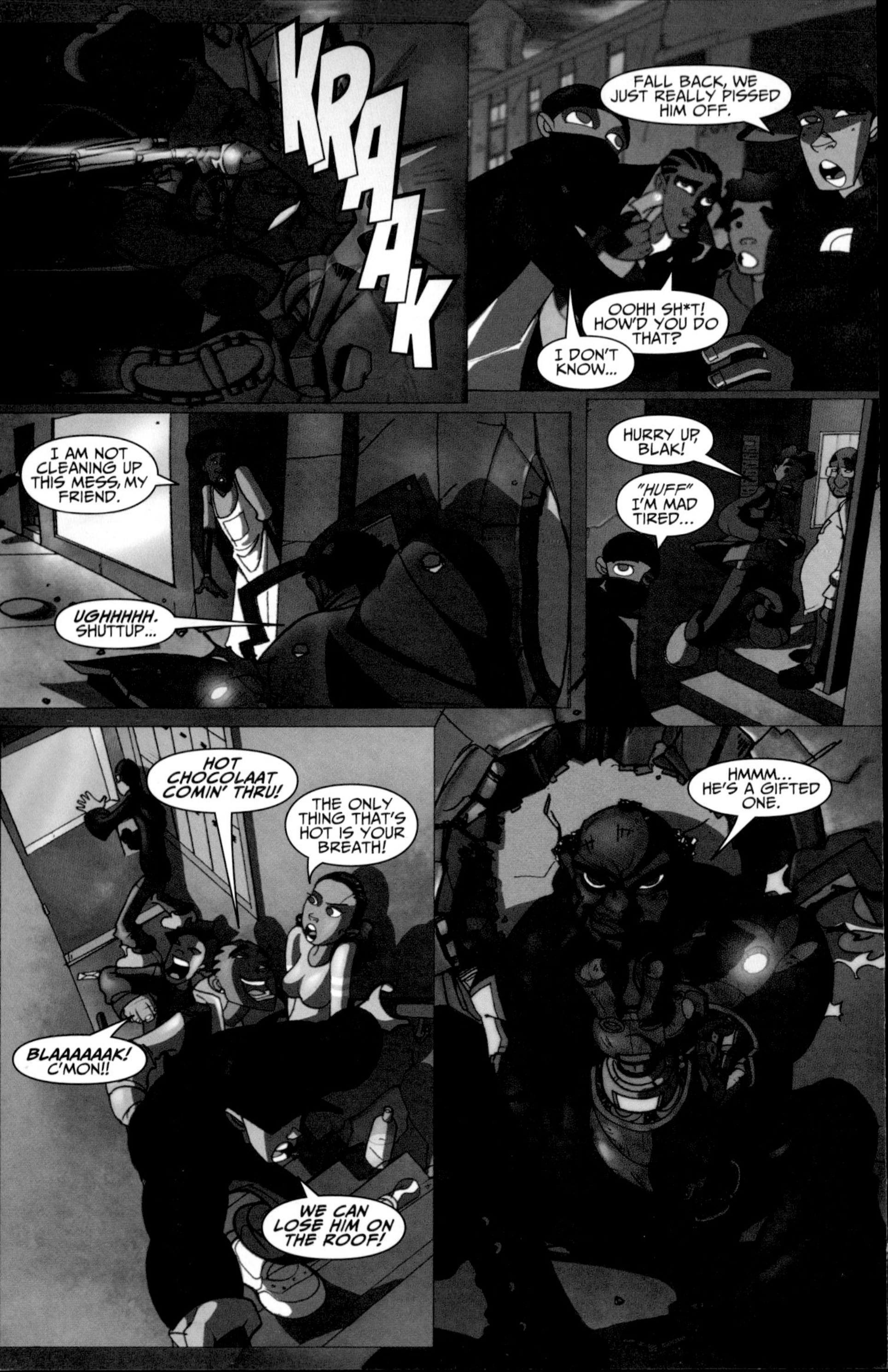
KRAAAK
FALL BACK, WE JUST REALLY PISSED HIM OFF.
OOHH SH*T! HOW'D YOU DO THAT?
I DON'T KNOW...
I AM NOT CLEANING UP THIS MESS, MY FRIEND.
UGHHHHH. SHUTTUP...
HURRY UP, BLAK!
"HUFF" I'M MAD TIRED...
HOT CHOCOLAAT COMIN' THRU!
THE ONLY THING THAT'S HOT IS YOUR BREATH!
BLAAAAAAK! C'MON!!
WE CAN LOSE HIM ON THE ROOF!
HMMM... HE'S A GIFTED ONE.

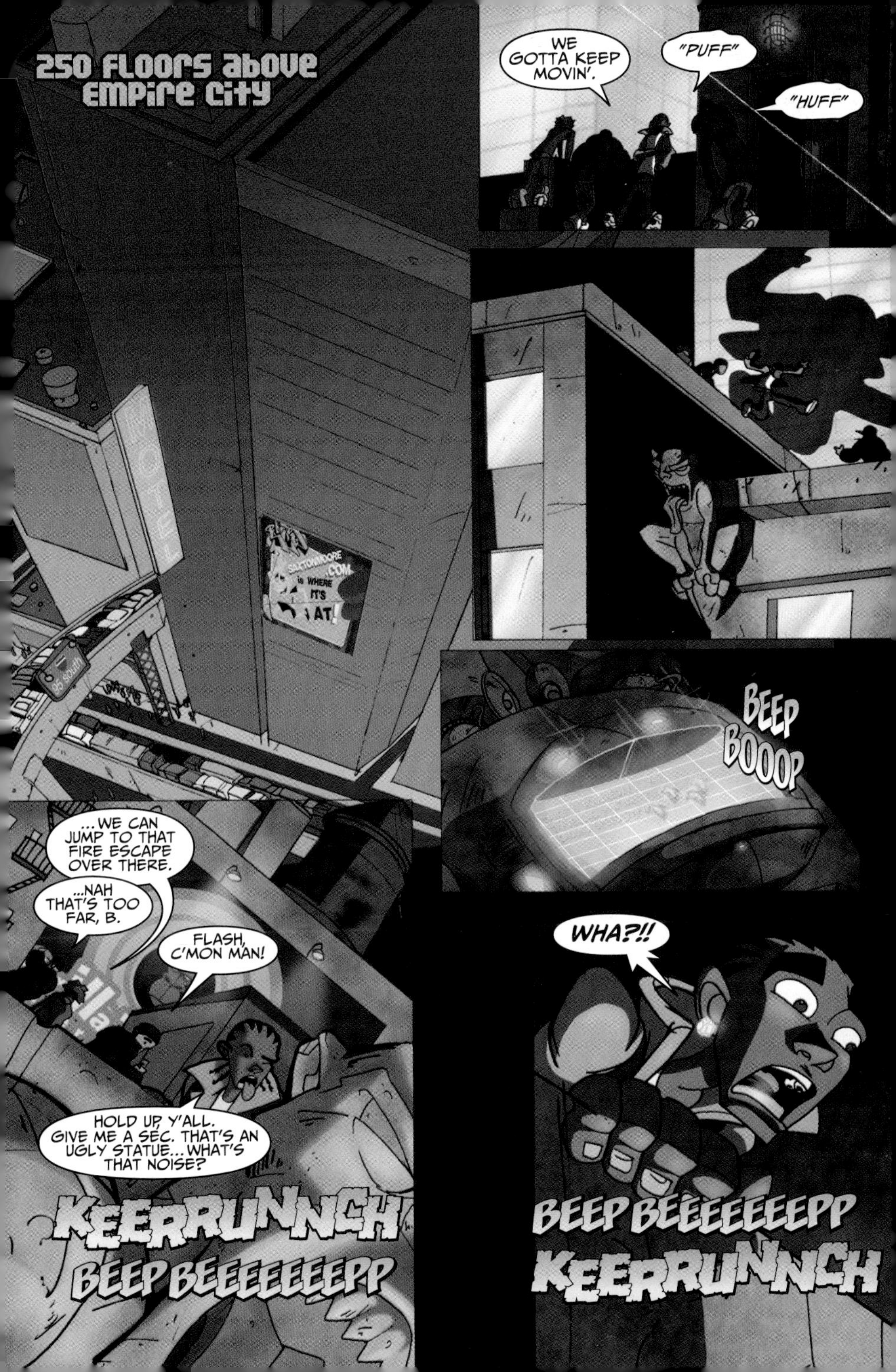
250 Floors above Empire City
WE GOTTA KEEP MOVIN'.
"PUFF"
"HUFF"
MOTEL
.COM is WHERE IT'S AT!
95 south
BEEP BOOOP
...WE CAN JUMP TO THAT FIRE ESCAPE OVER THERE.
...NAH THAT'S TOO FAR, B.
FLASH, C'MON MAN!
HOLD UP, Y'ALL. GIVE ME A SEC. THAT'S AN UGLY STATUE... WHAT'S THAT NOISE?
KEERRUNNCH
BEEP BEEEEEEEEPP
WHA?!!
BEEP BEEEEEEEEPP
KEERRUNNCH

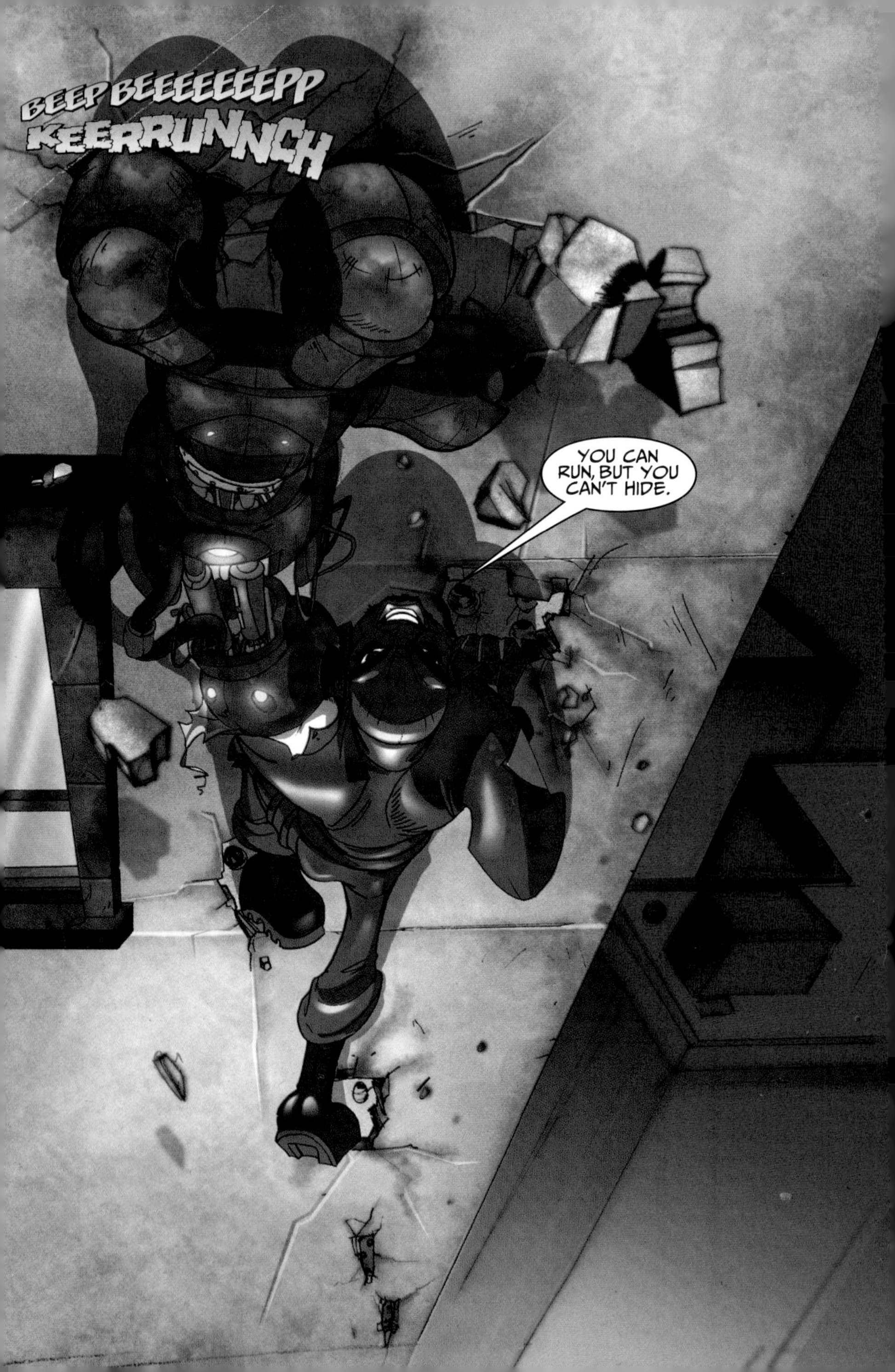
BEEP BEEEEEEEEPP
KEERRUNNCH
YOU CAN RUN, BUT YOU CAN'T HIDE.

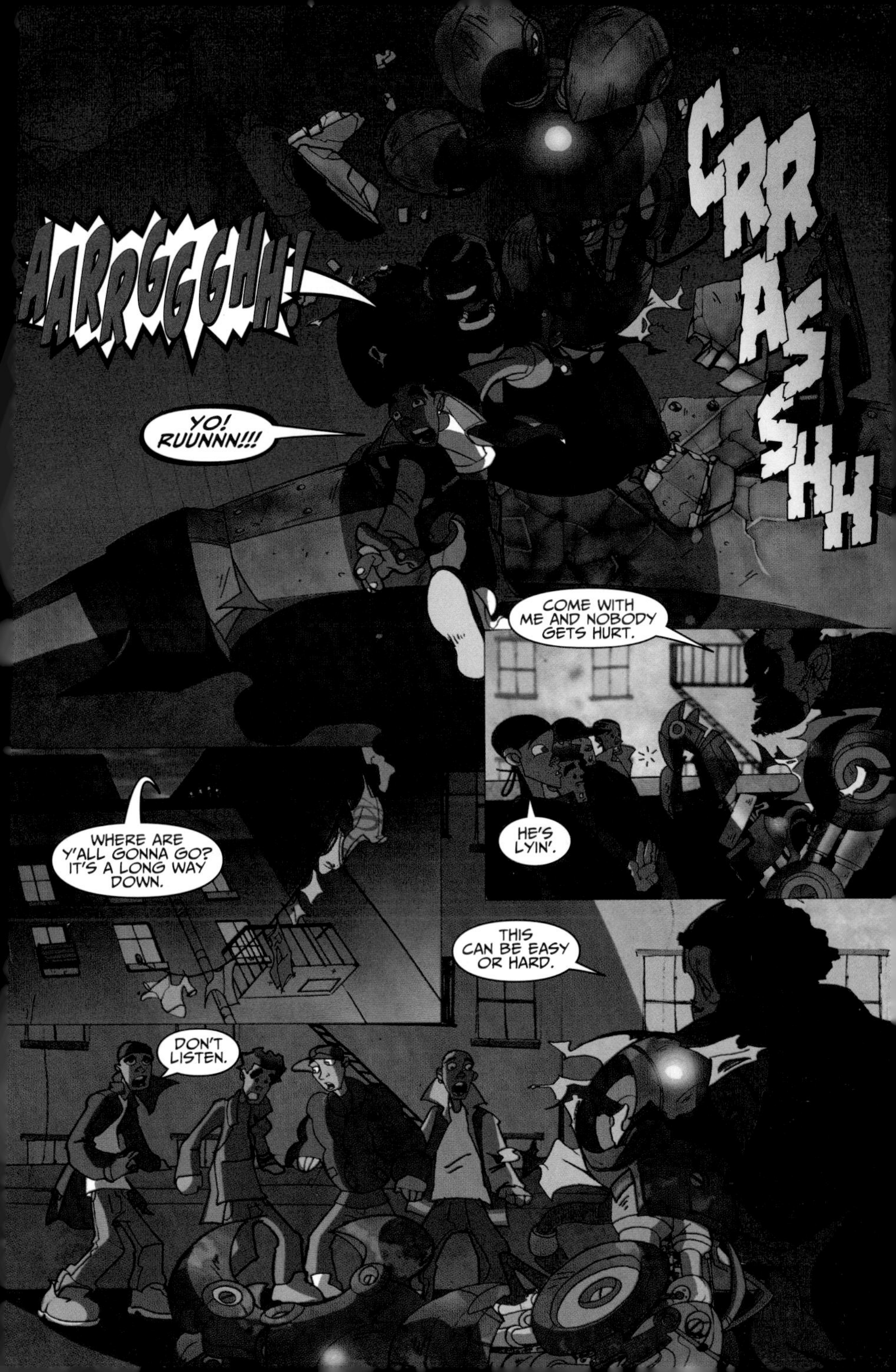
AARRGGGHH!
CRRASHH
YO! RUUNNN!!!
COME WITH ME AND NOBODY GETS HURT.
HE'S LYIN'.
WHERE ARE Y'ALL GONNA GO? IT'S A LONG WAY DOWN.
THIS CAN BE EASY OR HARD.
DON'T LISTEN.

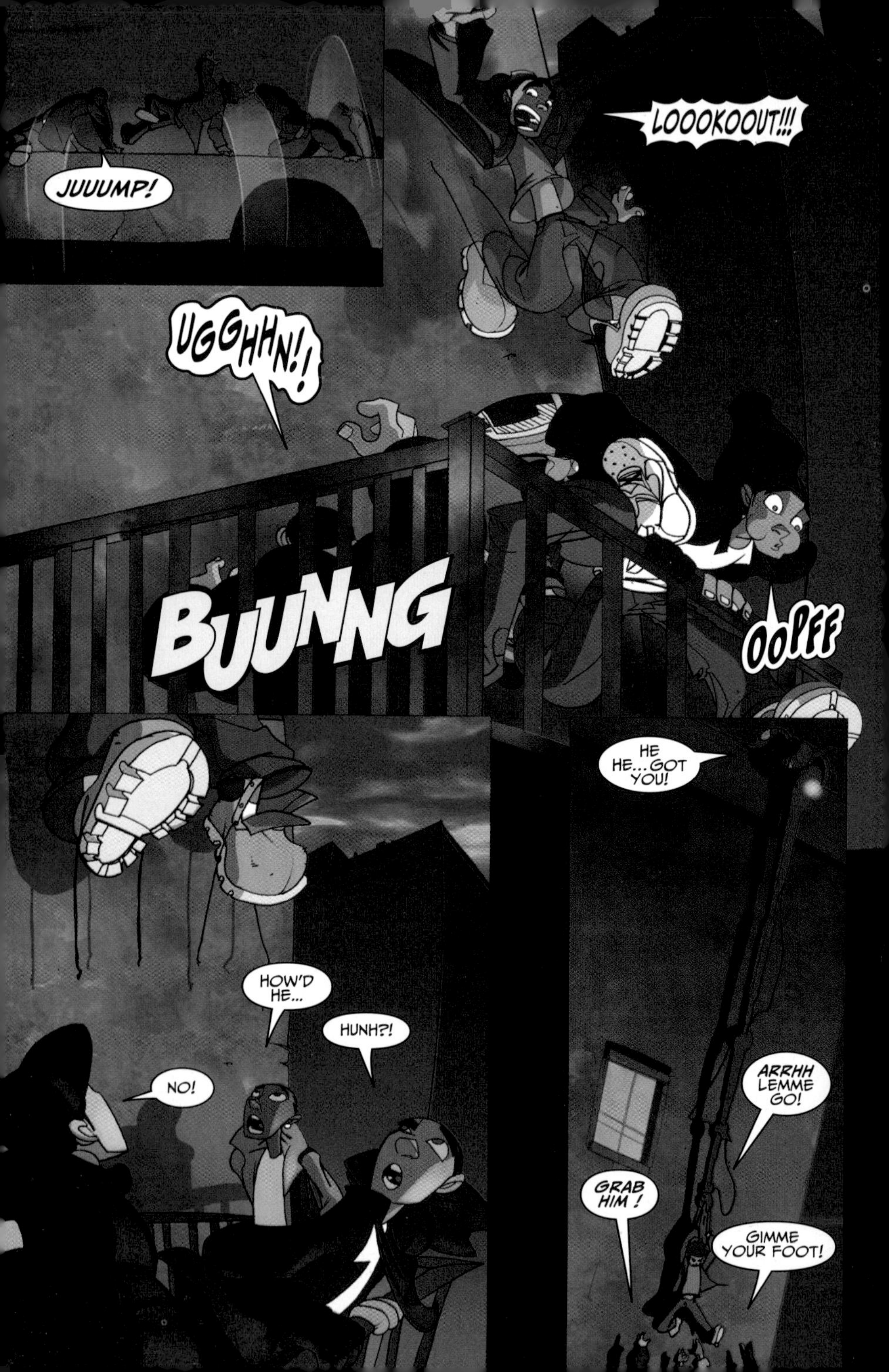
JUUUMP!
LOOOKOOUT!!!
UGGHHN!!
BUUNNG
OOPFF
HE
HE...GOT
YOU!
HOW'D
HE...
HUNH?!
NO!
ARRHH
LEMME
GO!
GRAB
HIM!
GIMME
YOUR FOOT!

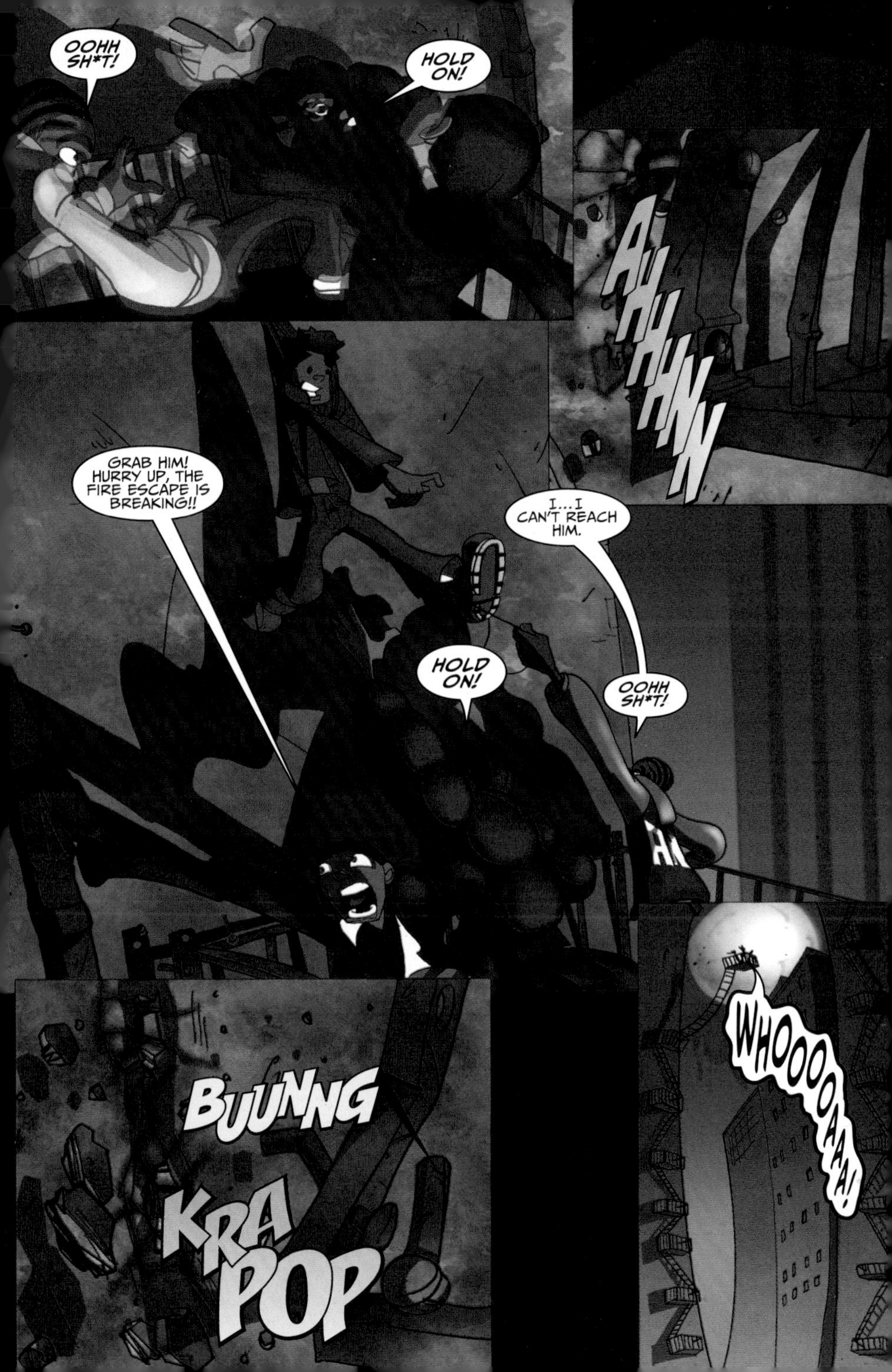
OOHH SH*T!
HOLD ON!
AHHHHNN
GRAB HIM! HURRY UP, THE FIRE ESCAPE IS BREAKING!!
I... I CAN'T REACH HIM.
HOLD ON!
OOHH SH*T!
BUUNNG
KRA POP
WHOOOOAAA!

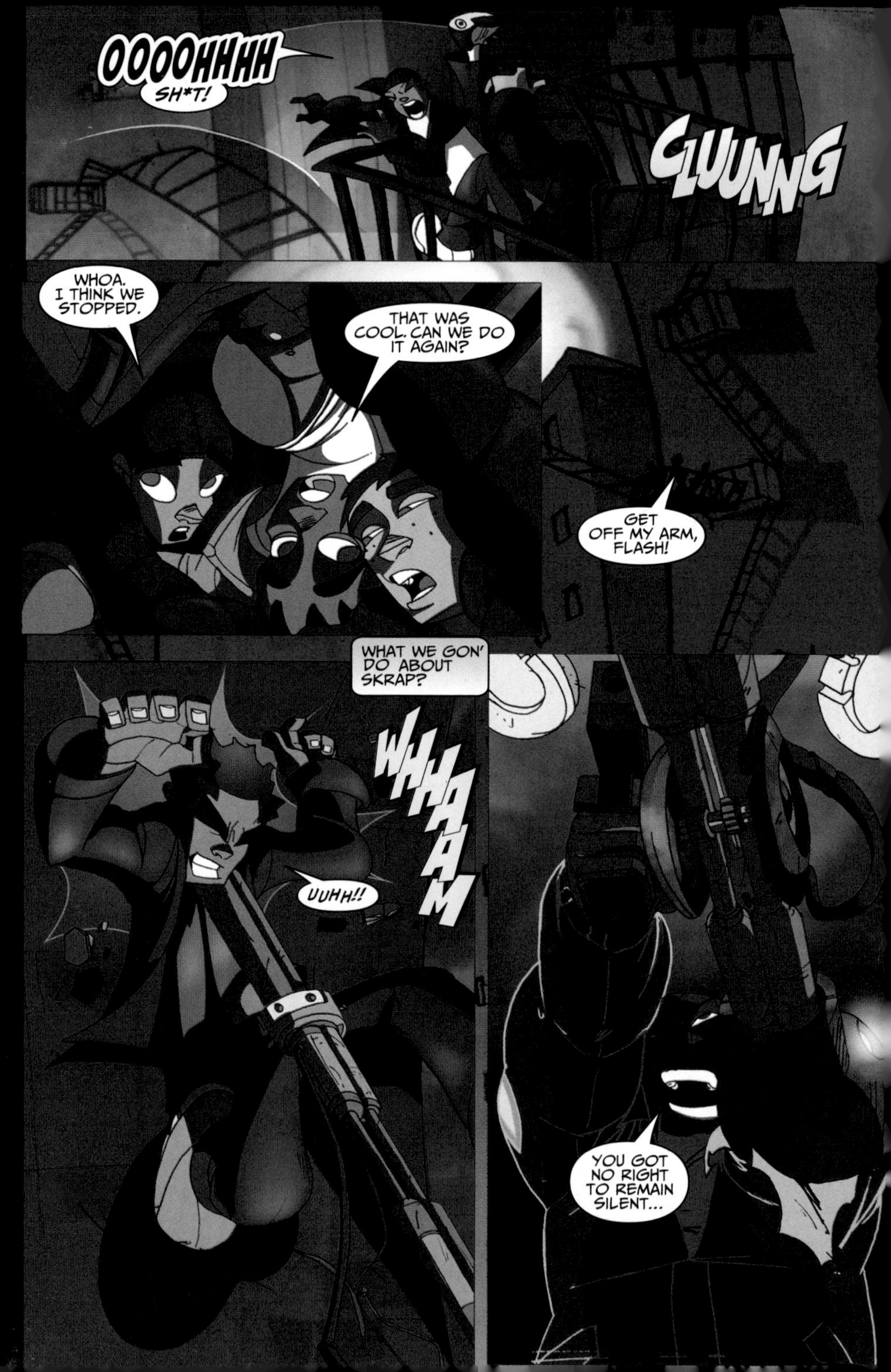
OOOOHHHH
SH*T!
CLUUNNG
WHOA. I THINK WE STOPPED.
THAT WAS COOL. CAN WE DO IT AGAIN?
GET OFF MY ARM, FLASH!
WHAT WE GON' DO ABOUT SKRAP?
WHHAAM
UUHH!!
YOU GOT NO RIGHT TO REMAIN SILENT...

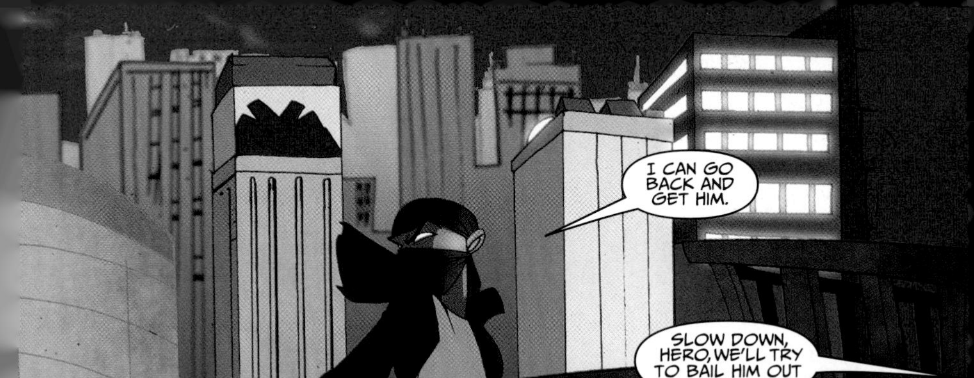
I CAN GO BACK AND GET HIM.
SLOW DOWN, HERO, WE'LL TRY TO BAIL HIM OUT LATER.

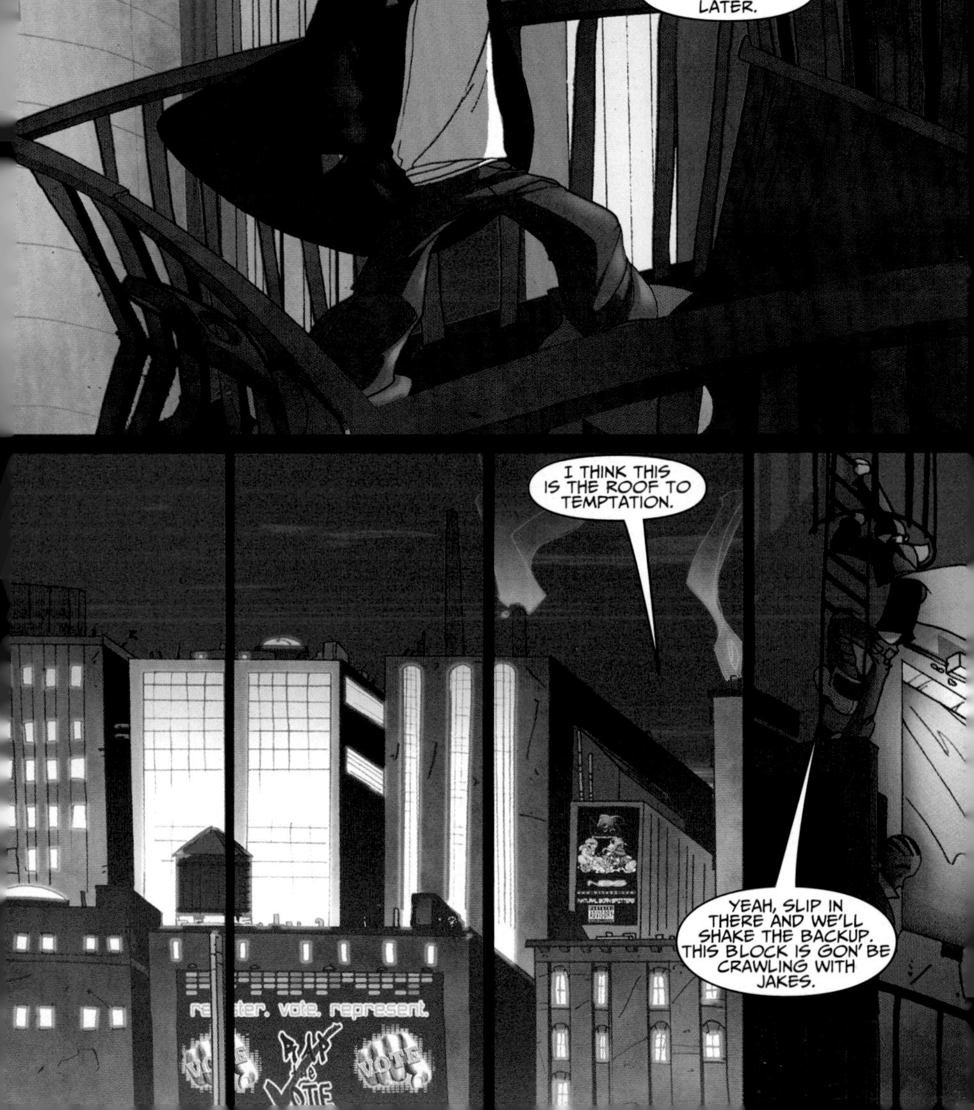
I THINK THIS IS THE ROOF TO TEMPTATION.
YEAH, SLIP IN THERE AND WE'LL SHAKE THE BACKUP. THIS BLOCK IS GON' BE CRAWLING WITH JAKES.

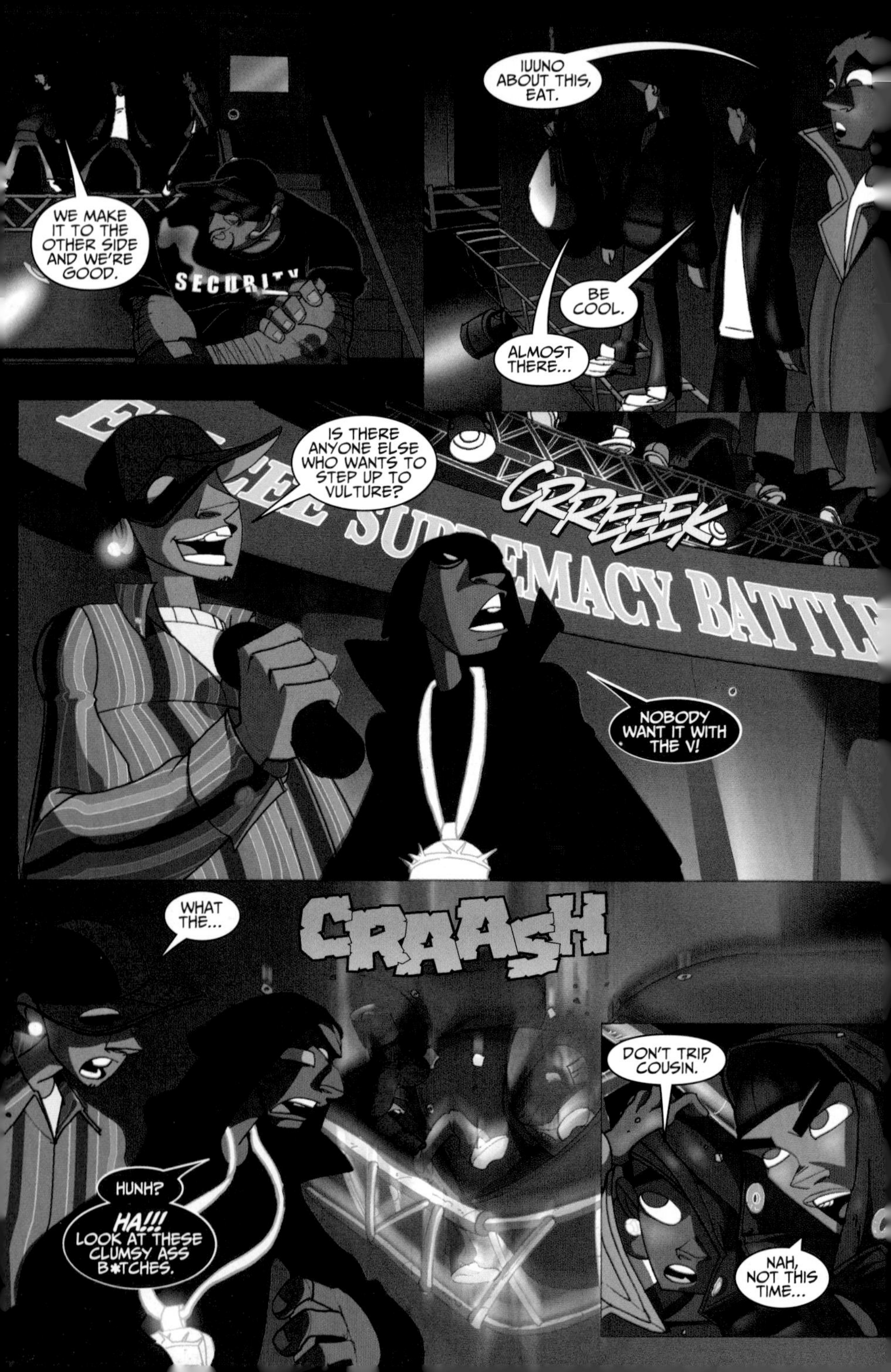
WE MAKE IT TO THE OTHER SIDE AND WE'RE GOOD.
IUUNO ABOUT THIS, EAT.
BE COOL.
ALMOST THERE...
IS THERE ANYONE ELSE WHO WANTS TO STEP UP TO VULTURE?
CRREEEK
NOBODY WANT IT WITH THE V!
WHAT THE...
CRAASH
HUNH?
HA!!! LOOK AT THESE CLUMSY ASS B*TCHES.
DON'T TRIP, COUSIN.
NAH, NOT THIS TIME...

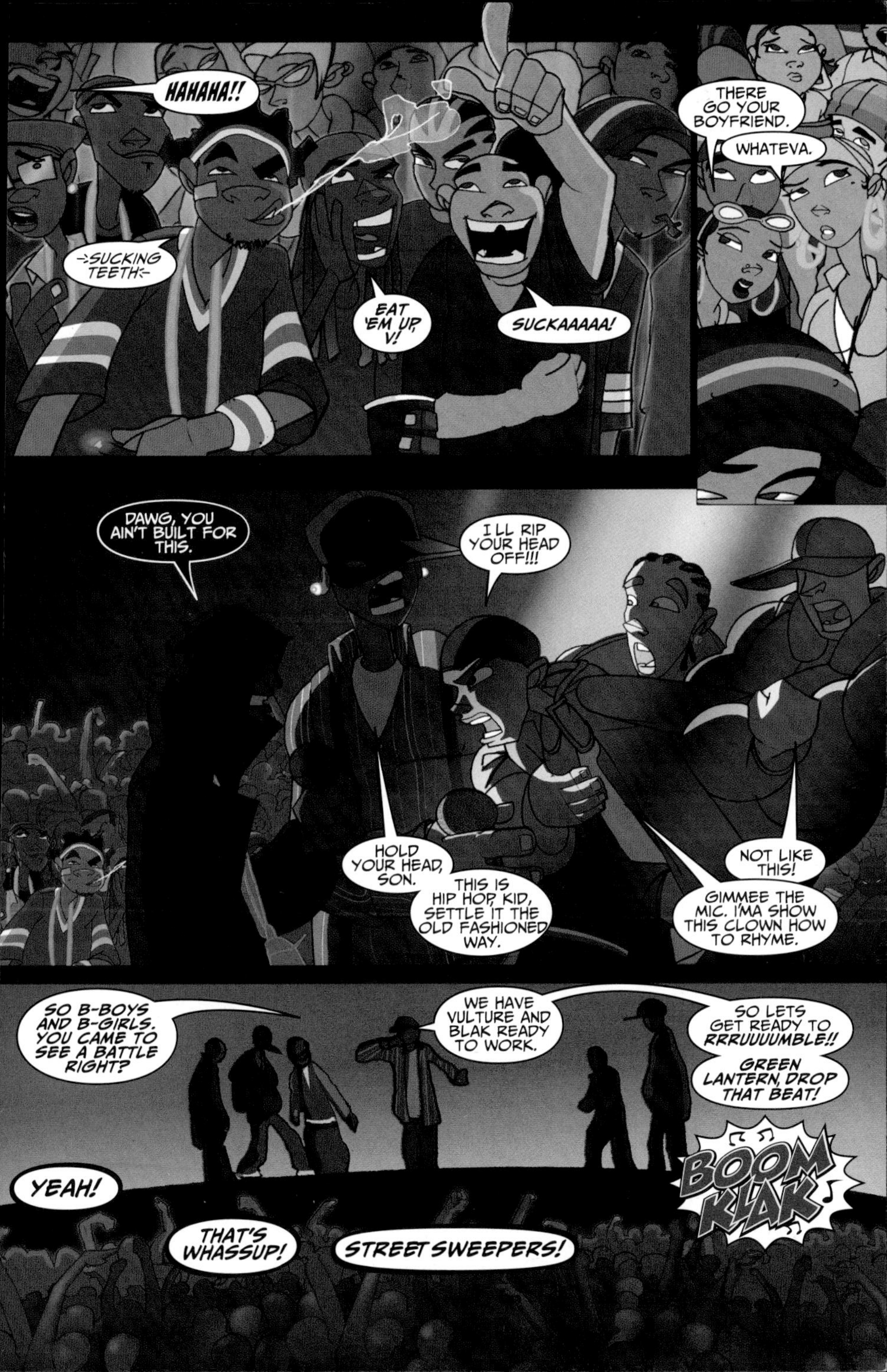

HAHAHA!!
-SUCKING TEETH-
EAT 'EM UP, V!
SUCKAAAAA!
THERE GO YOUR BOYFRIEND.
WHATEVA.
DAWG, YOU AIN'T BUILT FOR THIS.
I LL RIP YOUR HEAD OFF!!!
HOLD YOUR HEAD, SON.
THIS IS HIP HOP, KID, SETTLE IT THE OLD FASHIONED WAY.
NOT LIKE THIS!
GIMMEE THE MIC. I'MA SHOW THIS CLOWN HOW TO RHYME.
SO B-BOYS AND B-GIRLS. YOU CAME TO SEE A BATTLE RIGHT?
WE HAVE VULTURE AND BLAK READY TO WORK.
SO LETS GET READY TO RRRUUUUMBLE!!
GREEN LANTERN, DROP THAT BEAT!
BOOM KLAK
YEAH!
THAT'S WHASSUP!
STREET SWEEPERS!

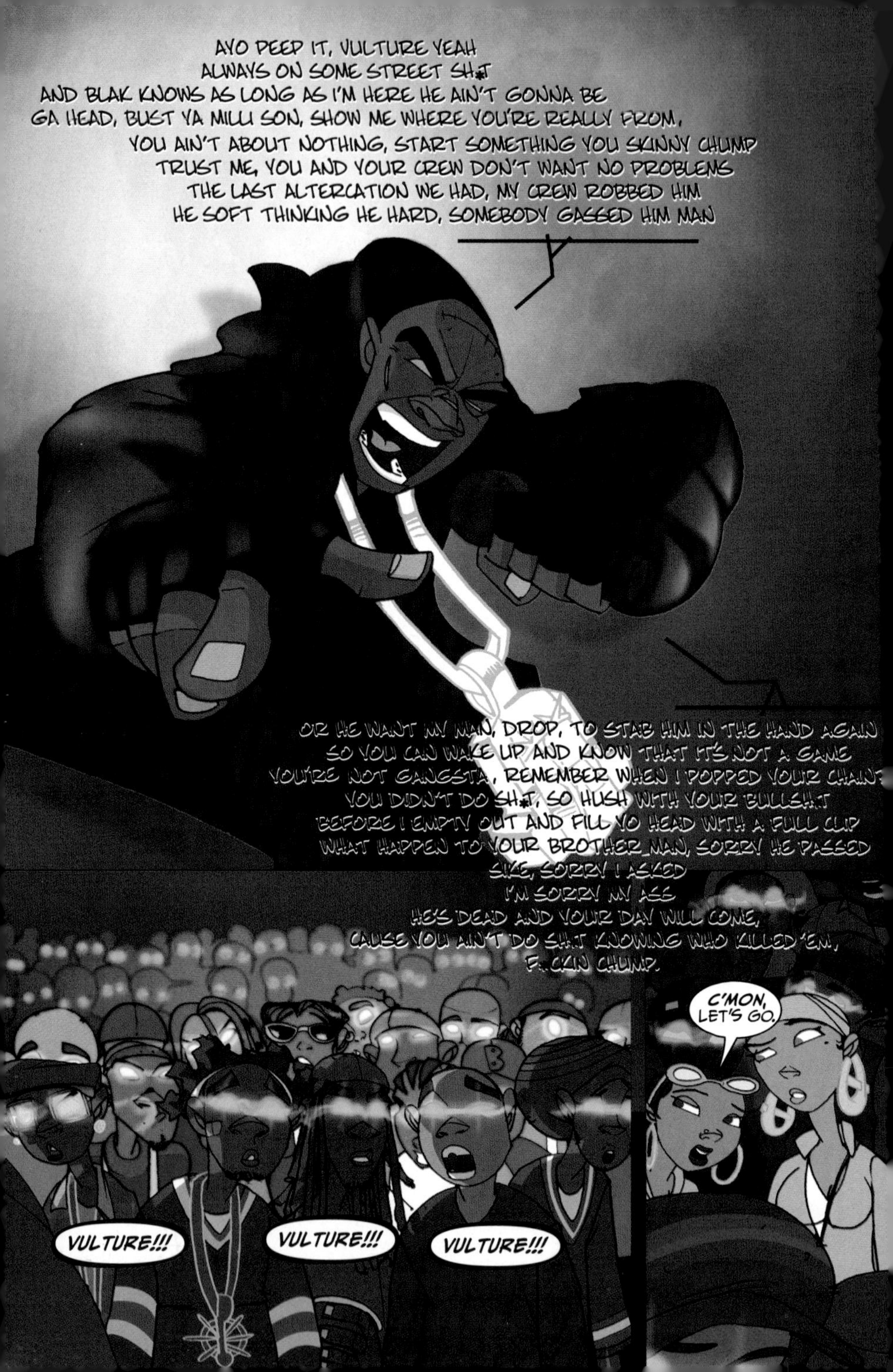
AYO PEEP IT, VULTURE YEAH
ALWAYS ON SOME STREET SH*T
AND BLAK KNOWS AS LONG AS I'M HERE HE AIN'T GONNA BE
GA HEAD, BUST YA MILLI SON, SHOW ME WHERE YOU'RE REALLY FROM.
YOU AIN'T ABOUT NOTHING, START SOMETHING YOU SKINNY CHUMP
TRUST ME, YOU AND YOUR CREW DON'T WANT NO PROBLEMS
THE LAST ALTERCATION WE HAD, MY CREW ROBBED HIM
HE SOFT THINKING HE HARD, SOMEBODY GASSED HIM MAN
OR HE WANT MY MAN, DROP, TO STAB HIM IN THE HAND AGAIN
SO YOU CAN WAKE UP AND KNOW THAT IT'S NOT A GAME
YOU'RE NOT GANGSTA, REMEMBER WHEN I POPPED YOUR CHAIN?
YOU DIDN'T DO SH*T, SO HUSH WITH YOUR BULLSH*T
BEFORE I EMPTY OUT AND FILL YO HEAD WITH A FULL CLIP
WHAT HAPPEN TO YOUR BROTHER_MAN, SORRY HE PASSED
SIKE, SORRY I ASKED
I'M SORRY MY ASS
HE'S DEAD AND YOUR DAY WILL COME,
CAUSE YOU AIN'T DO SH*T KNOWING WHO KILLED 'EM,
F*CKIN CHUMP.
C'MON, LET'S GO.
VULTURE!!!
VULTURE!!!
VULTURE!!!

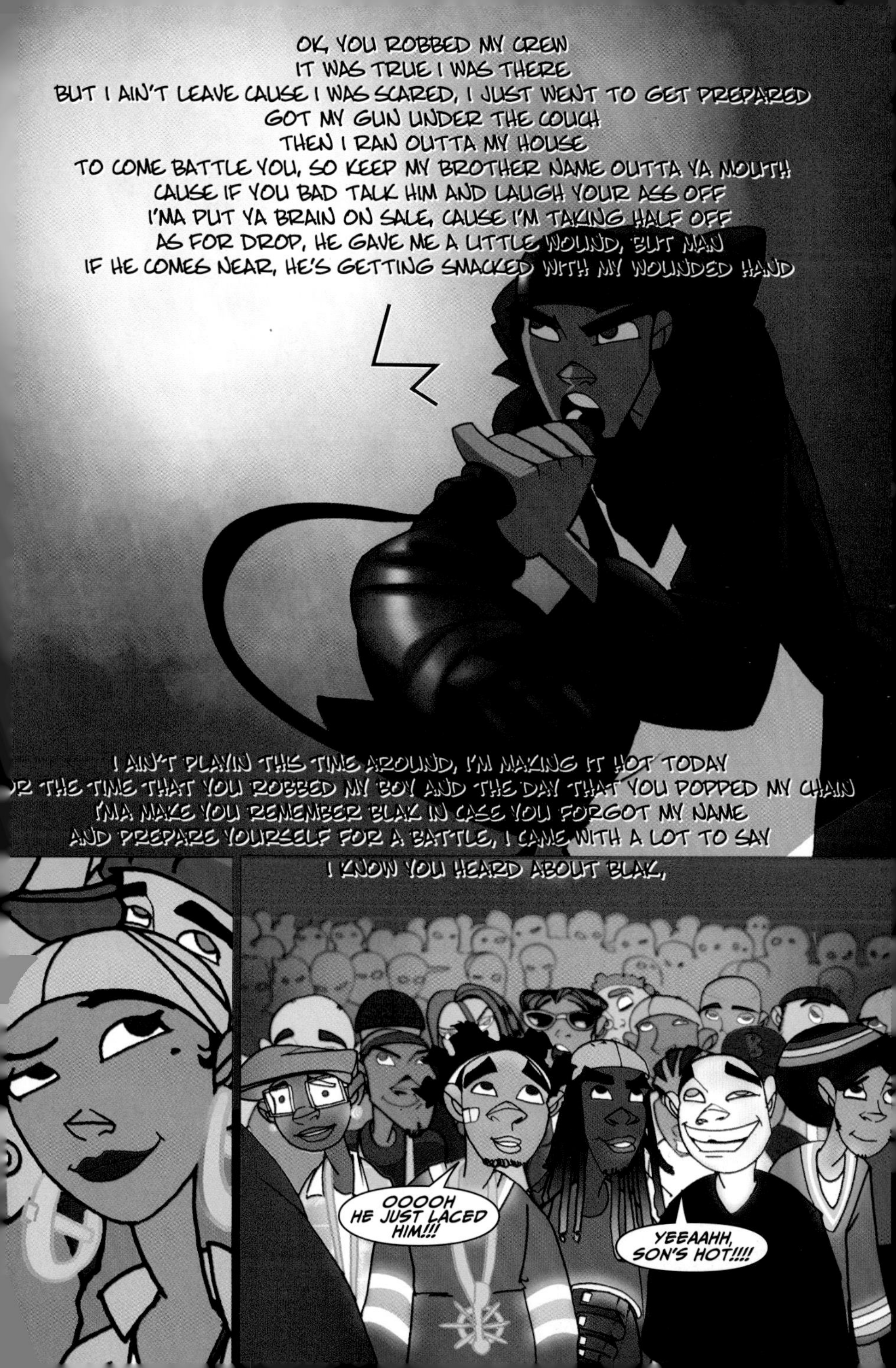
OK, YOU ROBBED MY CREW
IT WAS TRUE I WAS THERE
BUT I AIN'T LEAVE CAUSE I WAS SCARED, I JUST WENT TO GET PREPARED
GOT MY GUN UNDER THE COUCH
THEN I RAN OUTTA MY HOUSE
TO COME BATTLE YOU, SO KEEP MY BROTHER NAME OUTTA YA MOUTH
CAUSE IF YOU BAD TALK HIM AND LAUGH YOUR ASS OFF
I'MA PUT YA BRAIN ON SALE, CAUSE I'M TAKING HALF OFF
AS FOR DROP, HE GAVE ME A LITTLE WOUND, BUT MAN
IF HE COMES NEAR, HE'S GETTING SMACKED WITH MY WOUNDED HAND
I AIN'T PLAYIN THIS TIME AROUND, I'M MAKING IT HOT TODAY
R THE TIME THAT YOU ROBBED MY BOY AND THE DAY THAT YOU POPPED MY CHAIN
I'MA MAKE YOU REMEMBER BLAK IN CASE YOU FORGOT MY NAME
AND PREPARE YOURSELF FOR A BATTLE, I CAME WITH A LOT TO SAY
I KNOW YOU HEARD ABOUT BLAK,
OOOOH HE JUST LACED HIM!!!
YEEAAHH, SON'S HOT!!!!

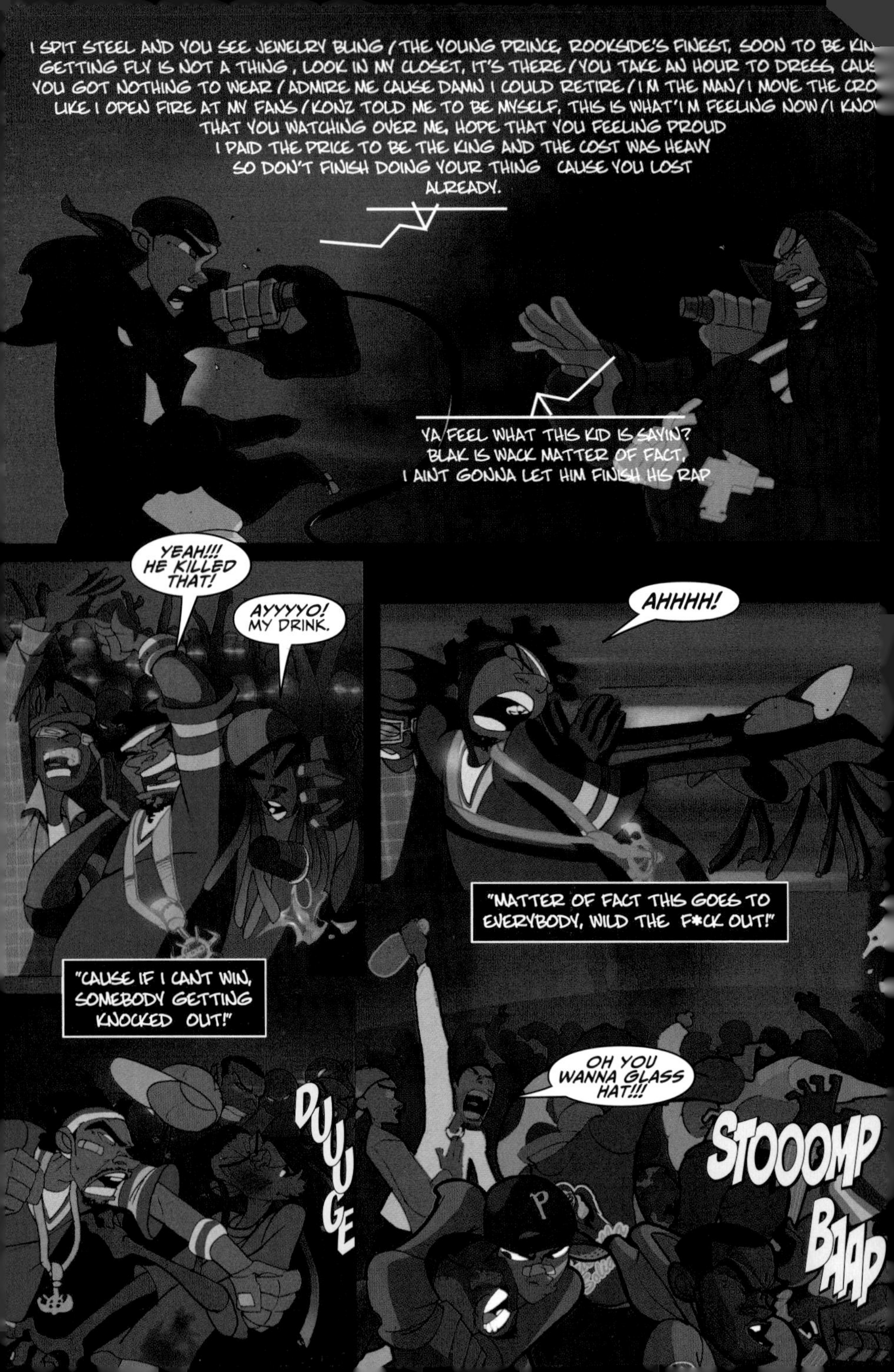
I SPIT STEEL AND YOU SEE JEWELRY BLING / THE YOUNG PRINCE, ROOKSIDE'S FINEST, SOON TO BE KIN
GETTING FLY IS NOT A THING, LOOK IN MY CLOSET, IT'S THERE / YOU TAKE AN HOUR TO DRESS CAUS
YOU GOT NOTHING TO WEAR / ADMIRE ME CAUSE DAMN I COULD RETIRE / I'M THE MAN / I MOVE THE CRO
LIKE I OPEN FIRE AT MY FANS / KONZ TOLD ME TO BE MYSELF, THIS IS WHAT I'M FEELING NOW / I KNO
THAT YOU WATCHING OVER ME, HOPE THAT YOU FEELING PROUD
I PAID THE PRICE TO BE THE KING AND THE COST WAS HEAVY
SO DON'T FINISH DOING YOUR THING CAUSE YOU LOST ALREADY.
YA FEEL WHAT THIS KID IS SAYIN? BLAK IS WACK MATTER OF FACT. I AINT GONNA LET HIM FINISH HIS RAP
YEAH!!! HE KILLED THAT!
AYYYYO! MY DRINK.
AHHHH!
"MATTER OF FACT THIS GOES TO EVERYBODY, WILD THE F*CK OUT!"
"CAUSE IF I CANT WIN, SOMEBODY GETTING KNOCKED OUT!"
OH YOU WANNA GLASS HAT!!!
DUUUGE
STOOOMP
BAAP

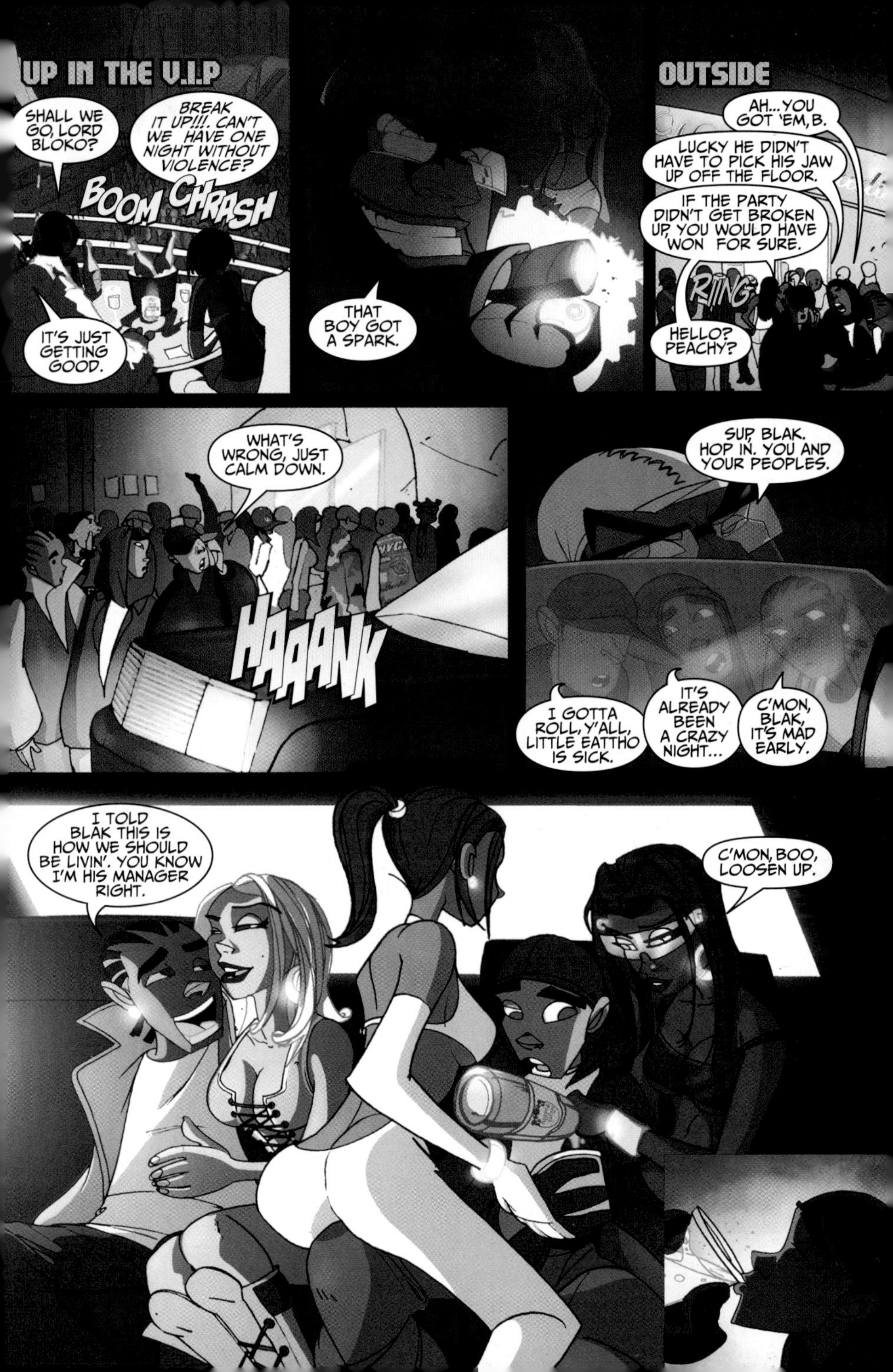
UP IN THE V.I.P
SHALL WE GO, LORD BLOKO?
BREAK IT UP!!!. CAN'T WE HAVE ONE NIGHT WITHOUT VIOLENCE?
BOOM CHRASH
IT'S JUST GETTING GOOD.
THAT BOY GOT A SPARK.
OUTSIDE
AH...YOU GOT 'EM, B.
LUCKY HE DIDN'T HAVE TO PICK HIS JAW UP OFF THE FLOOR.
IF THE PARTY DIDN'T GET BROKEN UP, YOU WOULD HAVE WON FOR SURE.
RIING
HELLO? PEACHY?
WHAT'S WRONG, JUST CALM DOWN.
HAAANK
SUP, BLAK. HOP IN. YOU AND YOUR PEOPLES.
I GOTTA ROLL, Y'ALL, LITTLE EATTHO IS SICK.
IT'S ALREADY BEEN A CRAZY NIGHT...
C'MON, BLAK, IT'S MAD EARLY.
I TOLD BLAK THIS IS HOW WE SHOULD BE LIVIN'. YOU KNOW I'M HIS MANAGER RIGHT.
C'MON, BOO, LOOSEN UP.

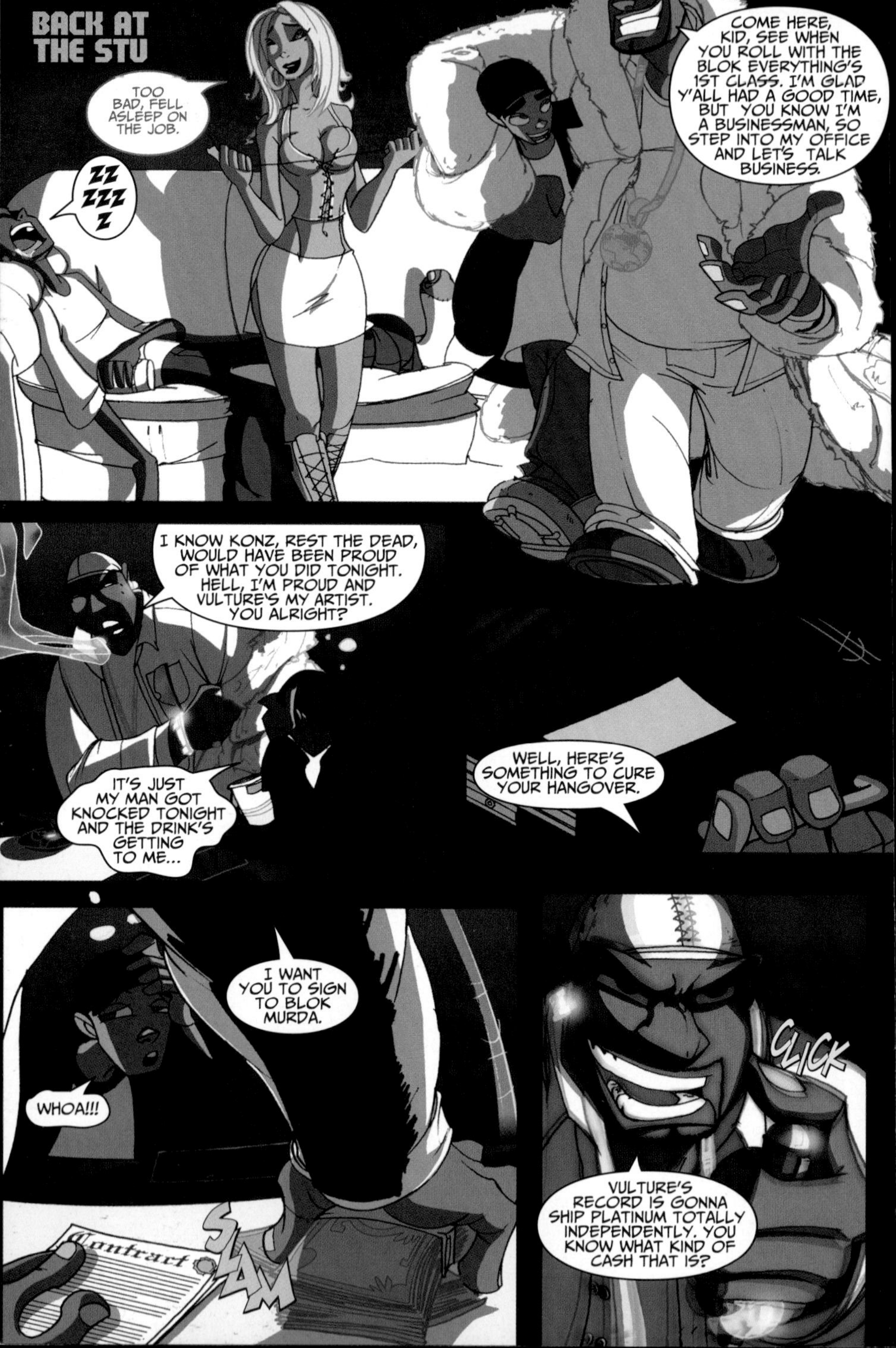
BACK AT THE STU
TOO BAD, FELL ASLEEP ON THE JOB.
ZZ ZZZ Z
COME HERE, KID, SEE WHEN YOU ROLL WITH THE BLOK EVERYTHING'S 1ST CLASS. I'M GLAD Y'ALL HAD A GOOD TIME, BUT YOU KNOW I'M A BUSINESSMAN, SO STEP INTO MY OFFICE AND LET'S TALK BUSINESS.
I KNOW KONZ, REST THE DEAD, WOULD HAVE BEEN PROUD OF WHAT YOU DID TONIGHT. HELL, I'M PROUD AND VULTURE'S MY ARTIST. YOU ALRIGHT?
IT'S JUST MY MAN GOT KNOCKED TONIGHT AND THE DRINK'S GETTING TO ME...
WELL, HERE'S SOMETHING TO CURE YOUR HANGOVER.
I WANT YOU TO SIGN TO BLOK MURDA.
WHOA!!!
Contract
SLAM
CLICK
VULTURE'S RECORD IS GONNA SHIP PLATINUM TOTALLY INDEPENDENTLY. YOU KNOW WHAT KIND OF CASH THAT IS?

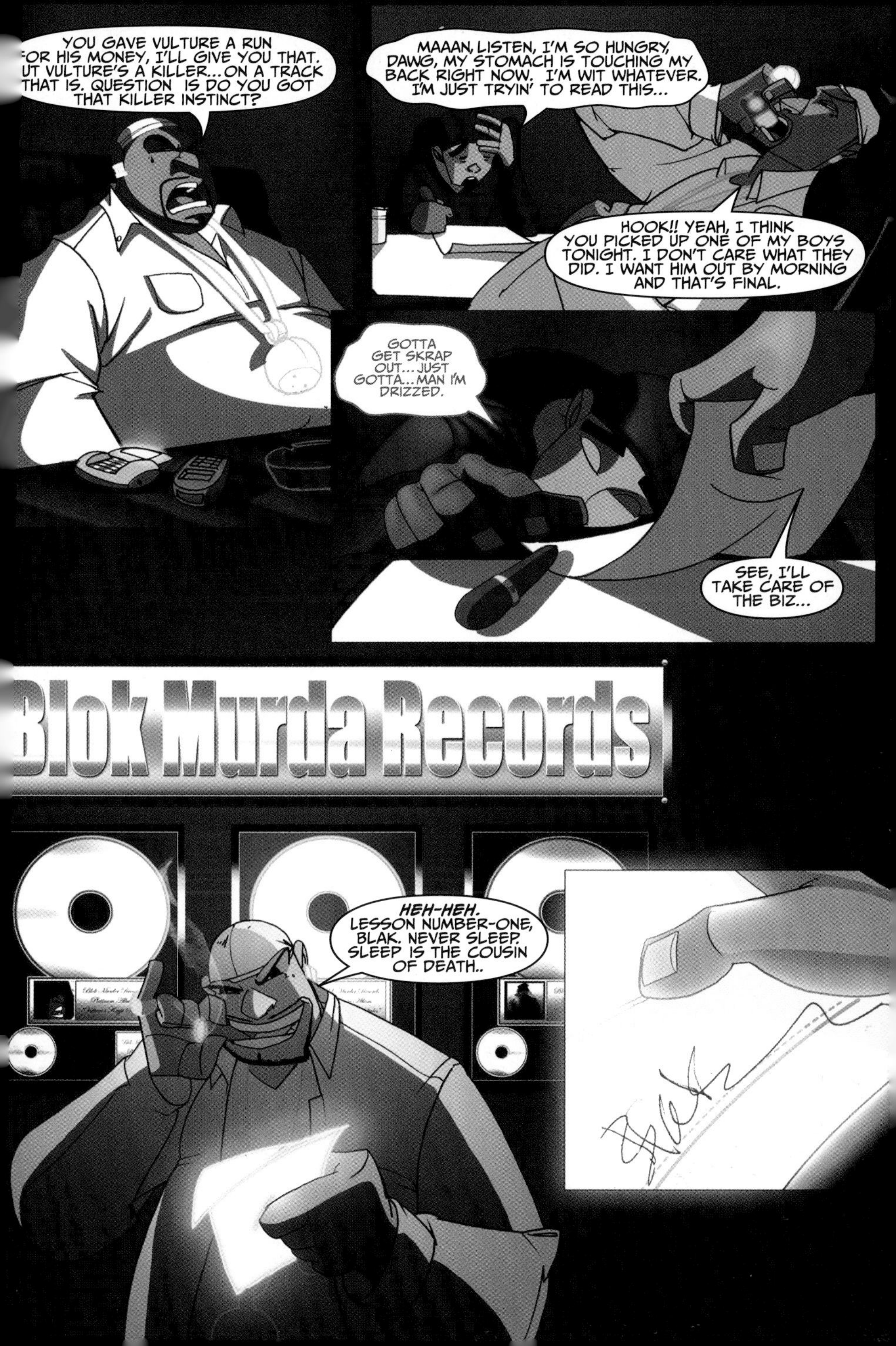
YOU GAVE VULTURE A RUN FOR HIS MONEY, I'LL GIVE YOU THAT. UT VULTURE'S A KILLER...ON A TRACK THAT IS. QUESTION IS DO YOU GOT THAT KILLER INSTINCT?
MAAAN, LISTEN, I'M SO HUNGRY, DAWG, MY STOMACH IS TOUCHING MY BACK RIGHT NOW. I'M WIT WHATEVER. I'M JUST TRYIN' TO READ THIS...
HOOK!! YEAH, I THINK YOU PICKED UP ONE OF MY BOYS TONIGHT. I DON'T CARE WHAT THEY DID. I WANT HIM OUT BY MORNING AND THAT'S FINAL.
GOTTA GET SKRAP OUT... JUST GOTTA... MAN I'M DRIZZED.
SEE, I'LL TAKE CARE OF THE BIZ...
Blok Murda Records
HEH-HEH. LESSON NUMBER-ONE, BLAK. NEVER SLEEP. SLEEP IS THE COUSIN OF DEATH..

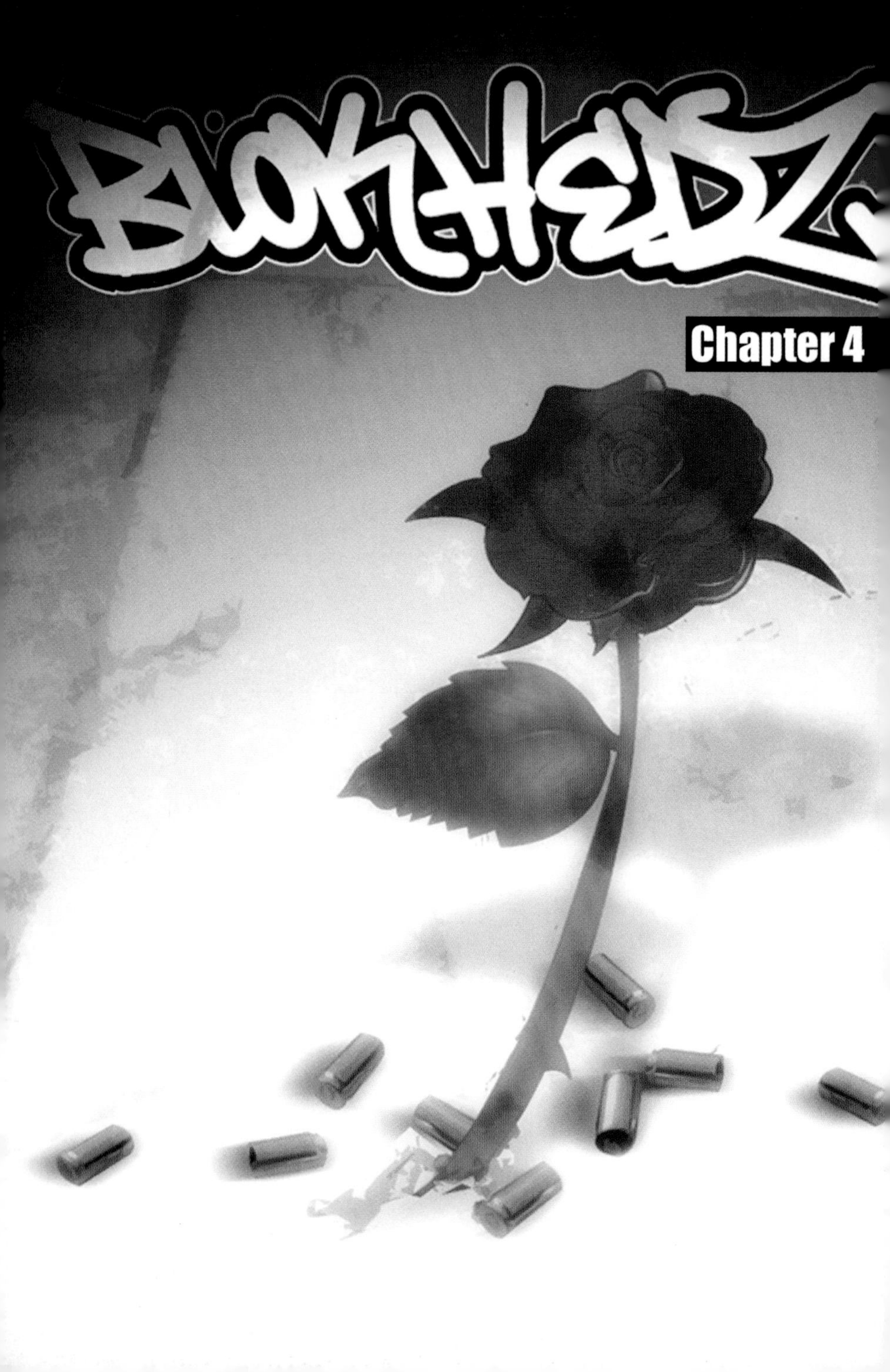
BLOKHEDZ
Chapter 4

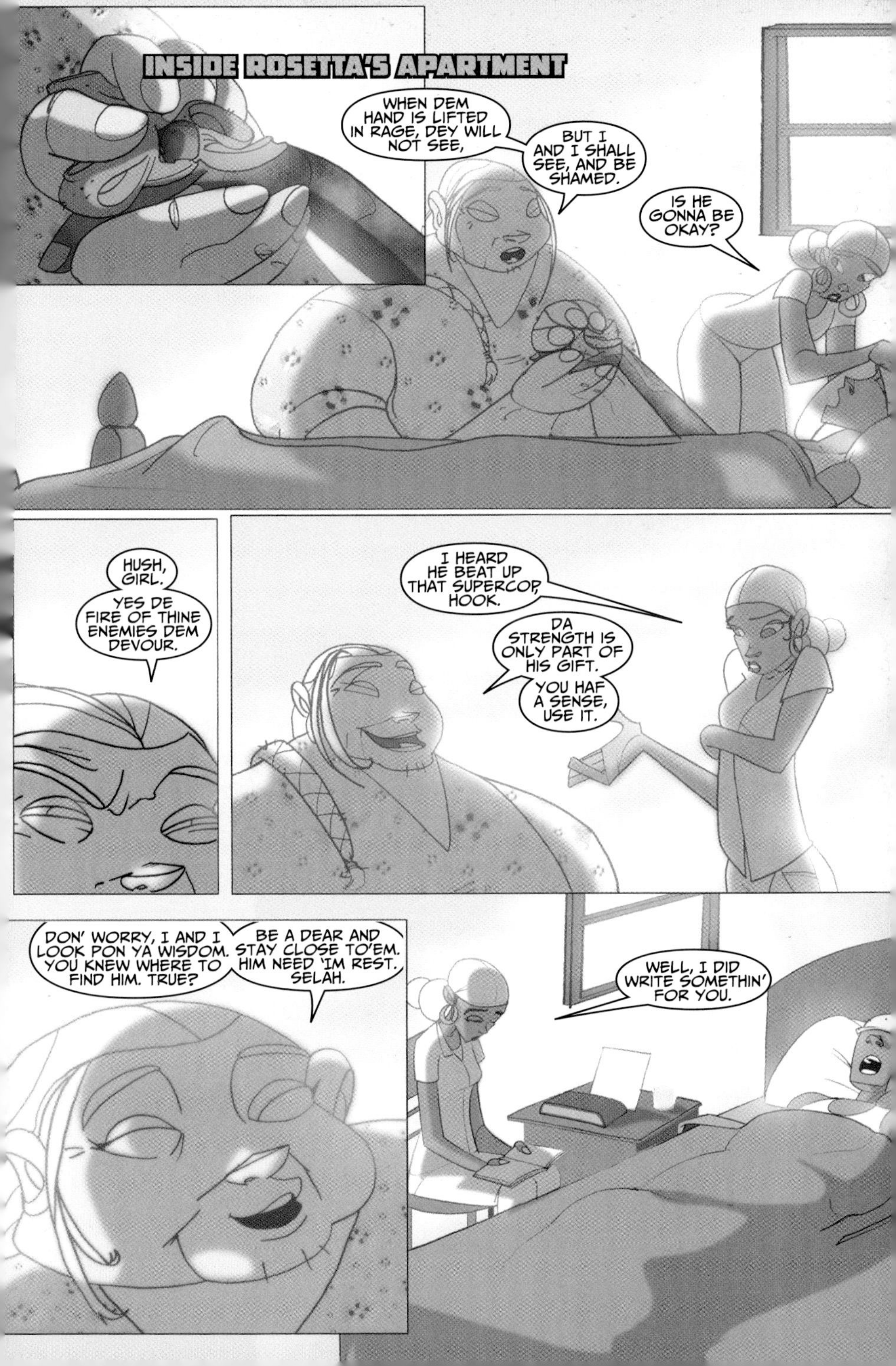
INSIDE ROSETTA'S APARTMENT
WHEN DEM HAND IS LIFTED IN RAGE, DEY WILL NOT SEE,
BUT I AND I SHALL SEE, AND BE SHAMED.
IS HE GONNA BE OKAY?
HUSH, GIRL.
YES DE FIRE OF THINE ENEMIES DEM DEVOUR.
I HEARD HE BEAT UP THAT SUPERCOP, HOOK.
DA STRENGTH IS ONLY PART OF HIS GIFT.
YOU HAF A SENSE, USE IT.
DON' WORRY, I AND I LOOK PON YA WISDOM. YOU KNEW WHERE TO FIND HIM. TRUE?
BE A DEAR AND STAY CLOSE TO'EM. HIM NEED 'IM REST. SELAH.
WELL, I DID WRITE SOMETHIN' FOR YOU.

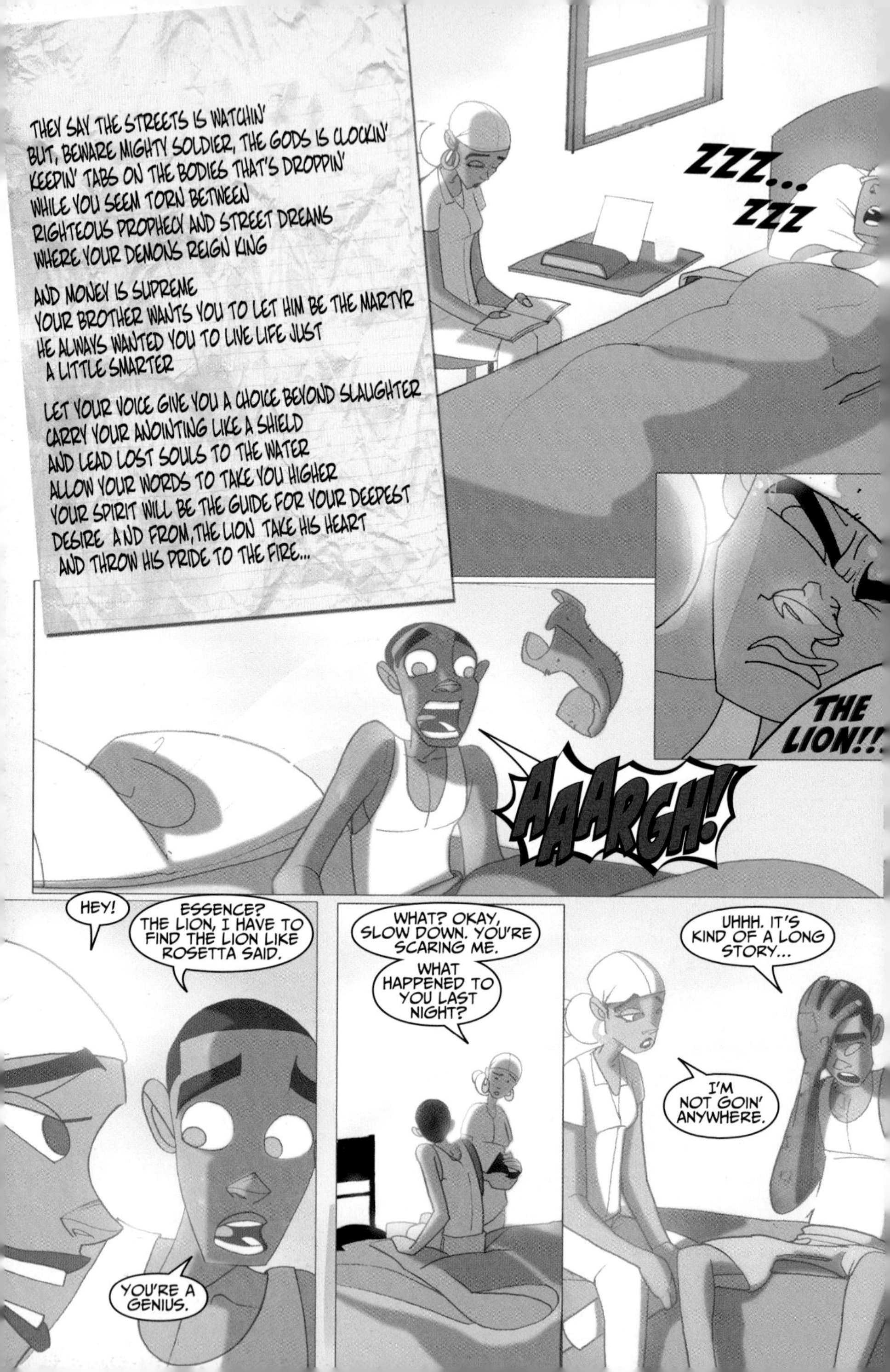
THEY SAY THE STREETS IS WATCHIN'
BUT, BEWARE MIGHTY SOLDIER, THE GODS IS CLOCKIN'
KEEPIN' TABS ON THE BODIES THAT'S DROPPIN'
WHILE YOU SEEM TORN BETWEEN
RIGHTEOUS PROPHECY AND STREET DREAMS
WHERE YOUR DEMONS REIGN KING
AND MONEY IS SUPREME
YOUR BROTHER WANTS YOU TO LET HIM BE THE MARTYR
HE ALWAYS WANTED YOU TO LIVE LIFE JUST A LITTLE SMARTER
LET YOUR VOICE GIVE YOU A CHOICE BEYOND SLAUGHTER
CARRY YOUR ANOINTING LIKE A SHIELD
AND LEAD LOST SOULS TO THE WATER
ALLOW YOUR WORDS TO TAKE YOU HIGHER
YOUR SPIRIT WILL BE THE GUIDE FOR YOUR DEEPEST DESIRE AND FROM, THE LION TAKE HIS HEART
AND THROW HIS PRIDE TO THE FIRE...
ZZZ... ZZZ
THE LION!!
AAARGH!
HEY!
ESSENCE? THE LION, I HAVE TO FIND THE LION LIKE ROSETTA SAID.
YOU'RE A GENIUS.
WHAT? OKAY, SLOW DOWN. YOU'RE SCARING ME.
WHAT HAPPENED TO YOU LAST NIGHT?
UHHH. IT'S KIND OF A LONG STORY...
I'M NOT GOIN' ANYWHERE.

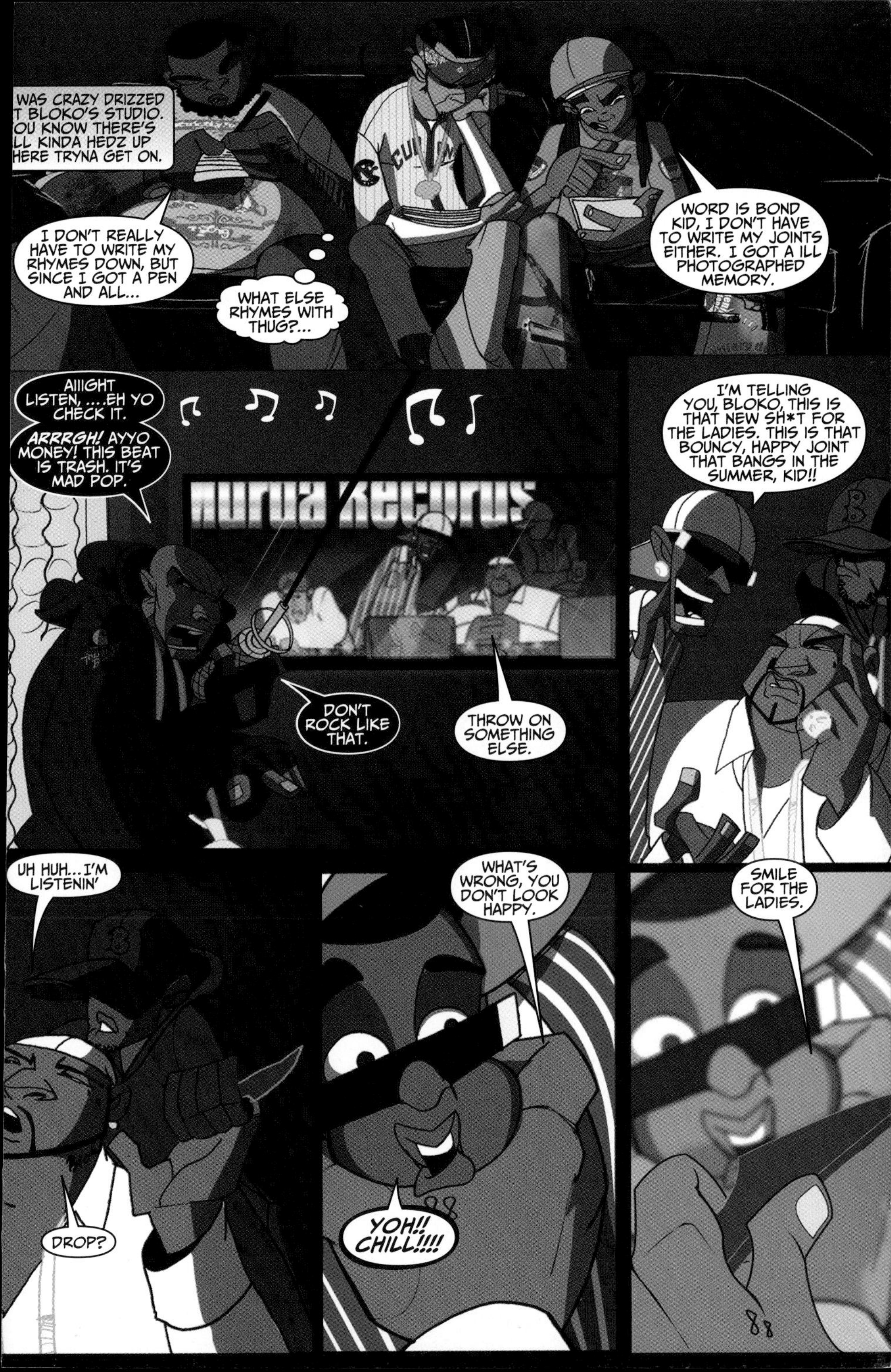
WAS CRAZY DRIZZED
T BLOKO'S STUDIO.
OU KNOW THERE'S
LL KINDA HEDZ UP
HERE TRYNA GET ON.
I DON'T REALLY HAVE TO WRITE MY RHYMES DOWN, BUT SINCE I GOT A PEN AND ALL...
WHAT ELSE RHYMES WITH THUG?...
WORD IS BOND KID, I DON'T HAVE TO WRITE MY JOINTS EITHER. I GOT A ILL PHOTOGRAPHED MEMORY.
AIIIGHT LISTEN, ...EH YO CHECK IT.
ARRRGH! AYYO MONEY! THIS BEAT IS TRASH. IT'S MAD POP.
I'M TELLING YOU, BLOKO, THIS IS THAT NEW SH*T FOR THE LADIES. THIS IS THAT BOUNCY, HAPPY JOINT THAT BANGS IN THE SUMMER, KID!!
DON'T ROCK LIKE THAT.
THROW ON SOMETHING ELSE.
UH HUH...I'M LISTENIN'
DROP?
WHAT'S WRONG, YOU DON'T LOOK HAPPY.
YOH!! CHILL!!!!
SMILE FOR THE LADIES.
88

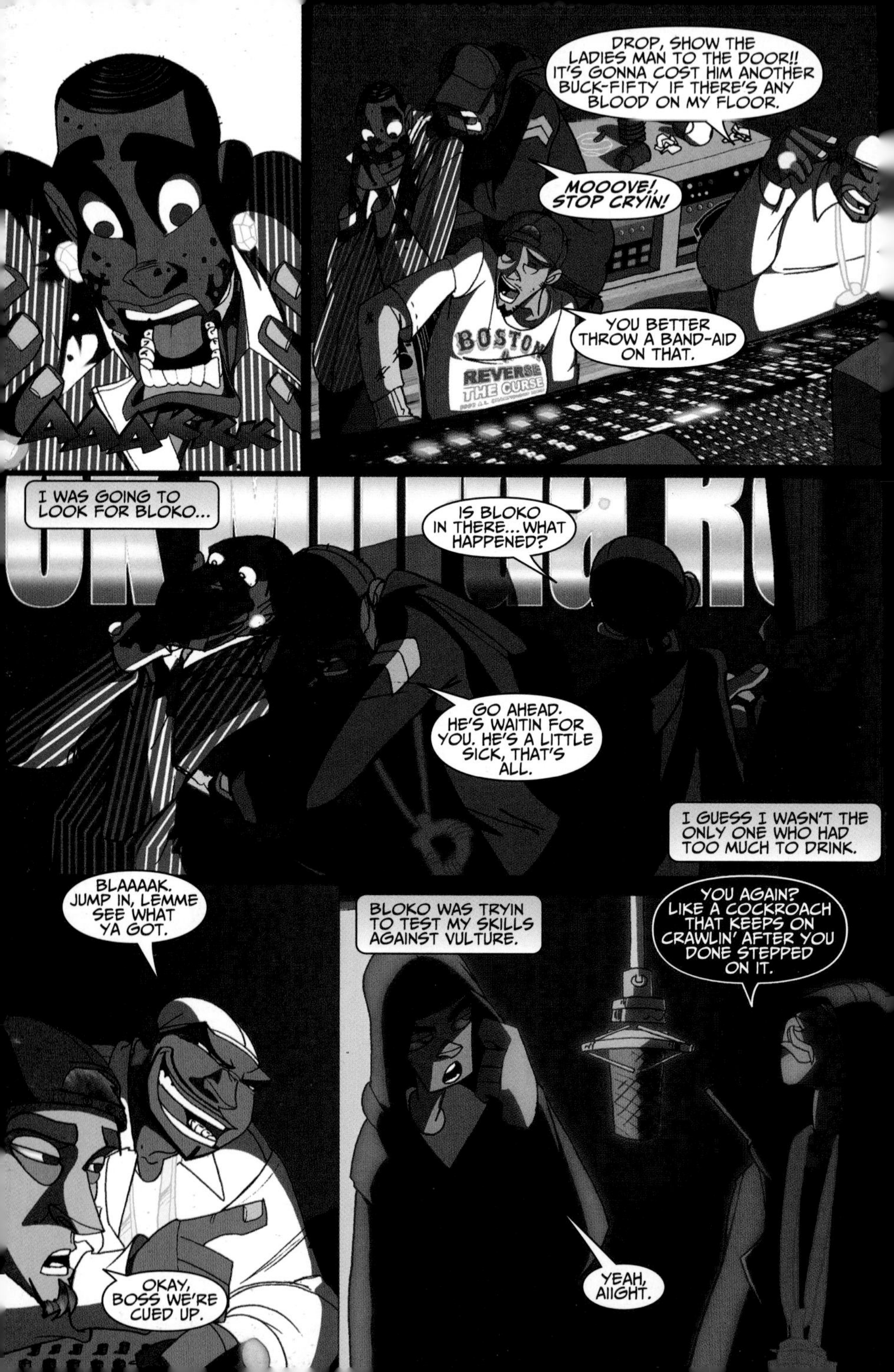
DROP, SHOW THE LADIES MAN TO THE DOOR!! IT'S GONNA COST HIM ANOTHER BUCK-FIFTY IF THERE'S ANY BLOOD ON MY FLOOR.
MOOOVE!, STOP CRYIN!
YOU BETTER THROW A BAND-AID ON THAT.
BOSTON
REVERSE THE CURSE
I WAS GOING TO LOOK FOR BLOKO...
IS BLOKO IN THERE...WHAT HAPPENED?
GO AHEAD. HE'S WAITIN FOR YOU. HE'S A LITTLE SICK, THAT'S ALL.
I GUESS I WASN'T THE ONLY ONE WHO HAD TOO MUCH TO DRINK.
BLAAAAK. JUMP IN, LEMME SEE WHAT YA GOT.
OKAY, BOSS WE'RE CUED UP.
BLOKO WAS TRYIN TO TEST MY SKILLS AGAINST VULTURE.
YOU AGAIN? LIKE A COCKROACH THAT KEEPS ON CRAWLIN' AFTER YOU DONE STEPPED ON IT.
YEAH, AIIGHT.

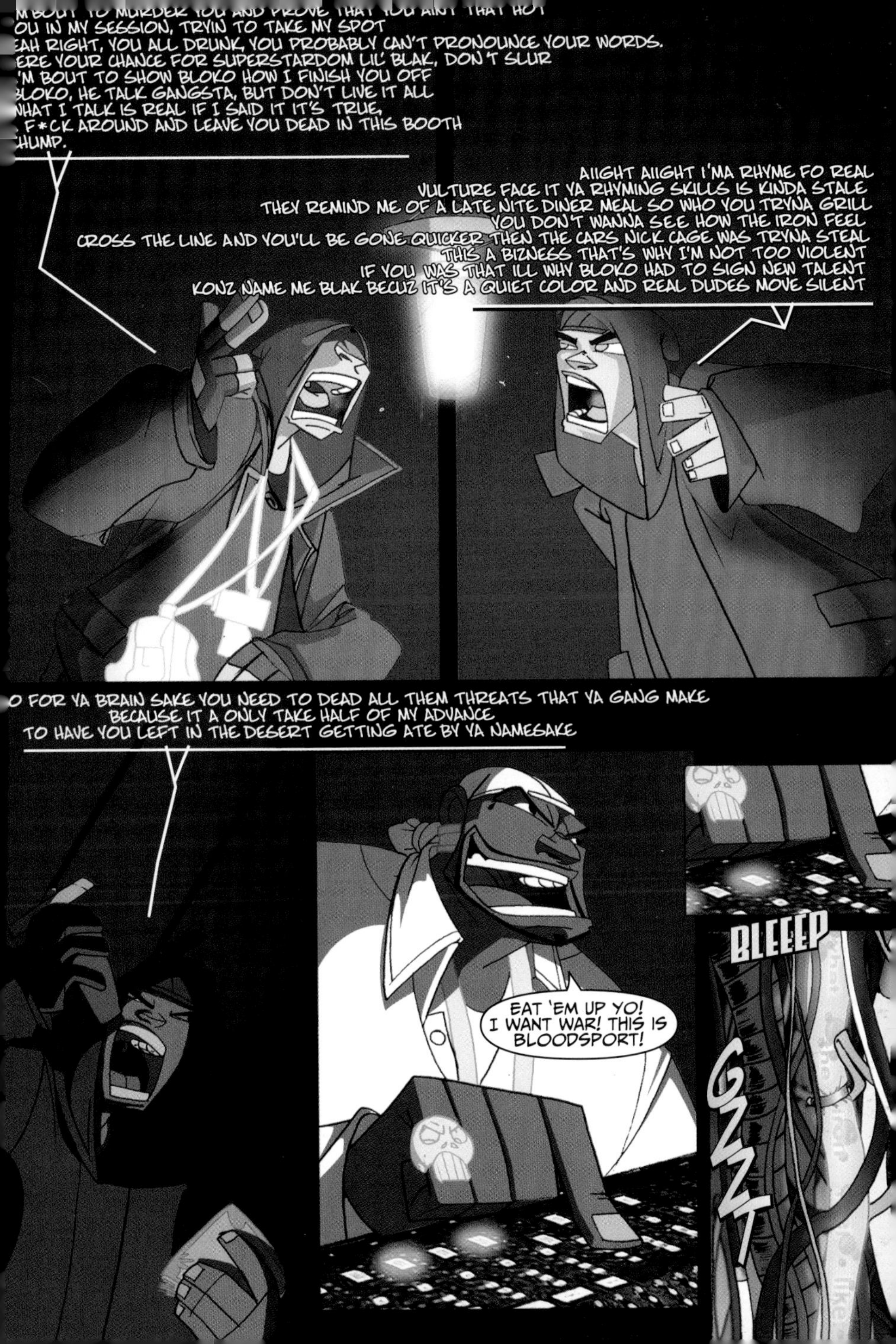
M BOUT TO MURDER YOU AND PROVE THAT YOU AINT THAT HOT
OU IN MY SESSION, TRYIN TO TAKE MY SPOT
EAH RIGHT, YOU ALL DRUNK, YOU PROBABLY CAN'T PRONOUNCE YOUR WORDS.
ERE YOUR CHANCE FOR SUPERSTARDOM LIL' BLAK, DON'T SLUR
'M BOUT TO SHOW BLOKO HOW I FINISH YOU OFF
BLOKO, HE TALK GANGSTA, BUT DON'T LIVE IT ALL
WHAT I TALK IS REAL IF I SAID IT IT'S TRUE,
F*CK AROUND AND LEAVE YOU DEAD IN THIS BOOTH
CHUMP.
AIIGHT AIIGHT I'MA RHYME FO REAL
VULTURE FACE IT YA RHYMING SKILLS IS KINDA STALE
THEY REMIND ME OF A LATE NITE DINER MEAL SO WHO YOU TRYNA GRILL
YOU DON'T WANNA SEE HOW THE IRON FEEL
CROSS THE LINE AND YOU'LL BE GONE QUICKER THEN THE CARS NICK CAGE WAS TRYNA STEAL
THIS A BIZNESS THAT'S WHY I'M NOT TOO VIOLENT
IF YOU WAS THAT ILL WHY BLOKO HAD TO SIGN NEW TALENT
KONZ NAME ME BLAK BECUZ IT'S A QUIET COLOR AND REAL DUDES MOVE SILENT
O FOR YA BRAIN SAKE YOU NEED TO DEAD ALL THEM THREATS THAT YA GANG MAKE
BECAUSE IT A ONLY TAKE HALF OF MY ADVANCE
TO HAVE YOU LEFT IN THE DESERT GETTING ATE BY YA NAMESAKE
EAT 'EM UP YO! I WANT WAR! THIS IS BLOODSPORT!
BLEEEP
GZZZT!

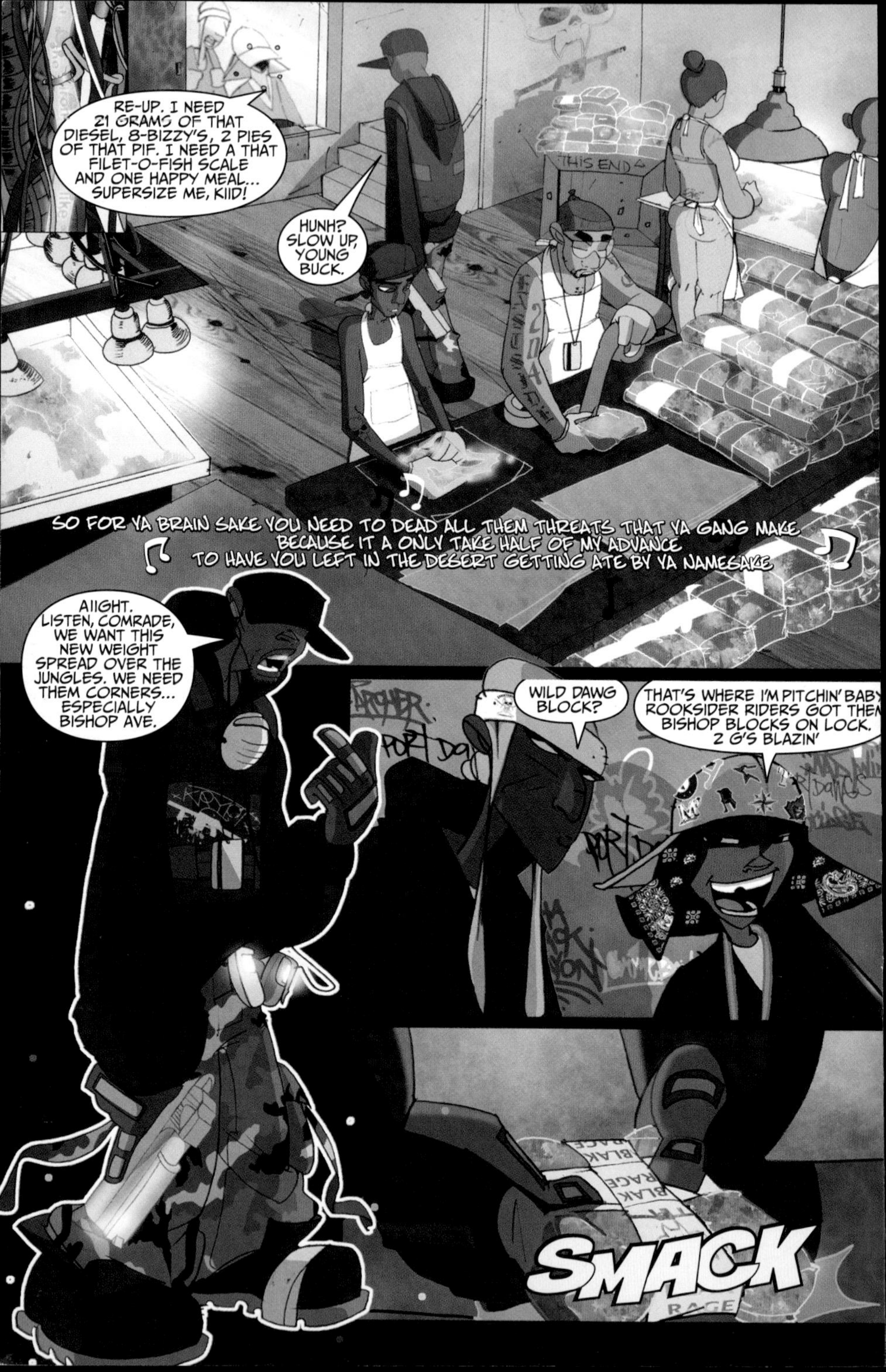
RE-UP. I NEED 21 GRAMS OF THAT DIESEL, 8-BIZZY'S, 2 PIES OF THAT PIF. I NEED A THAT FILET-O-FISH SCALE AND ONE HAPPY MEAL... SUPERSIZE ME, KIID!
HUNH? SLOW UP, YOUNG BUCK.
SO FOR YA BRAIN SAKE YOU NEED TO DEAD ALL THEM THREATS THAT YA GANG MAKE
BECAUSE IT A ONLY TAKE HALF OF MY ADVANCE
TO HAVE YOU LEFT IN THE DESERT GETTING ATE BY YA NAMESAKE
AIIGHT. LISTEN, COMRADE, WE WANT THIS NEW WEIGHT SPREAD OVER THE JUNGLES. WE NEED THEM CORNERS... ESPECIALLY BISHOP AVE.
WILD DAWG BLOCK?
THAT'S WHERE I'M PITCHIN' BABY ROOKSIDER RIDERS GOT THEM BISHOP BLOCKS ON LOCK. 2 G'S BLAZIN'
THIS END
SMACK

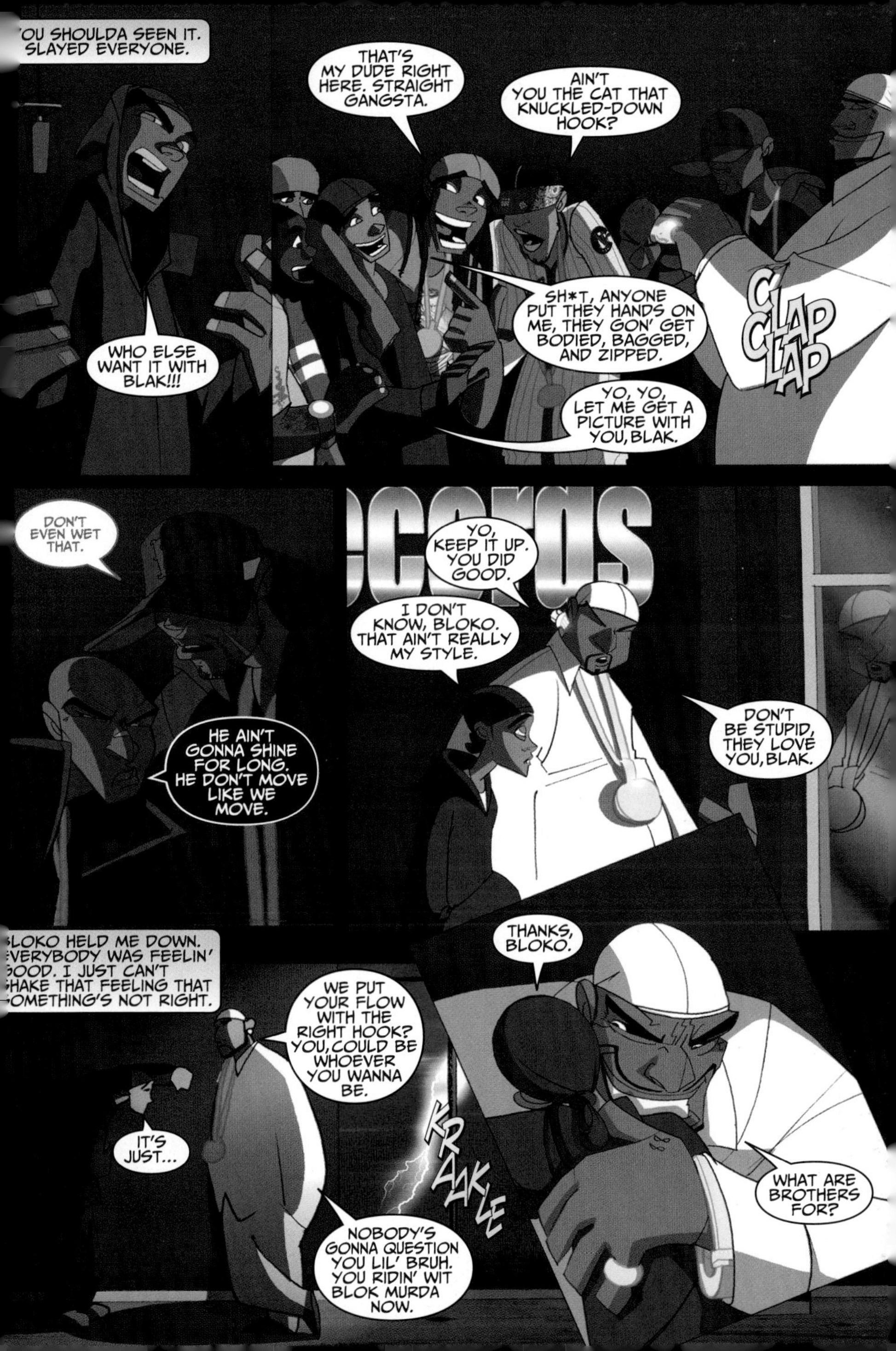
YOU SHOULDA SEEN IT. SLAYED EVERYONE.
WHO ELSE WANT IT WITH BLAK!!!
THAT'S MY DUDE RIGHT HERE. STRAIGHT GANGSTA.
AIN'T YOU THE CAT THAT KNUCKLED-DOWN HOOK?
SH*T, ANYONE PUT THEY HANDS ON ME, THEY GON' GET BODIED, BAGGED, AND ZIPPED.
YO, YO, LET ME GET A PICTURE WITH YOU, BLAK.
CLAP CLAP
DON'T EVEN WET THAT.
HE AIN'T GONNA SHINE FOR LONG. HE DON'T MOVE LIKE WE MOVE.
YO, KEEP IT UP. YOU DID GOOD.
I DON'T KNOW, BLOKO. THAT AIN'T REALLY MY STYLE.
DON'T BE STUPID, THEY LOVE YOU, BLAK.
BLOKO HELD ME DOWN. EVERYBODY WAS FEELIN' GOOD. I JUST CAN'T SHAKE THAT FEELING THAT SOMETHING'S NOT RIGHT.
WE PUT YOUR FLOW WITH THE RIGHT HOOK? YOU, COULD BE WHOEVER YOU WANNA BE.
IT'S JUST...
NOBODY'S GONNA QUESTION YOU LIL' BRUH. YOU RIDIN' WIT BLOK MURDA NOW.
KRAAKLE
THANKS, BLOKO.
WHAT ARE BROTHERS FOR?

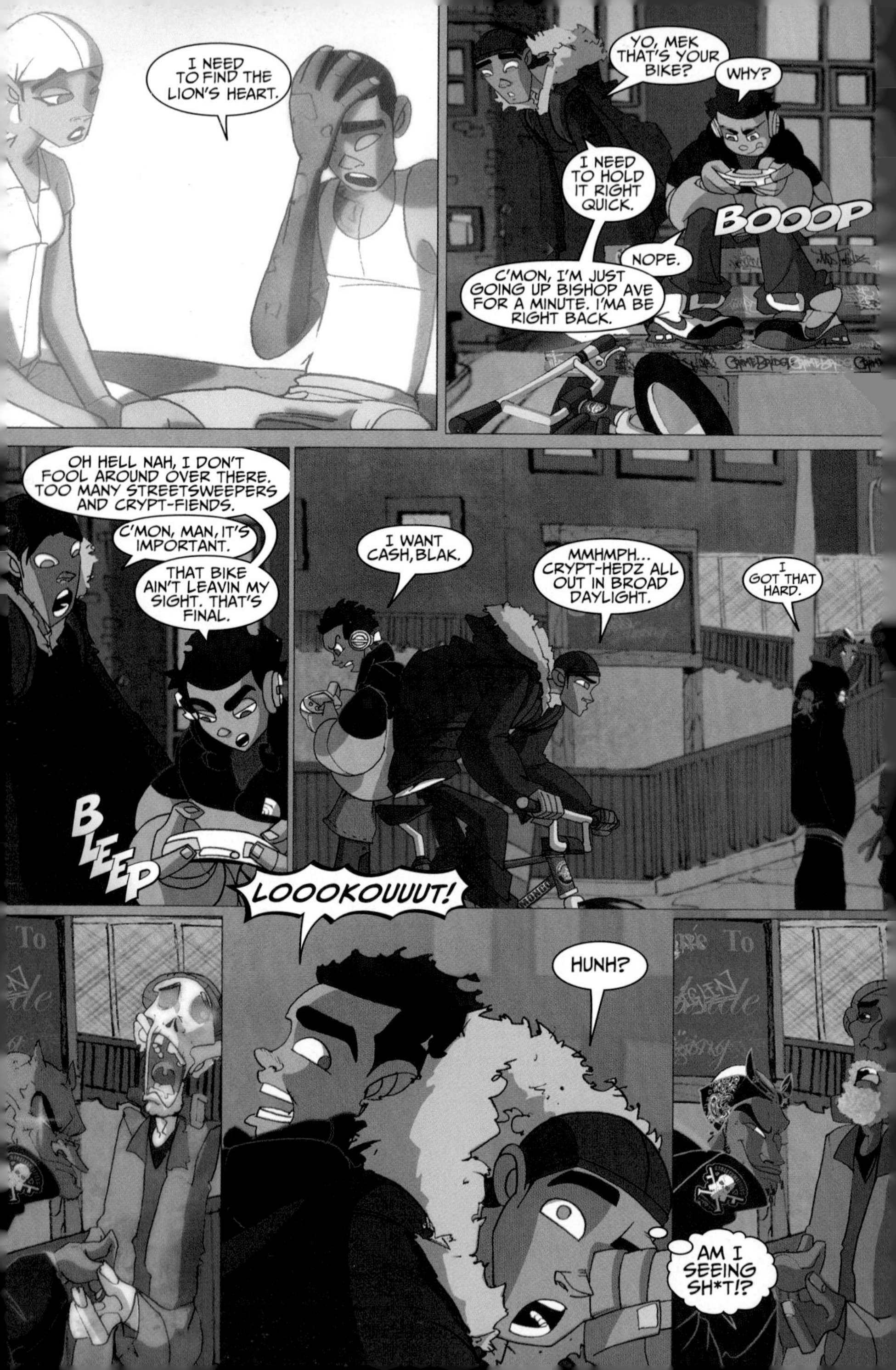

I NEED TO FIND THE LION'S HEART.
YO, MEK THAT'S YOUR BIKE?
WHY?
I NEED TO HOLD IT RIGHT QUICK.
BOOOP
NOPE.
C'MON, I'M JUST GOING UP BISHOP AVE FOR A MINUTE. I'MA BE RIGHT BACK.
OH HELL NAH, I DON'T FOOL AROUND OVER THERE. TOO MANY STREETSWEEPERS AND CRYPT-FIENDS.
C'MON, MAN, IT'S IMPORTANT.
THAT BIKE AIN'T LEAVIN MY SIGHT. THAT'S FINAL.
BLEEP
I WANT CASH, BLAK.
MMHMPH... CRYPT-HEDZ ALL OUT IN BROAD DAYLIGHT.
I GOT THAT HARD.
LOOOKOUUUT!
HUNH?
AM I SEEING SH*T!?

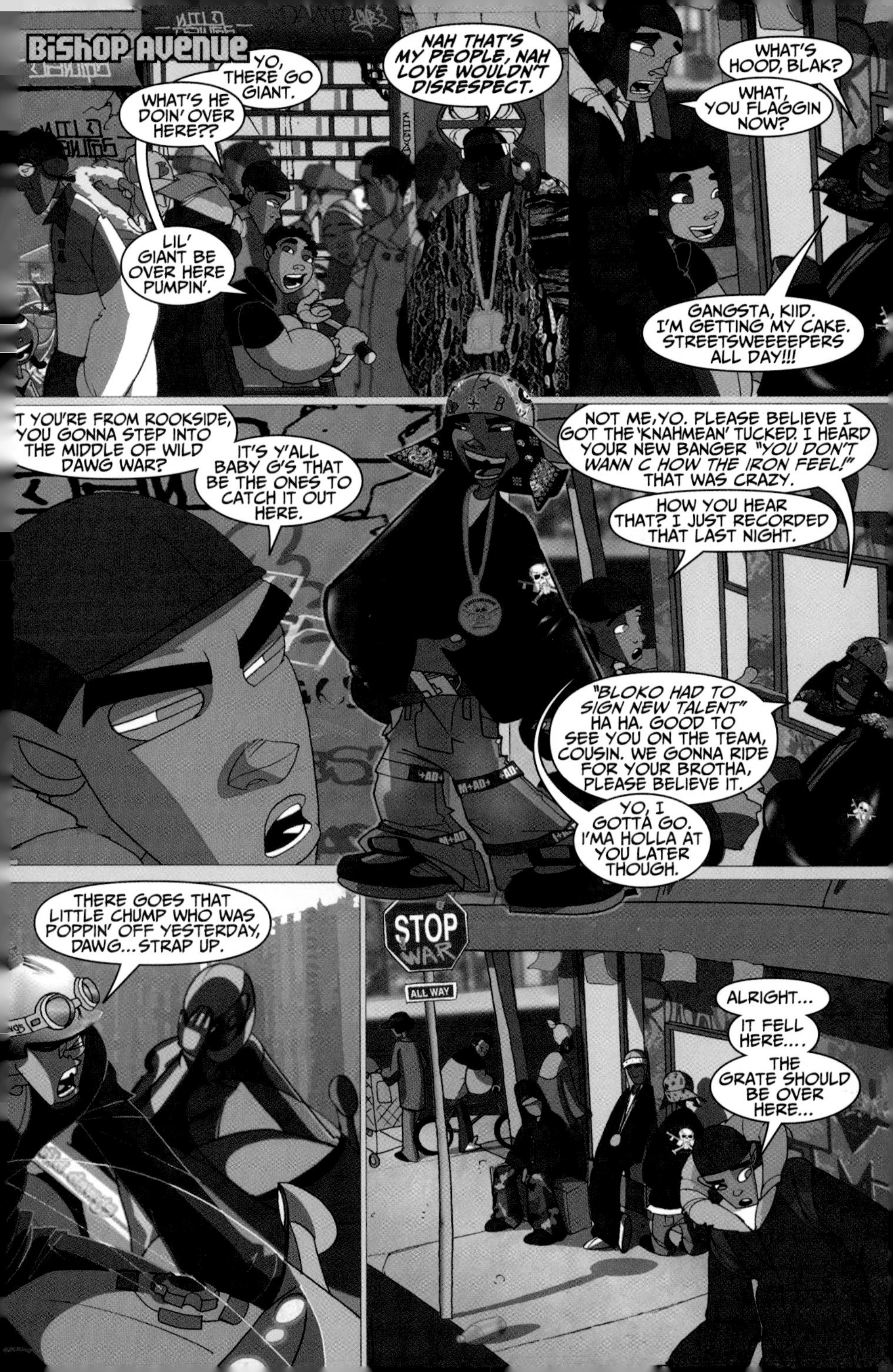
BISHOP AVENUE
YO, THERE GO GIANT.
WHAT'S HE DOIN' OVER HERE??
LIL' GIANT BE OVER HERE PUMPIN'.
NAH THAT'S MY PEOPLE, NAH LOVE WOULDN'T DISRESPECT.
WHAT'S HOOD, BLAK?
WHAT, YOU FLAGGIN NOW?
GANGSTA, KIID. I'M GETTING MY CAKE. STREETSWEEEEPERS ALL DAY!!!
T YOU'RE FROM ROOKSIDE, YOU GONNA STEP INTO THE MIDDLE OF WILD DAWG WAR?
IT'S Y'ALL BABY G'S THAT BE THE ONES TO CATCH IT OUT HERE.
NOT ME, YO. PLEASE BELIEVE I GOT THE 'KNAHMEAN' TUCKED. I HEARD YOUR NEW BANGER "YOU DON'T WANN C HOW THE IRON FEEL!" THAT WAS CRAZY.
HOW YOU HEAR THAT? I JUST RECORDED THAT LAST NIGHT.
"BLOKO HAD TO SIGN NEW TALENT" HA HA. GOOD TO SEE YOU ON THE TEAM, COUSIN. WE GONNA RIDE FOR YOUR BROTHA, PLEASE BELIEVE IT.
YO, I GOTTA GO. I'MA HOLLA AT YOU LATER THOUGH.
THERE GOES THAT LITTLE CHUMP WHO WAS POPPIN' OFF YESTERDAY, DAWG...STRAP UP.
STOP WAR
ALL WAY
ALRIGHT...
IT FELL HERE....
THE GRATE SHOULD BE OVER HERE...

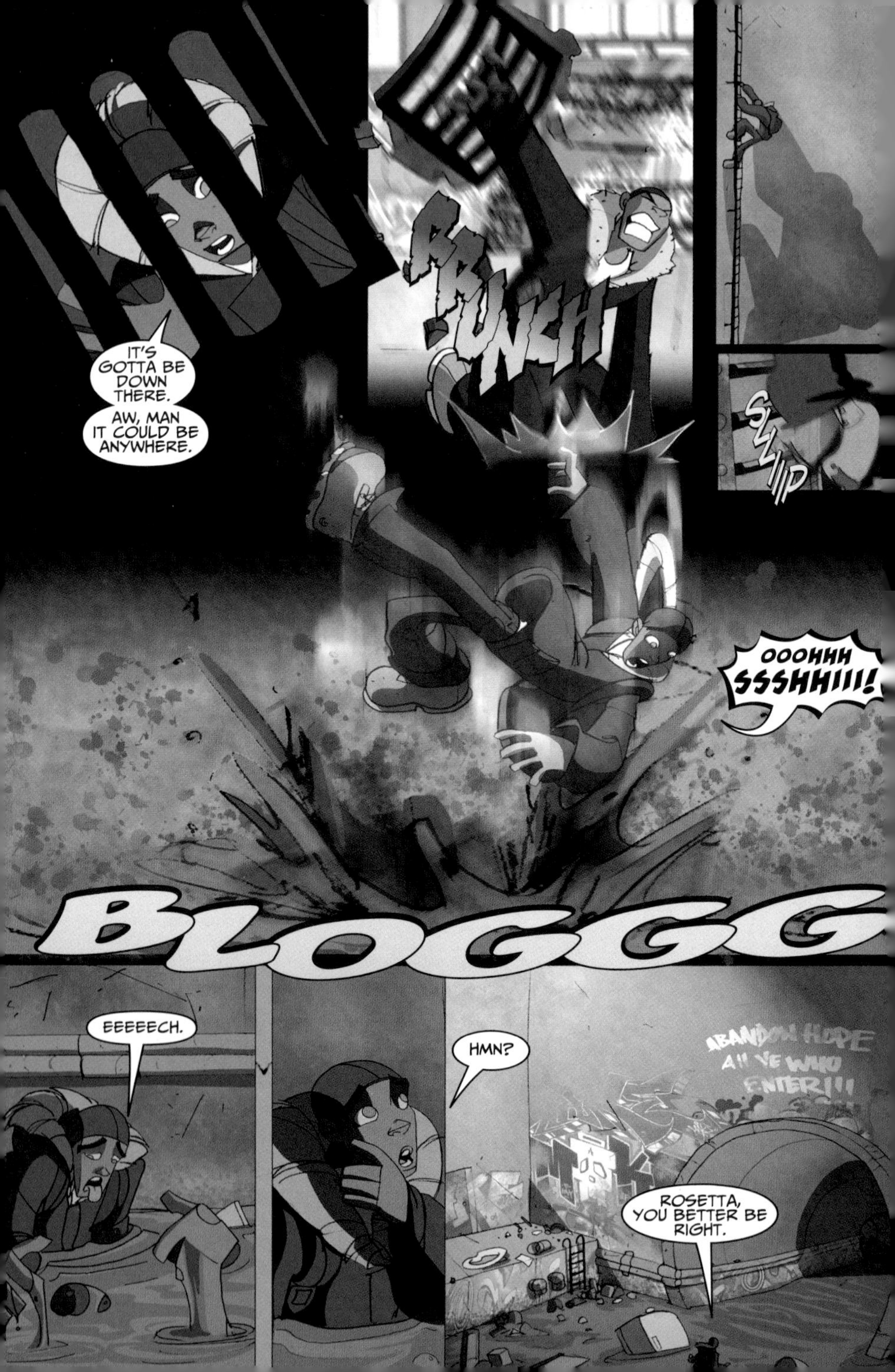
IT'S GOTTA BE DOWN THERE.
AW, MAN IT COULD BE ANYWHERE.
BRUNCH
SLLIP
OOOHHH SSSHHIII!
BLOGGG
EEEEECH.
HMN?
ABANDON HOPE ALL YE WHO ENTER!!!
ROSETTA, YOU BETTER BE RIGHT.

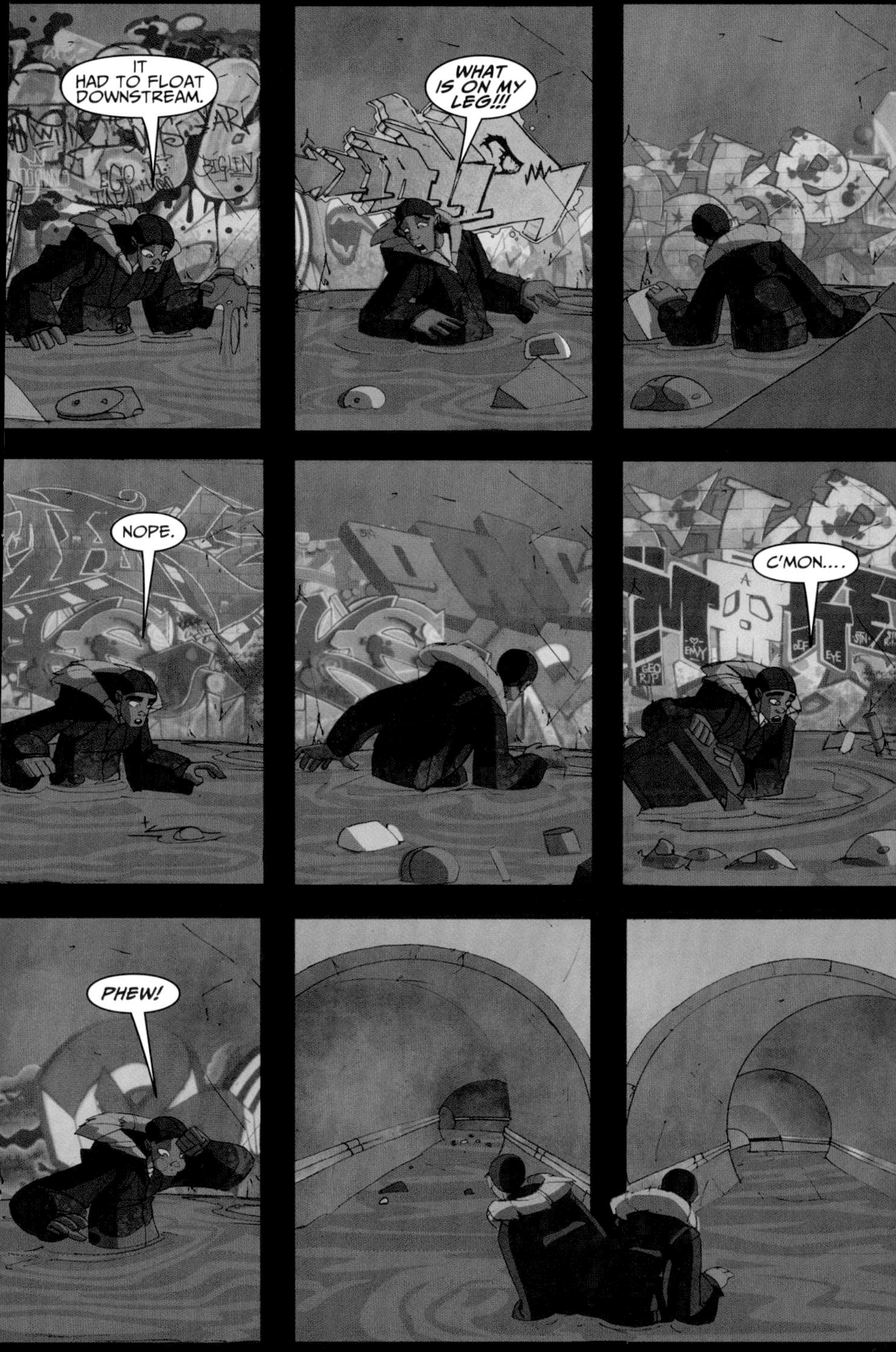
IT HAD TO FLOAT DOWNSTREAM.
WHAT IS ON MY LEG!!!
NOPE.
C'MON....
PHEW!

OKAY, THROUGH THIS TUNNEL HERE... AND.

HUFF
PUFF

OH HELL NAH!

ABANDON HOPE ALL YE WHO ENTER!!!

SH*T!!! I'M BACK IN THE SEWER!

DO NOT OPEN

I'M NEVER GONNA FIND IT. I'M GONNA DIE DOWN HERE.

UNNH?

GRRRGLE

WHOOOSH

SPLOOOSH

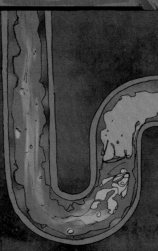

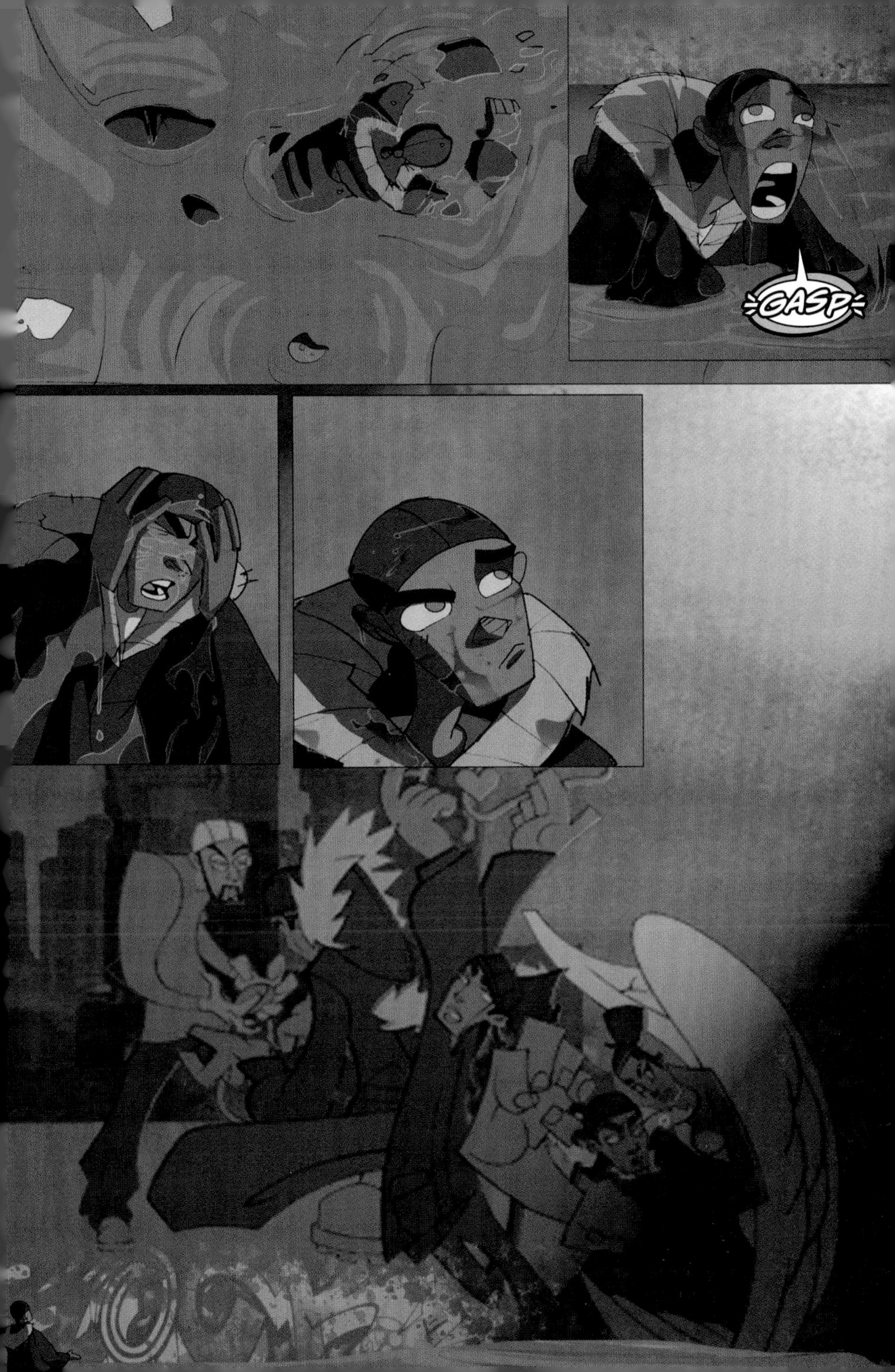
GASP

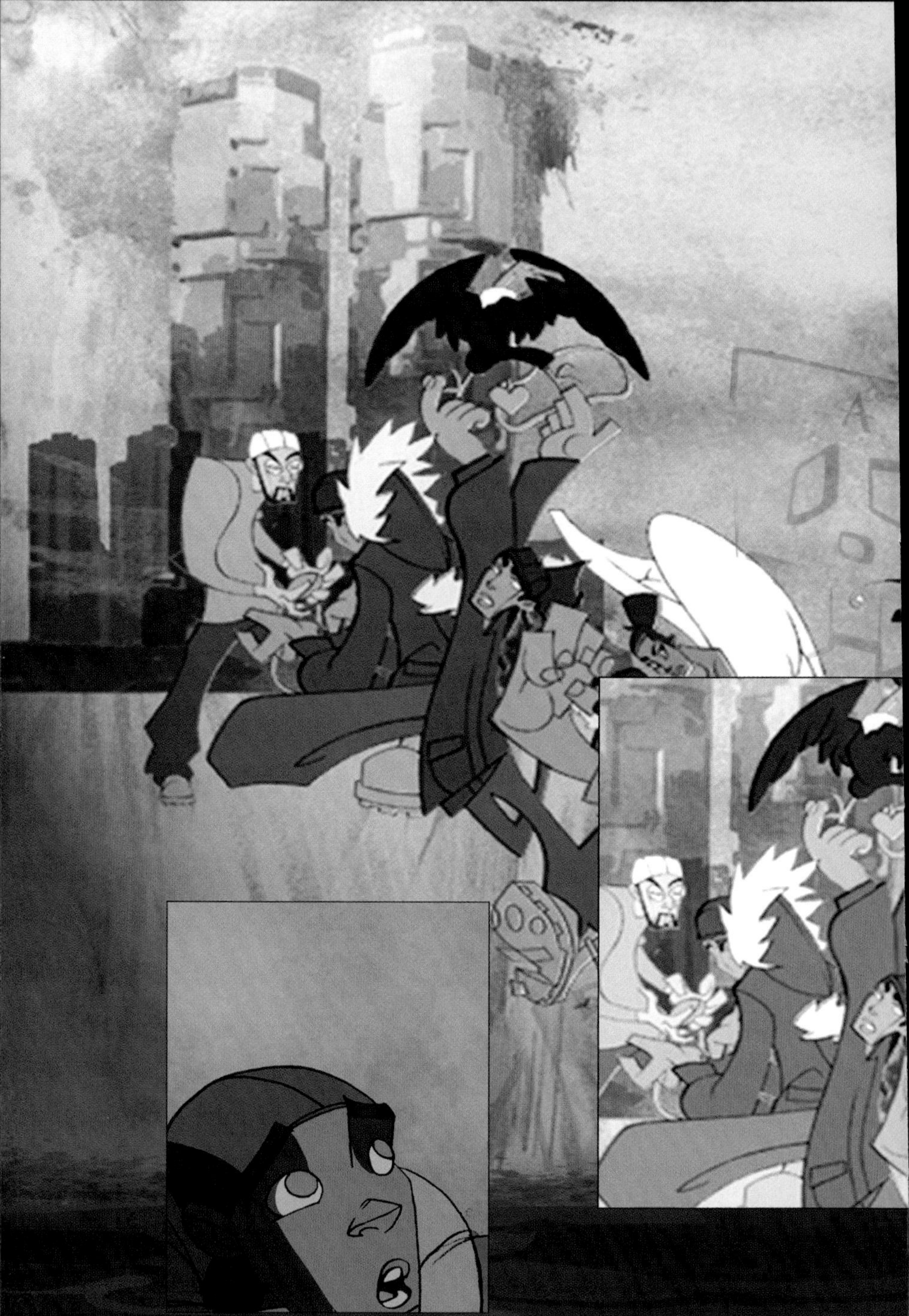

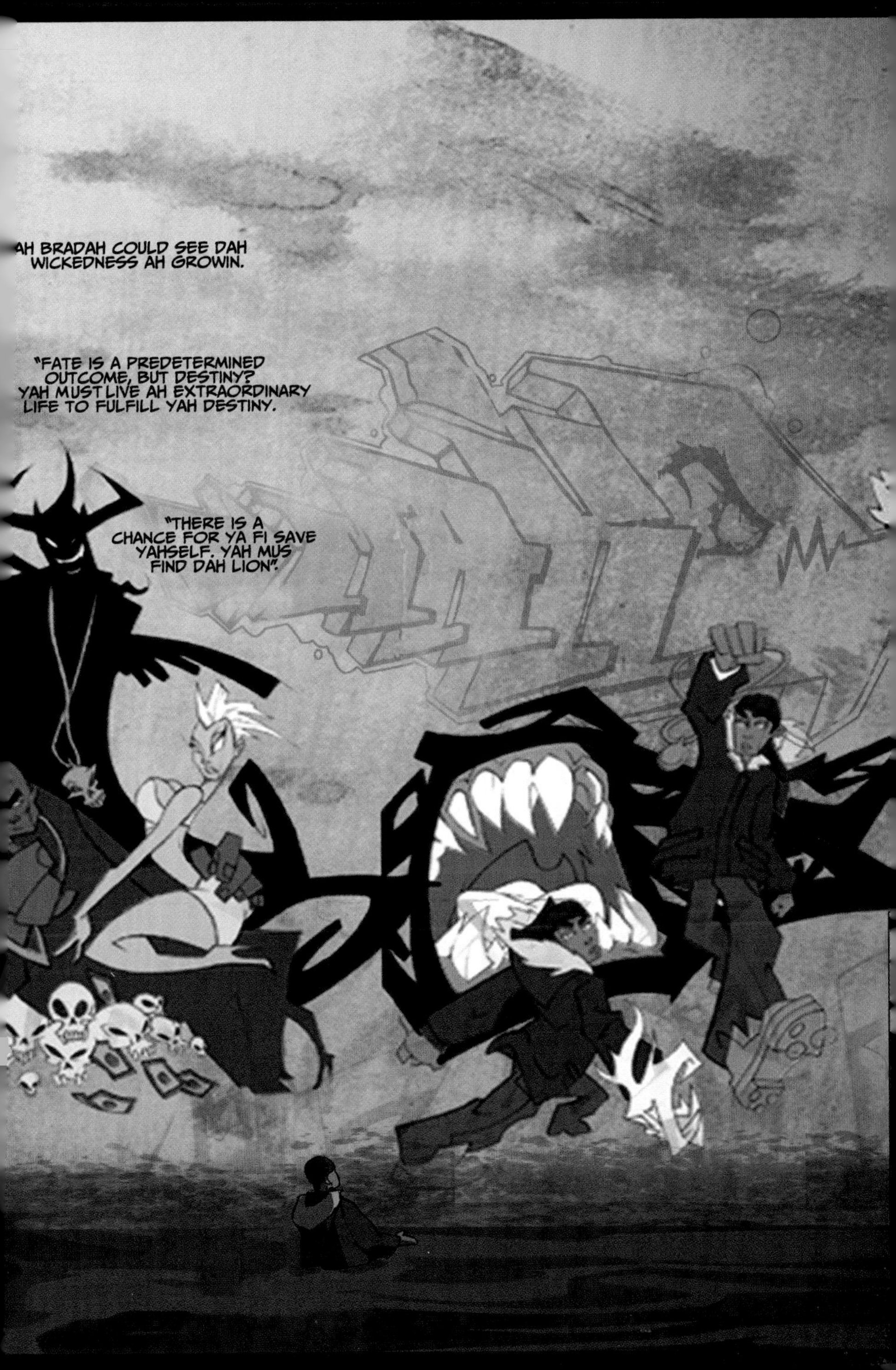
AH BRADAH COULD SEE DAH WICKEDNESS AH GROWIN.
"FATE IS A PREDETERMINED OUTCOME, BUT DESTINY? YAH MUST LIVE AH EXTRAORDINARY LIFE TO FULFILL YAH DESTINY.
"THERE IS A CHANCE FOR YA FI SAVE YAHSELF. YAH MUS FIND DAH LION".

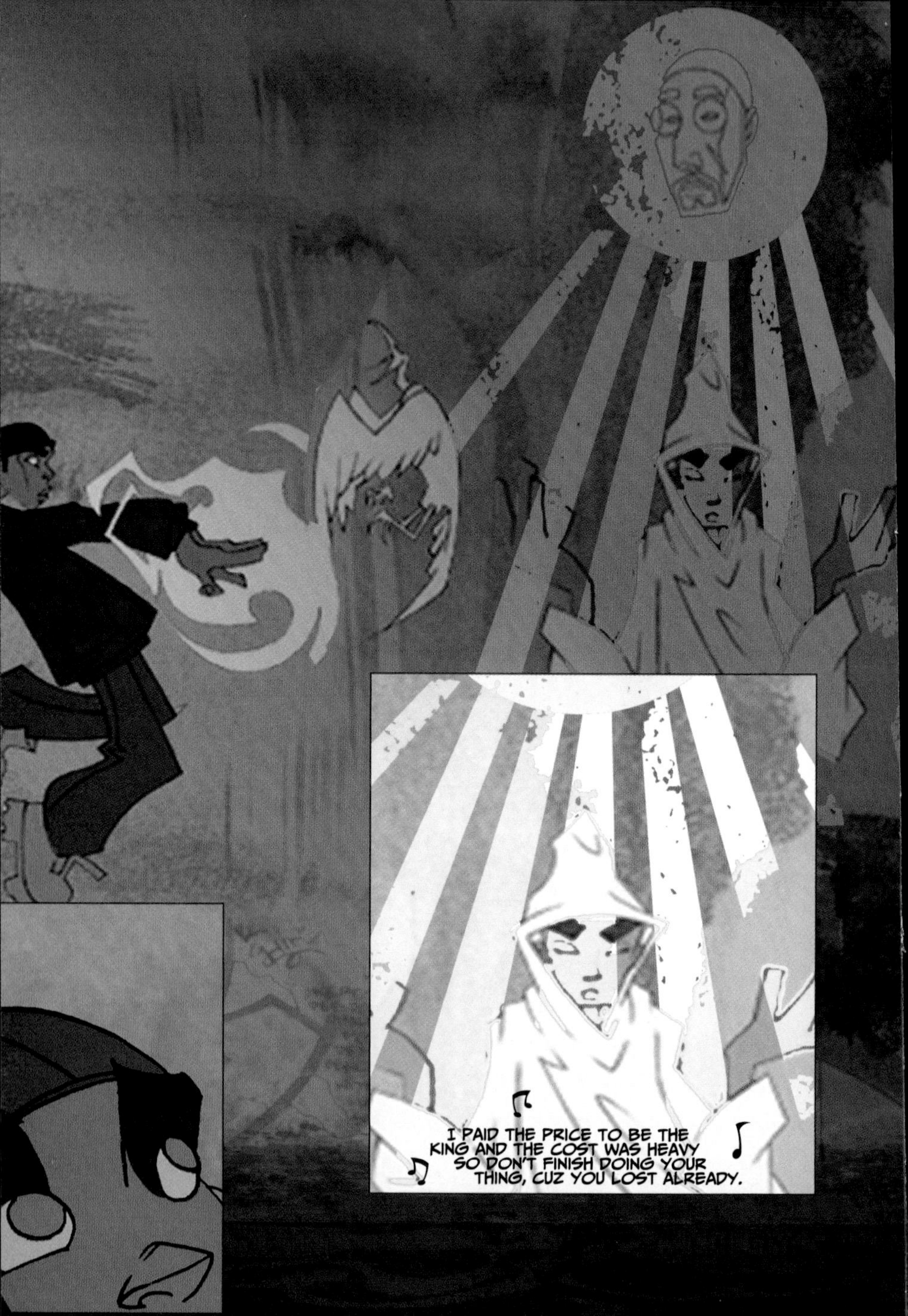
I PAID THE PRICE TO BE THE
KING AND THE COST WAS HEAVY
SO DON'T FINISH DOING YOUR
THING, CUZ YOU LOST ALREADY.

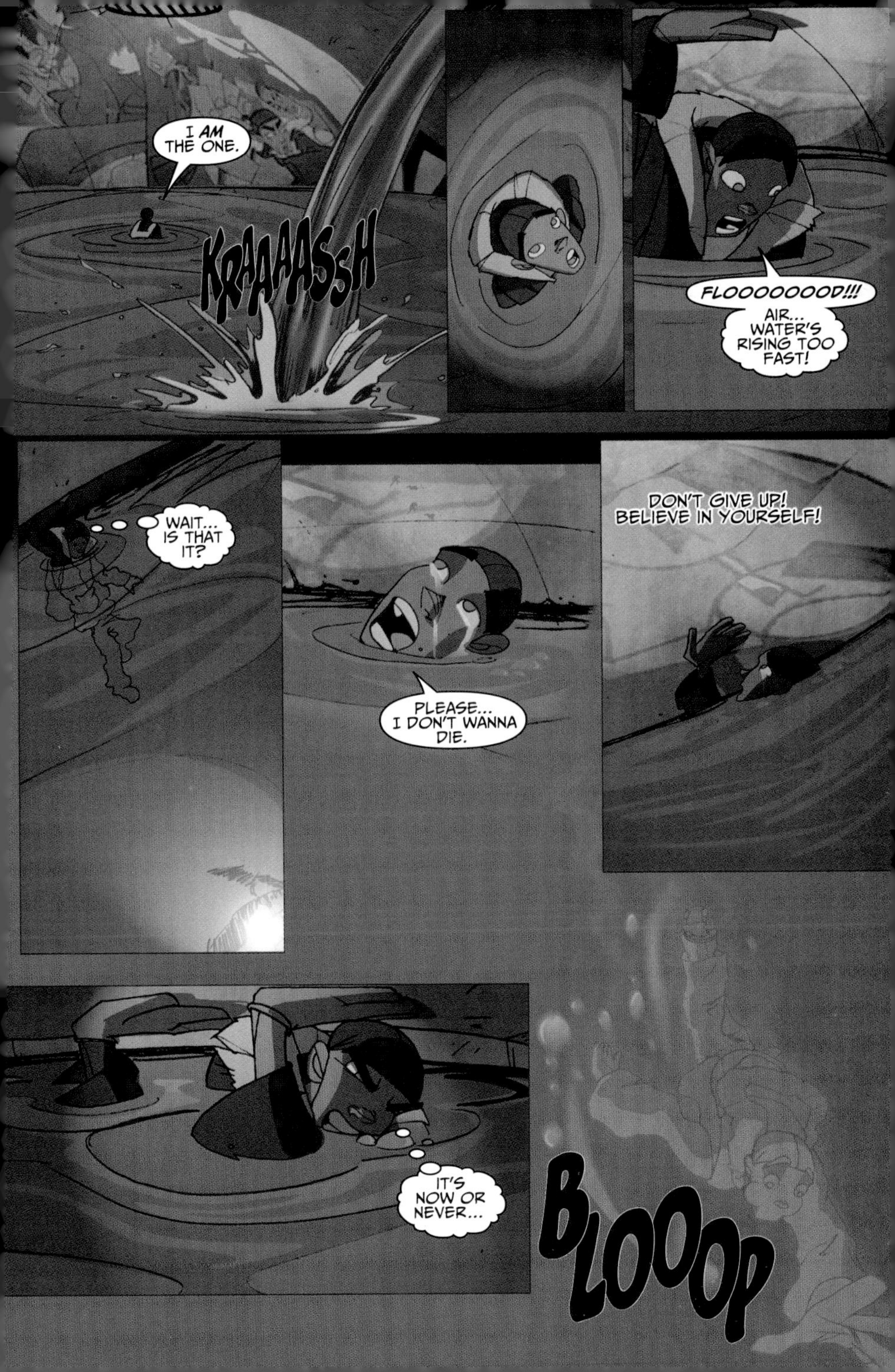
I *AM* THE ONE.
KRAAAASsH
FLOOOOOOOD!!!
AIR... WATER'S RISING TOO FAST!
WAIT... IS THAT IT?
PLEASE... I DON'T WANNA DIE.
DON'T GIVE UP! BELIEVE IN YOURSELF!
IT'S NOW OR NEVER...
BLOOOP

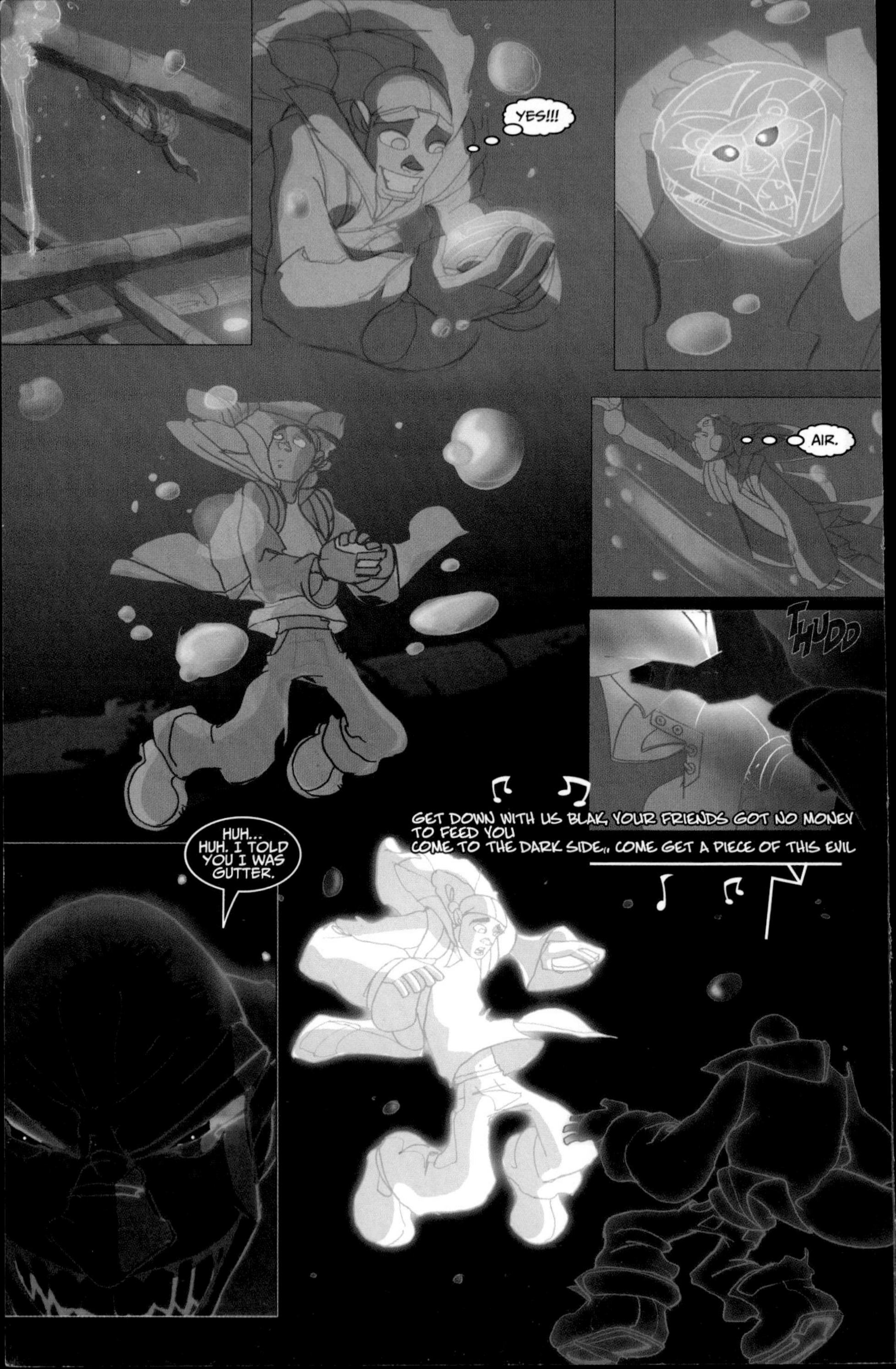
YES!!!
AIR.
THUDD
HUH... HUH. I TOLD YOU I WAS GUTTER.
GET DOWN WITH US BLAK, YOUR FRIENDS GOT NO MONEY TO FEED YOU
COME TO THE DARK SIDE,, COME GET A PIECE OF THIS EVIL

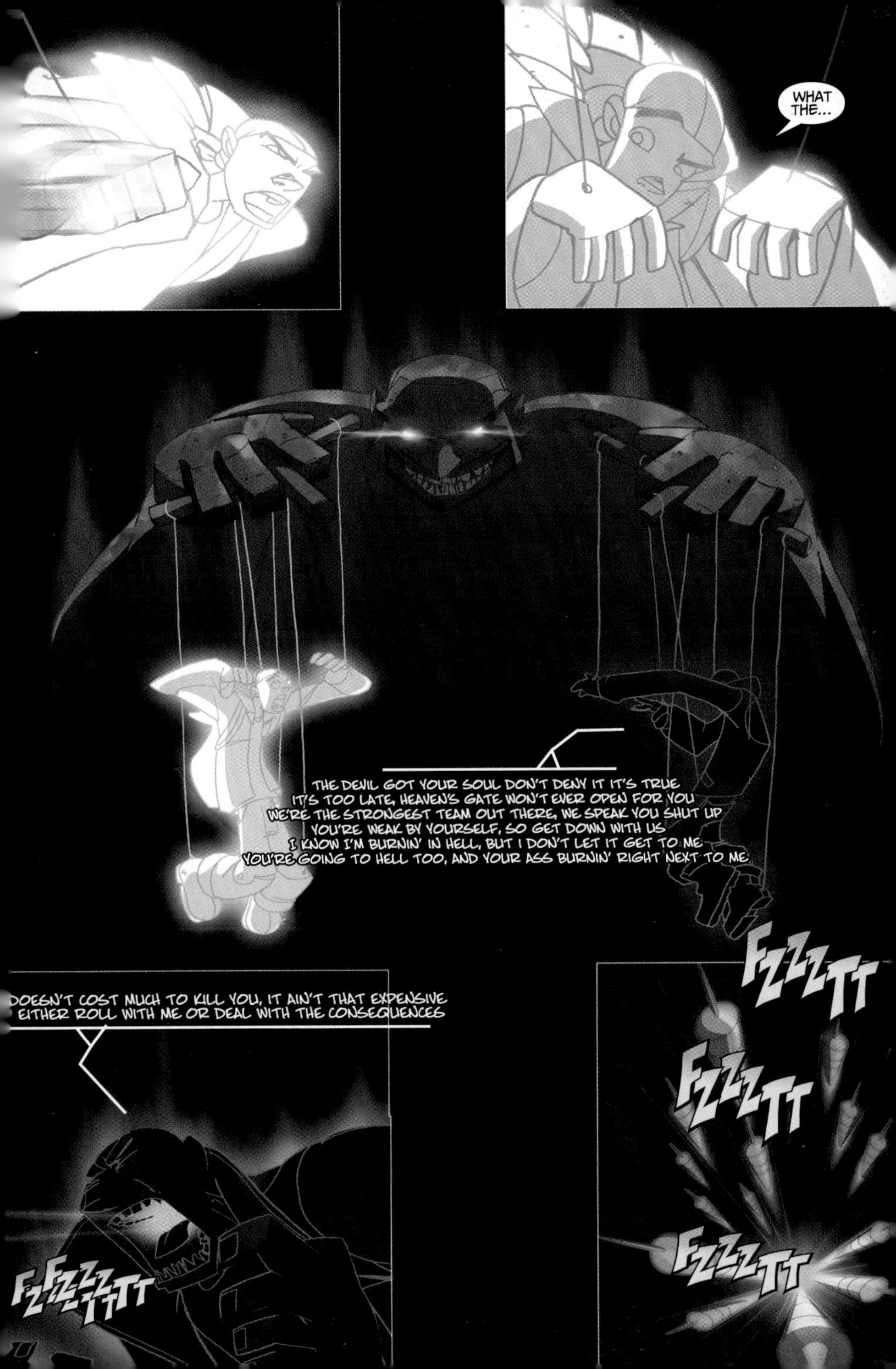
WHAT THE...
THE DEVIL GOT YOUR SOUL DON'T DENY IT IT'S TRUE
IT'S TOO LATE, HEAVEN'S GATE WON'T EVER OPEN FOR YOU
WE'RE THE STRONGEST TEAM OUT THERE, WE SPEAK YOU SHUT UP
YOU'RE WEAK BY YOURSELF, SO GET DOWN WITH US
I KNOW I'M BURNIN' IN HELL, BUT I DON'T LET IT GET TO ME
YOU'RE GOING TO HELL TOO, AND YOUR ASS BURNIN' RIGHT NEXT TO ME
DOESN'T COST MUCH TO KILL YOU, IT AIN'T THAT EXPENSIVE
EITHER ROLL WITH ME OR DEAL WITH THE CONSEQUENCES
FZZZZTT
FZZZZTT
FZZZZTT

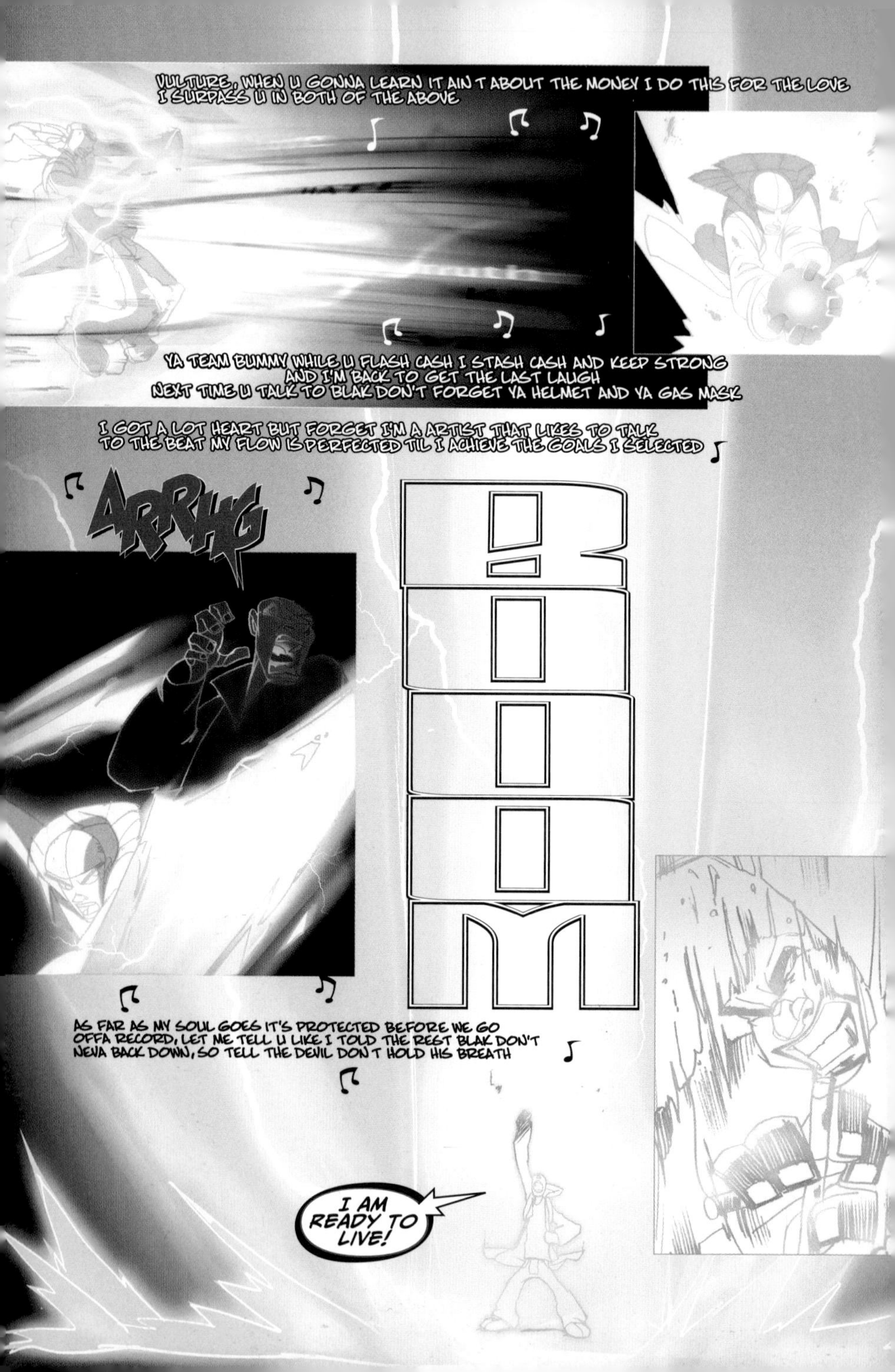
VULTURE, WHEN U GONNA LEARN IT AIN T ABOUT THE MONEY I DO THIS FOR THE LOVE
I SURPASS U IN BOTH OF THE ABOVE
YA TEAM BUMMY WHILE U FLASH CASH I STASH CASH AND KEEP STRONG
AND I'M BACK TO GET THE LAST LAUGH
NEXT TIME U TALK TO BLAK DON'T FORGET YA HELMET AND YA GAS MASK
I GOT A LOT HEART BUT FORGET I'M A ARTIST THAT LIKES TO TALK
TO THE BEAT MY FLOW IS PERFECTED TIL I ACHIEVE THE GOALS I SELECTED
ARRHG
BOOOM
AS FAR AS MY SOUL GOES IT'S PROTECTED BEFORE WE GO
OFFA RECORD, LET ME TELL U LIKE I TOLD THE REST BLAK DON'T
NEVA BACK DOWN, SO TELL THE DEVIL DON T HOLD HIS BREATH
I AM READY TO LIVE!

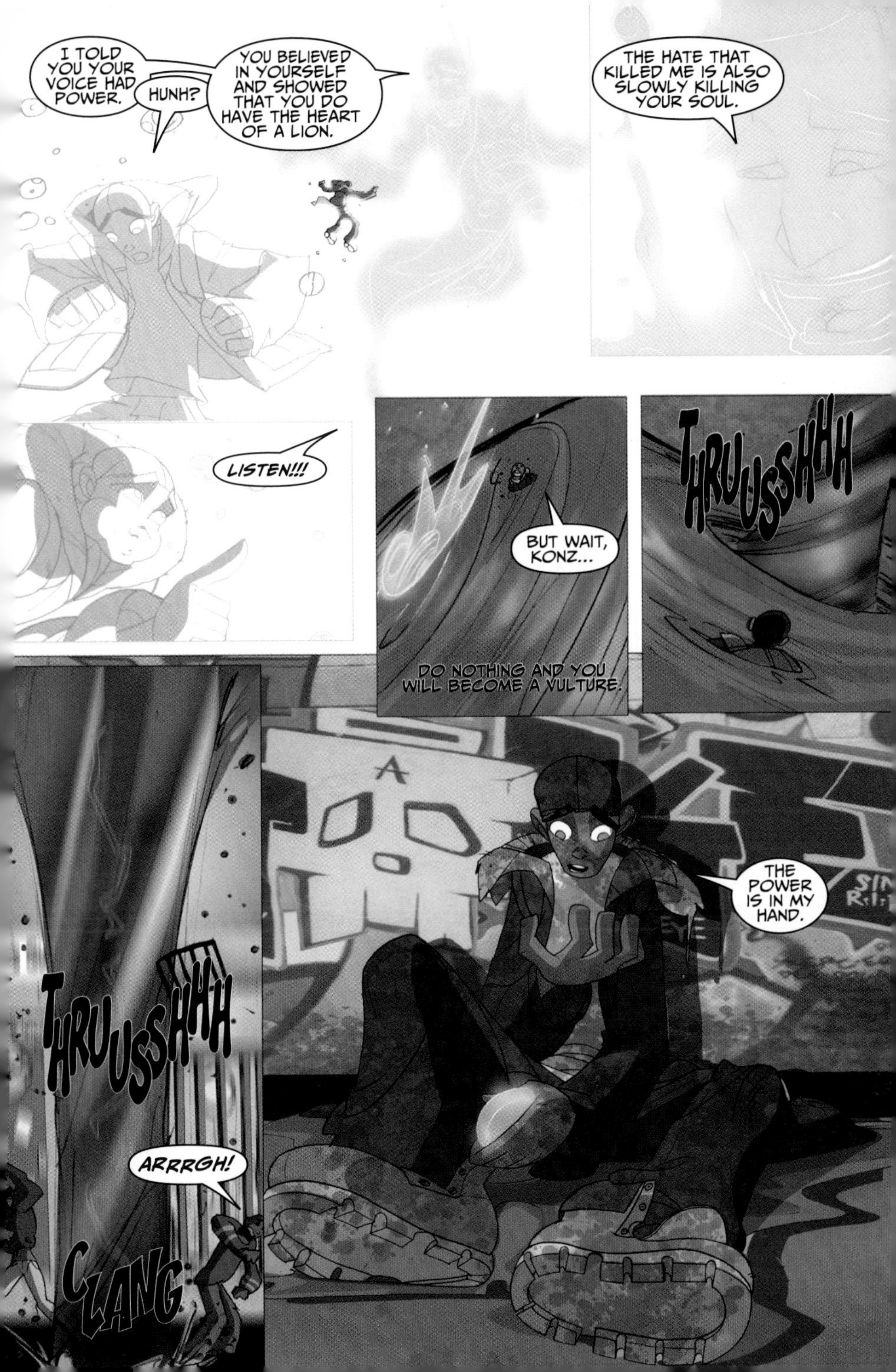
I TOLD YOU YOUR VOICE HAD POWER.
HUNH?
YOU BELIEVED IN YOURSELF AND SHOWED THAT YOU DO HAVE THE HEART OF A LION.
THE HATE THAT KILLED ME IS ALSO SLOWLY KILLING YOUR SOUL.
LISTEN!!!
BUT WAIT, KONZ...
DO NOTHING AND YOU WILL BECOME A VULTURE.
THRUUSSHHH
THRUUSSHHH
THE POWER IS IN MY HAND.
ARRRGH!
CLANG

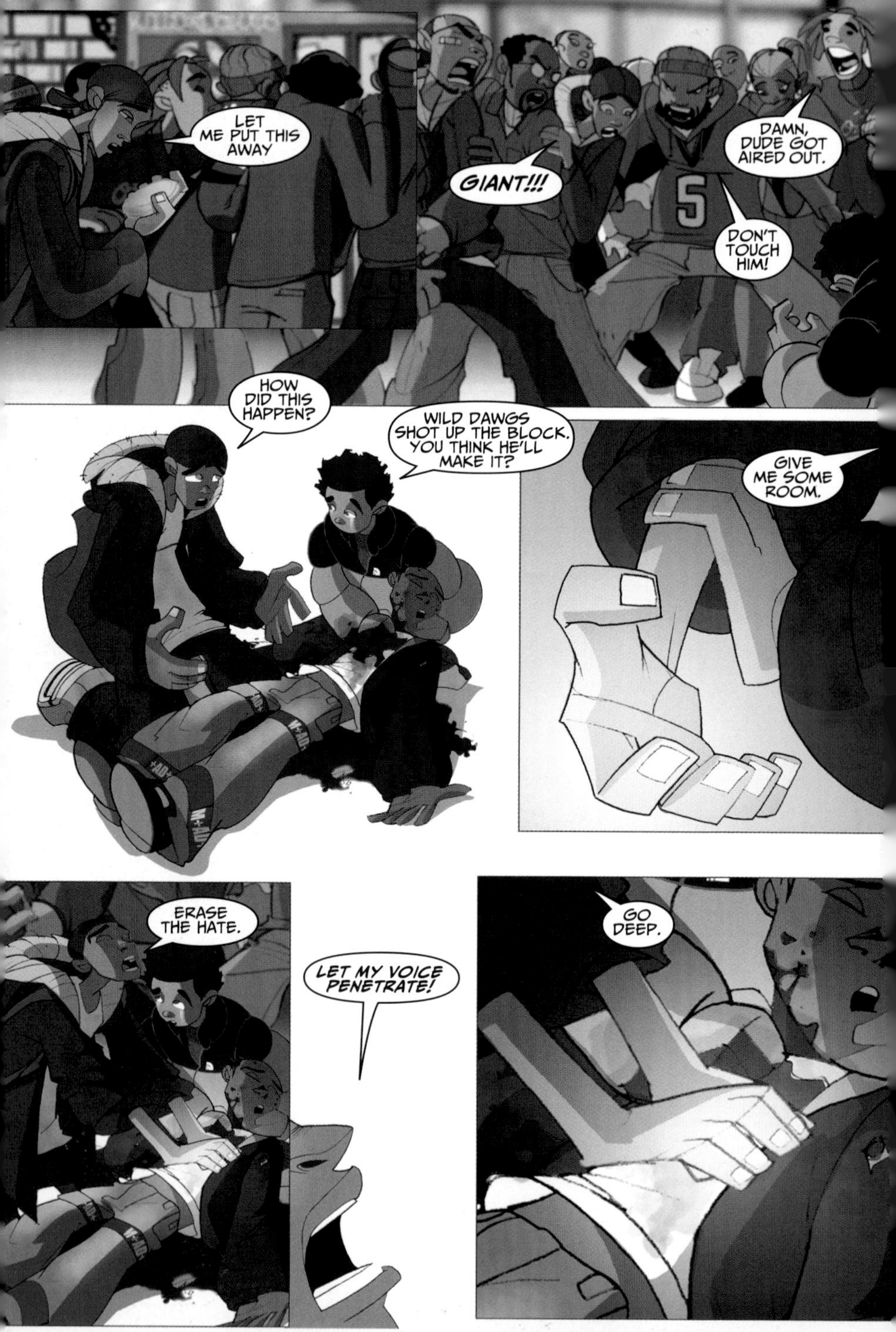
LET ME PUT THIS AWAY
GIANT!!!
DAMN, DUDE GOT AIRED OUT.
DON'T TOUCH HIM!
HOW DID THIS HAPPEN?
WILD DAWGS SHOT UP THE BLOCK. YOU THINK HE'LL MAKE IT?
GIVE ME SOME ROOM.
ERASE THE HATE.
LET MY VOICE PENETRATE!
GO DEEP.

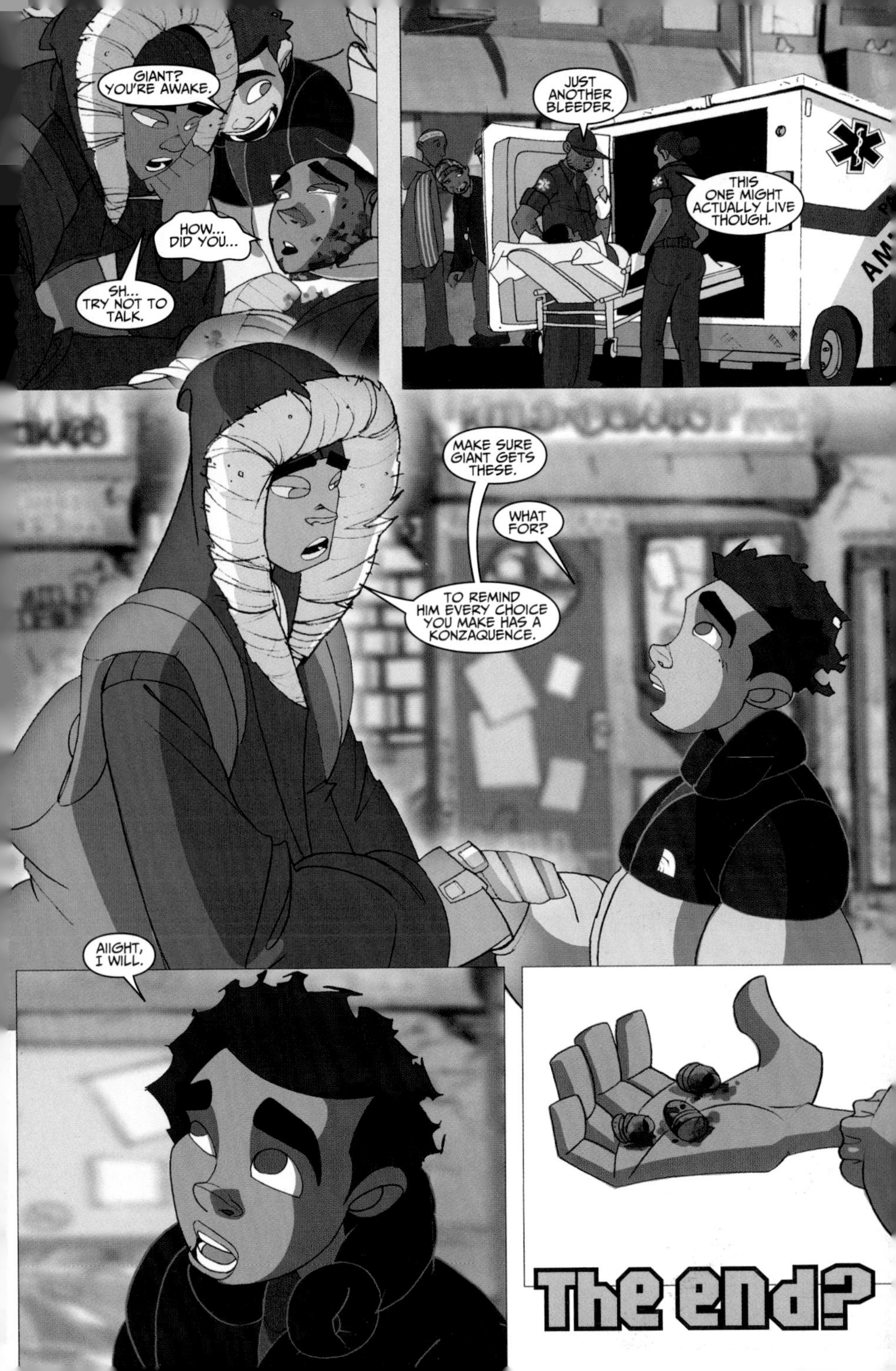
GIANT? YOU'RE AWAKE.
HOW... DID YOU...
SH... TRY NOT TO TALK.
JUST ANOTHER BLEEDER.
THIS ONE MIGHT ACTUALLY LIVE THOUGH.
MAKE SURE GIANT GETS THESE.
WHAT FOR?
TO REMIND HIM EVERY CHOICE YOU MAKE HAS A KONZAQUENCE.
AIIGHT, I WILL.
The end?

slang glossary

5-O: (pronounced "Five - Oh") The police.

Aiight: Okay. All right. Acceptable or agreeable.

Baby-G: Baby gangster. Young reputable thug.

Back in the day: In the past.

Bodied: The act of taking a life, or ones own life being taken.

Buck 50: To cut one a person the side of the face, resulting in a gash that requires 150 stitches.

Can't see: Non-threatening, as in direct competition.

Ceelo: Dice game involving 3 die.

Crib: Home. Place of residence.

Crypt: An illegal substance in Empire City with the addictive-qualites of crack, but consumed like weed. Known to give users a greenish tint of the eyes.

Dip: To go away from, as a place.

Dope: 1. Aesthetically pleasing to the eyes or ears. 2. Illegal drugs.

Doin' dirt: To take part in illegal activities.

Down low: Inconspicuous. Low profile.

Drizzed: An intoxicated state. Drunk.

Empty out: The firing of a weapon until contents of its cartridge are exhausted.

Fall back: To ease up. To conduct oneself in a less agressive manner.

Flagging: To signify one's group affiliation by the display of items or colors that are used to identify a specific group of individuals.

Flow: The fluidity of one's syntax while rapping a verse or song.

Fly: Aesthetically pleasing to the eye. To adorn onslelf with attractive and or expensive new clothing.

Gassed: (To gas) To cater and inflate an individual's ego with false pretense.

Get touched: The act of being physically harmed or causing physical harm to another.

Ghost: To leave from a place. The act of going.

Hating: Resentful and envious, as of someone's success.

Headcrack: A term in ceelo, as a winning roll of the dice.

Ho: An overly promiscuous person.

Hold it down: Take care of responsibilities. To protect. Derived from the phrase "hold down the fort".

Ill: 1. Very impressive. Aesthetically pleasing. 2. Extremely cruel.

Iron: Firearm.

Jake: The police.

Knahmean: "Do you know what I mean."

Knocked: To get arrested.

Mac: A mac 10 or mac 11. A type of semi-automatic machine gun.

Mad: In excess. Very. To a high degree. Extremely.

Milli: A firearm. Derived from "millimeter," the unit of measurement used to determine the circumference of a guns barrel.

Murk: The act of taking a life, or one's own life being taken.

Pitching: The act of selling (usually refers to illegal drugs).

Pumping: The act of selling (usually refers to illegal drugs).

Ratchet: A firearm.

Run it: To unwillingly give up a personal possession.

Straight off the top: 1. An impromptu performance, related to rapping. 2. Totally improvisational.

Weight: A large amount of an illegal substance.

Wild out: To misbehave. To act in an unrully manner.

Whip: An automobile.

BLOKHEDZ

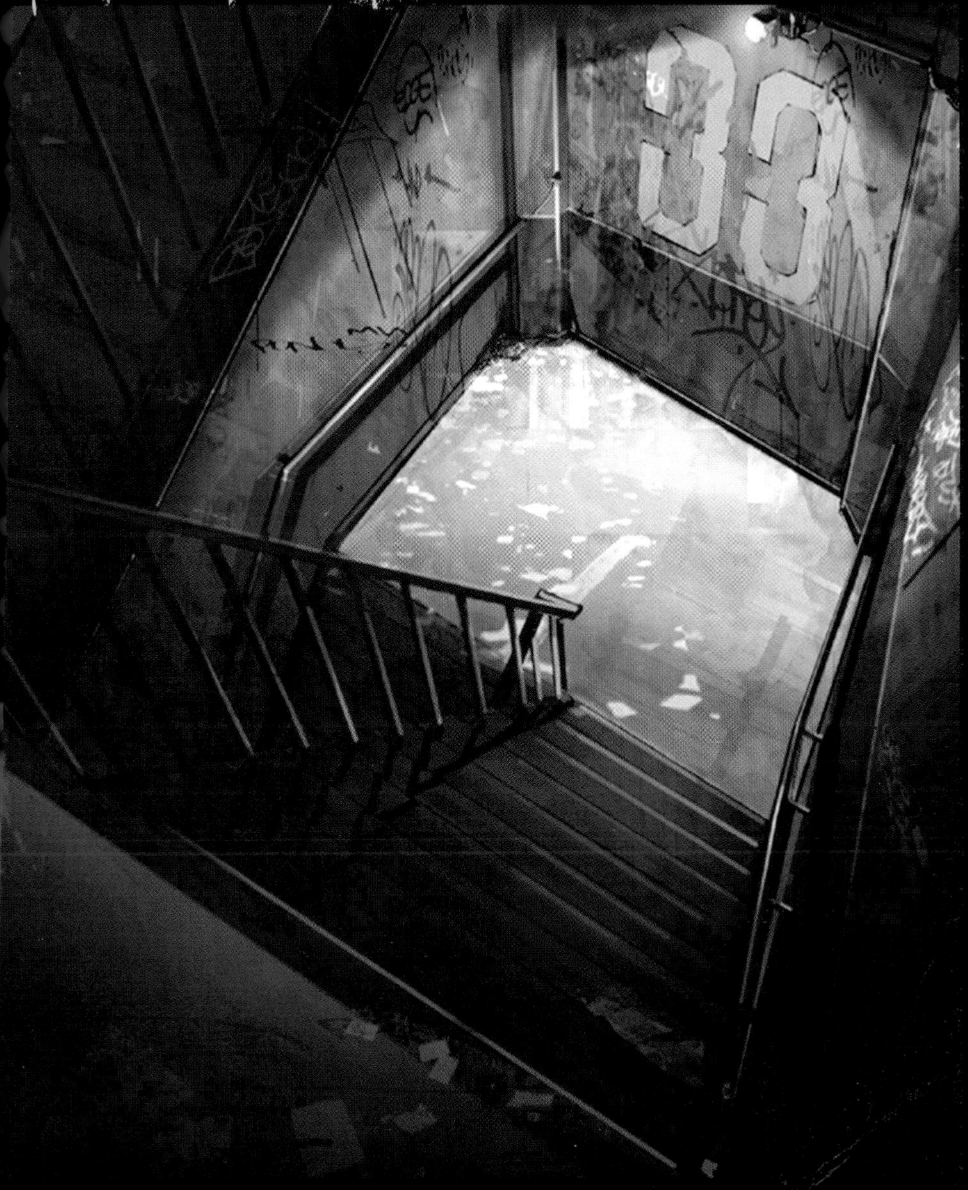

Background painting of a
Monarch projects hallway.

concept painting: Maverix studios

BLOKHEDZ

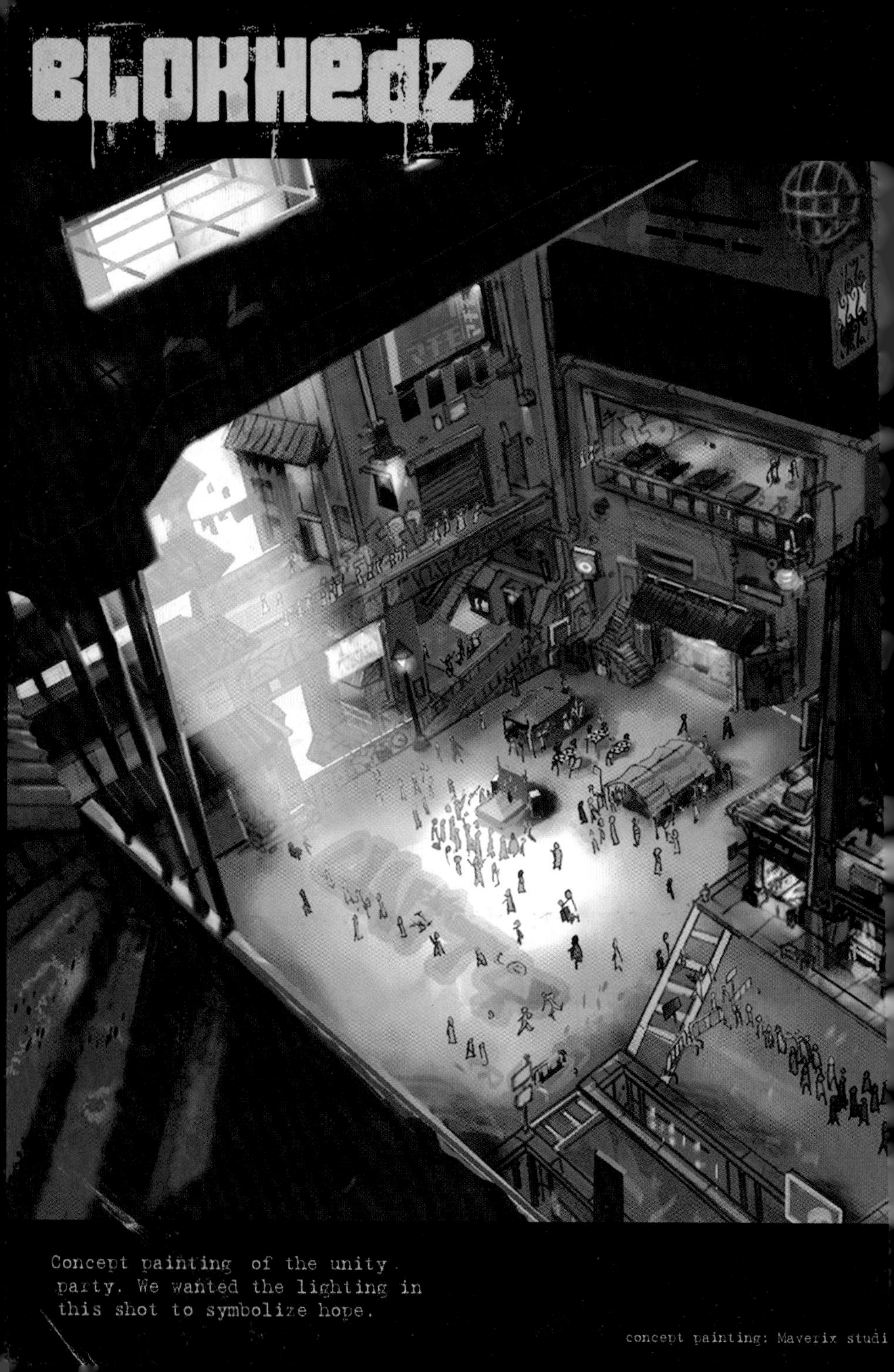

Concept painting of the unity party. We wanted the lighting in this shot to symbolize hope.

concept painting: Maverix studi

BLOKHEDZ

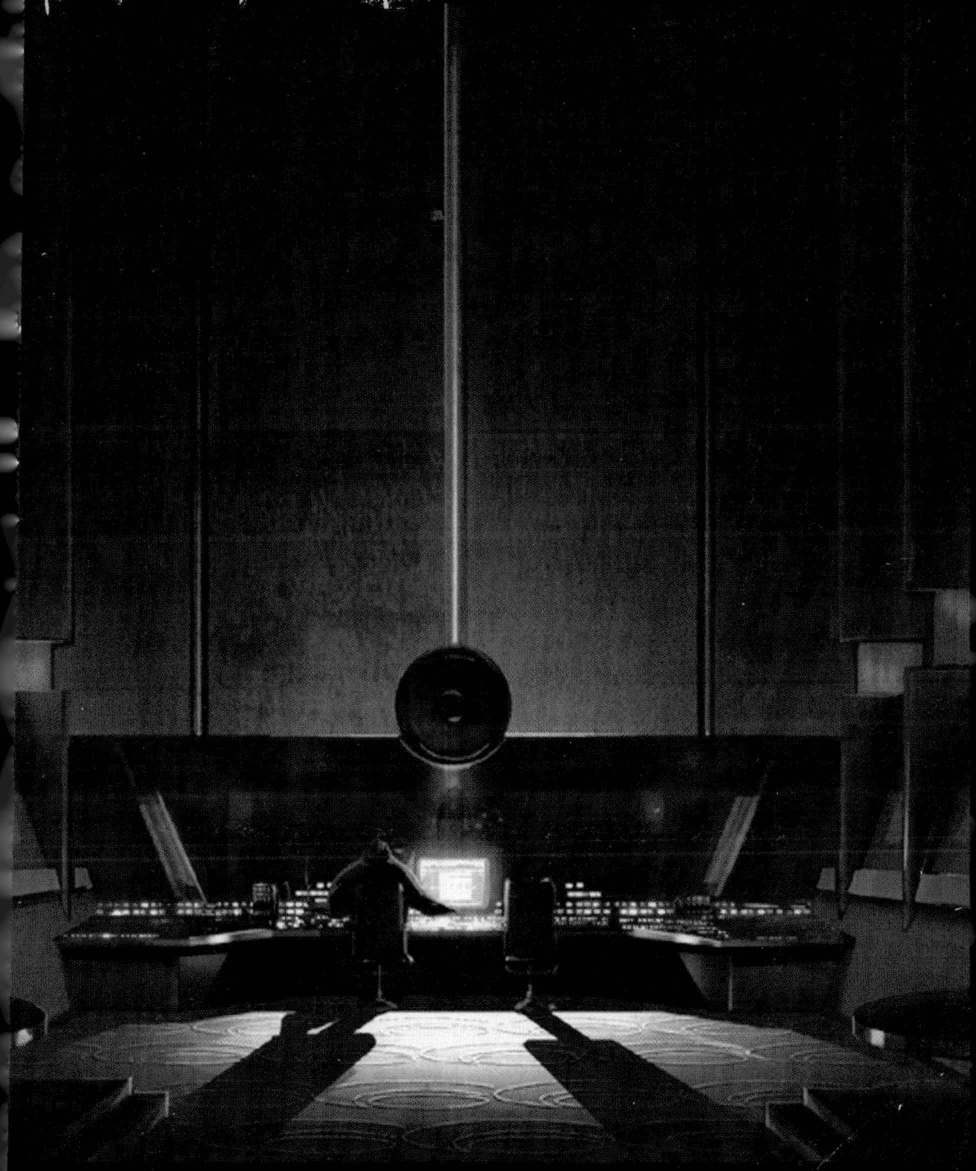

elopmental painting of
k Murder Studios

concept painting: Maverix studios

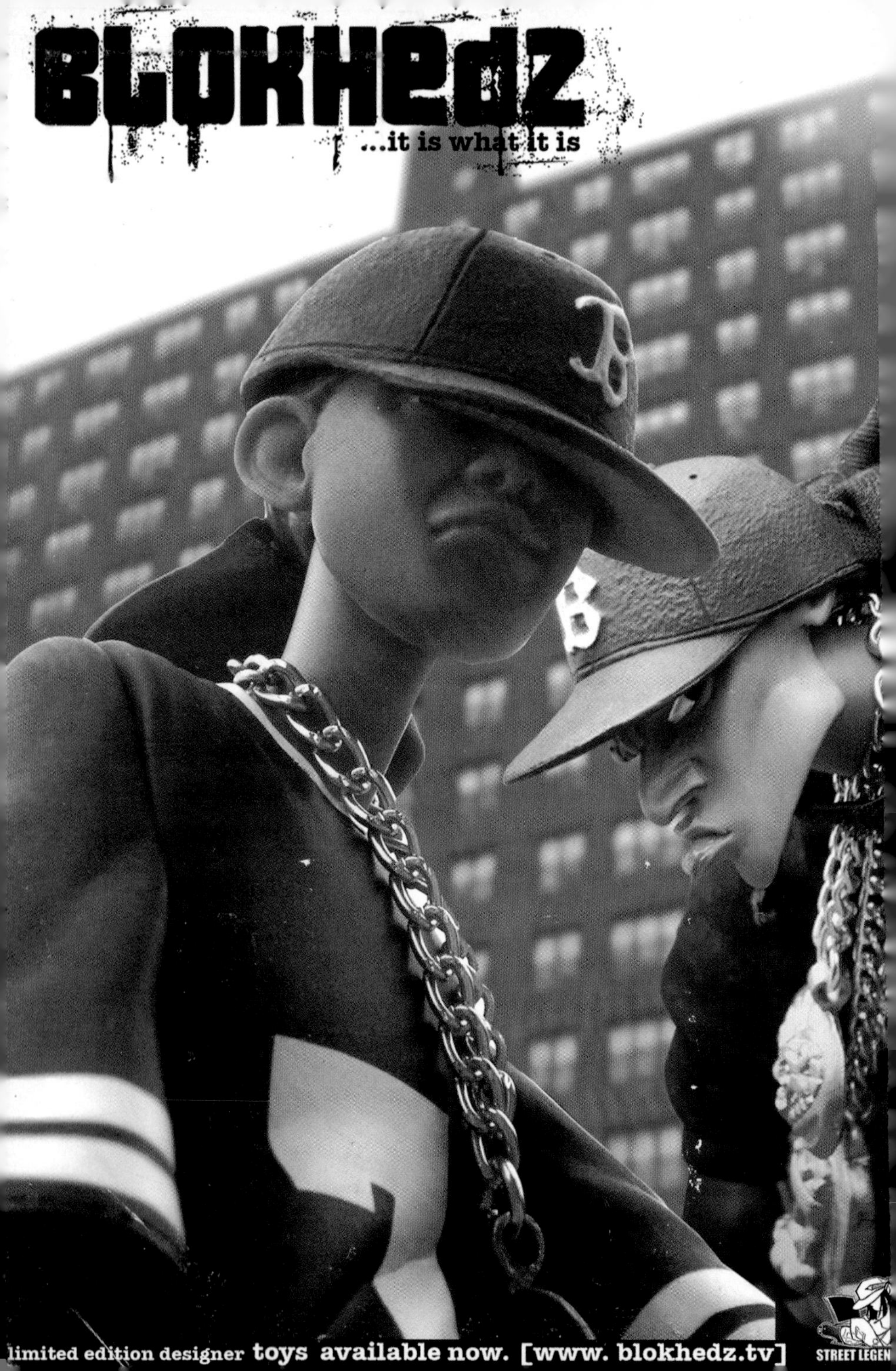
BLOKHEdZ
...it is what it is
limited edition designer toys available now. [www. blokhedz.tv]
STREET LEGEN